THE CIVIL WAR REMINISCENCES OF
MAJOR SILAS T. GRISAMORE, C.S.A.

THE CIVIL WAR REMINISCENCES OF
MAJOR SILAS T. GRISAMORE, C.S.A.

Edited, with an Introduction, by ARTHUR W. BERGERON, JR.

LOUISIANA STATE UNIVERSITY PRESS   *Baton Rouge and London*

Originally published in slightly different form under the title
*Reminiscences of Uncle Silas: A History of the Eighteenth
Louisiana Infantry Regiment* (1981), by Le Comite des Archives
de la Louisiane.

02 01 00 99 98 97 96 95 94 93   5 4 3 2 1

Designer: Amanda McDonald Key
Typeface: Trump
Typesetter: G&S Typesetters, Inc.
Printer and binder: Thomson-Shore, Inc.

Library of Congress Cataloging-in-Publication Data

The Civil War reminiscences of Major Silas T. Grisamore, Confederate
   States Army / edited with an introduction by Arthur W. Bergeron, Jr.
      p.   cm.
   Includes bibliographical references and index.
   ISBN 0-8071-1817-6 (alk. paper)
   1. Silas, Uncle, 1825–1897.   2. United States—History—Civil War,
1861–1865—Personal narratives, Confederate.   3. Confederate States
of America. Army. Louisiana Infantry Regiment, 18th.
   4. Louisiana—History—Civil War, 1861–1865—Personal narratives
   5. Soldiers—Louisiana—Thibodaux—Biography.   6. Thibodaux (La.)—
Biography.   I. Bergeron, Arthur W.
E565 18th.S55C58   1993
973.7'4263'092—dc20
[B]   92-37038
                                                              CIP

The editor of this volume offers grateful acknowledgment to
Loretta Gilibert for permission to quote from the diary of
Elphege LeBoeuf, 1861–1862.

CONTENTS

Illustrations

In the April 27, 1867, edition of the *Weekly Thibodaux Sentinel*, there appeared the first of a continuing series of articles entitled "Reminiscences." Silas T. Grisamore wrote these articles under the name "Uncle Silas," and his column appeared over a period of four years, ending in the December 2, 1871, edition. Grisamore's reminiscences described his activities as both a Confederate company officer and a staff officer during the American Civil War.

The story told in these articles contains many facts of interest and numerous amusing stories. Grisamore had a flair for writing and often included in his narrative humorous episodes from his wartime experience. The reader will find that he often used an only slightly veiled tongue-in-cheek style when discussing people and events. The primary importance of Grisamore's memoir is that it emphasized the operations in Louisiana of the military unit to which he belonged. Unfortunately, the war in Louisiana produced few diaries and memoirs by the state's own soldiers; hence, Grisamore's reminiscences fill a gap in the war's literature. He provides items of information found in no other sources, for example, the status of General Alfred Mouton during the Battle of Labadieville and the actions of General Henry H. Sibley at the Battle of Bisland. In many instances, Grisamore recorded details on the service of his regiment's soldiers (enlistment and discharge dates, illnesses, battle casualties, etc.) not available in the official records.

Grisamore's accounts of the operations of the supportive services of the army enhance the interest provided by his story of the shooting war. During much of his career in the army, Grisamore acted as a quartermaster officer. As such, he had responsibility for supplying food and clothing to the soldiers in the field, providing tents or other shelters, transporting all of these items on campaigns, and purchasing or seizing wagons. Grisamore's description of the trials and tribulations of the quartermaster adds real significance to the history he wrote.

Unfortunately, three installments of Grisamore's "Reminiscences" are missing from extant copies of the *Sentinel*. One of the missing columns is not crucial to the story, but two are: one dealing with the Battle of Labadieville on October 27, 1862, and the other describing the surrender of the troops of the Trans-Mississippi Department in May, 1865. Later articles written by Grisamore permitted a reconstruction of his account of the fight at Labadieville, so his "Reminiscences" now stand practically complete.

Grisamore undoubtedly wrote his "Reminiscences" with the aid of a diary, for his account contains an almost day-by-day reconstruction of events. No evidence of the existence of such a diary has surfaced, however, and its loss is a tragic one. The only Grisamore diary available covers the years 1846 to 1853. A typescript of this journal forms a part of the William Littlejohn (Litt) Martin Collection, deposited in the Manuscript Collection of Nicholls State University.

Grisamore's reminiscences are presented here substantially as they appeared in the *Sentinel*. In several instances, material originally printed out of sequence or later as separate installments has been placed at points in the memoir where it enhances the story or fills in gaps of missing information. I have retained Grisamore's paragraphing but have divided the entire narrative into chapters at points where such breaks seemed appropriate. Because the primary purpose of a document like this is to inform, the text should be easy to read and clear. In keeping with this aim, I have corrected minor spelling and punctuation errors.

ACKNOWLEDGMENTS

A number of people aided me in putting together both the original edition of this volume and this new edition. The original edition was published in 1981 by Le Comite des Archives de la Louisiane under the title *Reminiscences of Uncle Silas: A History of the Eighteenth Louisiana Infantry Regiment.* The late T. Harry Williams, former Boyd Professor of History at Louisiana State University, read the original draft and made several excellent suggestions on improvements. He also offered constant encouragement during my early, unsuccessful attempts to get Silas Grisamore's narrative into print. Philip D. Uzee of Nicholls State University assisted me in locating material in the archives there, especially the typescript of Grisamore's prewar diary. Mrs. Arthur Boland of New Orleans kindly shared biographical data on Leopold L. Armant, one of her ancestors. Loretta Gilibert of Aurora, Colorado, provided a typescript of a diary kept by an ancestor who served in the 18th Louisiana Infantry. She also allowed me to quote from it.

Several people contributed or assisted in obtaining the photographs used as illustrations. In particular, I want to thank Bettie Wurzlow of Schriever, Claude J. Knobloch of Thibodaux, Wilbur E. Meneray of Tulane University Library, Bernard Eble of Confederate Memorial Hall in New Orleans, Bruce Turner of the University of Southwestern Louisiana Archives, and Carol A. Mathias of Nicholls State University. Bobbie Young of Baton Rouge drew the maps for this edition.

As always, the staff of Louisiana State University Press have made the process of getting this manuscript into print as effortless and enjoyable as possible. I want to express my appreciation to Margaret Dalrymple, John Easterly, Catherine Landry, and Julie Schorfheide of the Press. My copy editor, Lois Geehr, did a fine job in preparing the manuscript for publication.

Finally, I want to thank my wife, Phyllis, and my daughter, Kathleen, for their patience, understanding, and support.

Introduction

Silas T. Grisamore was born March 8, 1825, in Clark County in southern Indiana, about nine miles from Louisville, Kentucky. He attended public school in that county and later spent two or three sessions in the Charlestown Academy at Charlestown, Indiana, while working as a teacher elsewhere to earn his tuition. On October 23, 1846, Grisamore and a cousin, Dr. James H. Hazard, boarded a steamer bound for Louisiana, where Grisamore's brother had lived for several years. Grisamore hoped to make a living as a teacher, and Dr. Hazard planned to open his medical practice in Natchez, Mississippi. The cousins arrived at Donaldsonville on November 3, and Grisamore soon settled near Napoleonville. For a short time, Grisamore tutored a young lady on a nearby plantation.

On January 4, 1847, Grisamore began teaching at a private school. He worked hard at his task until the term ended in August. Grisamore took a short vacation to his home in Indiana, but when he returned to Louisiana he found that he had no future as a teacher. Unemployed until December, 1847, Grisamore finally hired on as an overseer on a plantation owned by a man named Sims. This job lasted only nine months. Grisamore sought employment unsuccessfully until early 1849. In March of that year, he began selling various goods from a flatboat on Bayou Lafourche.

Grisamore had succeeded well enough in his new occupation after a year's time that he bought his own flatboat, the *Gen. Satisfaction No. 1*. He would buy his goods in New Orleans for resale on the bayou. In his diary, Grisamore recorded: "My stock consists of Provisions, Groceries, Liquors, Dry Goods, Fancy articles, Hardware, Stoneware, Woodware, Crockery, Shoes, Boots, Hats, Tinware." He even had two youths working for him. Finally, in 1857, Grisamore settled permanently in Thibodaux, where he opened a copper, tin, and sheet iron business with John Larkin. Two years later, Larkin sold his interest to W. H. Ragan and George Westbrooks, and the firm from then on went by the name S. T. Grisamore & Co.

As a young man, Grisamore found himself drawn toward the Whig party. He wrote in his diary on November 7, 1848: "To day I gave my first vote for President and Vice President. I voted for Taylor and Fillmore. Whig from principle, I have always preferred Henry Clay to any living man for the highest office in the gift of the people. . . . Taylor I considered, as the saying is, a pill easier to swallow than Cass." When the Whig party broke up after 1854, Grisamore apparently became a Democrat, but in the election of 1860 he supported John Bell, the Union party candidate. He opposed secession, but when Louisiana left the Union he cast his lot with his adopted state.

Grisamore joined the Lafourche Creoles (a volunteer company) as fifth sergeant, and the company was mustered into state service on September 16, 1861. The unit went to New Orleans later that month and was sent to Camp Moore on October 4. The next day, Grisamore became first sergeant of the company when it joined the 18th Louisiana Infantry Regiment as Company G. This regiment received orders to go to Camp Roman at Carrollton for training. On December 17, the members of the company elected Grisamore as junior second lieutenant of their unit. The regiment moved to Camp Benjamin on Gentilly Ridge in early January, 1862, and continued its drill and instruction.

The fall of Fort Henry, Tennessee, caused the Confederate government to order reinforcements to that state. Grisamore and his regiment left New Orleans and arrived at Corinth, Mississippi, on February 18. The 18th Louisiana fought its first skirmish of the war at Pittsburg Landing on the Tennessee River on March 1. After the regiment returned to Corinth, Colonel Alfred Mouton appointed Grisamore acting quartermaster, undoubtedly because of his background as a merchant. He was in charge of the regiment's wagons during the march toward Shiloh. On the morning that the battle opened (April 6), he left the train and joined his company. The 18th Louisiana was not engaged until early that afternoon and then conducted an assault against a stronger enemy force at about 3 P.M. Grisamore got through the battle without even a bullet mark on his uniform. Toward the end of the next day's fighting, he became company commander because the captain and other lieutenants had all been wounded. He also took charge of the remnants of another company and led both companies back to Corinth during the retreat.

Grisamore continued as commander of the two companies until

mid-May. His only active duty in the field came when he led the men during a skirmish at Farmington on May 9. He soon received word from Richmond of his appointment, dated April 30, as assistant quartermaster in the Provisional Army. When the 18th Louisiana was reorganized under the Conscript Act, Grisamore was elected first lieutenant of Company G on May 13. He refused the rank of captain and insisted upon the reelection of Captain J. Kleber Gourdain, who was then absent, sick and wounded. After the elections, he turned over command of the company to the new second lieutenant and resumed his duties as acting quartermaster of the regiment. Grisamore acted briefly as lieutenant colonel of the 18th Louisiana during the closing stages of the siege of Corinth because illnesses had taken all captains off duty.

When the Army of the Mississippi retreated from Corinth toward Tupelo, Grisamore resumed his quartermaster duties full time. The illness of Captain Clerville T. Patin resulted in Grisamore's becoming acting commissary officer as well for a couple of weeks. Instead of accompanying the army on its march toward Kentucky, the 18th Louisiana was detached as a garrison at Pollard, Alabama, near Mobile. Grisamore had taken his wagons to Chattanooga and did not rejoin his unit until about September 1. There Colonel Leopold L. Armant appointed him captain. Grisamore did not receive confirmation of this promotion from the authorities in Richmond until the following February.

The 18th Louisiana received orders to report for duty in the Trans-Mississippi Department and left Pollard on October 2. Ten days later, the men arrived at New Iberia. Thus began their and Grisamore's long association with Major General Richard Taylor's Army of Western Louisiana. Though his duties required him to remain in the rear, Grisamore took every opportunity he could to visit the front lines during the various military operations in south Louisiana. His only extended absence from the army occurred in late 1863, when illness forced him to go on leave from September until December. In his reminiscences, he filled in the activities of the regiment he had not witnessed from information given him by men who had participated in the numerous battles and skirmishes.

Brigadier General Alfred Mouton made Grisamore the acting quartermaster of his Louisiana infantry brigade on January 30, 1864. In April, following the Battle of Mansfield, Brigadier General Henry Gray, who then commanded the brigade, appointed Grisamore major and assistant quartermaster of the brigade. He held this position until the end of the war. In July and August, 1864, Grisamore served briefly as acting quartermaster of Brigadier General Camille J. Polignac's division (formerly Mouton's) during the absence of the division quartermaster. Brigadier General Allen Thomas named Grisamore post quartermaster at Alexandria in late January, 1865. When the brigade left Alexandria for Natchitoches in April, he gave up this position and again became brigade quartermaster. The Confederate forces at Natchitoches and Mansfield disbanded in May when the men received word that General Edmund Kirby Smith was about to surrender the department to Union forces. Grisamore received his parole at Washington, Louisiana, in June, 1865, while on his way home.

At Thibodaux, he found his business in a state of ruin. After a few months' service as deputy sheriff of Lafourche Parish, Grisamore returned to his mercantile business to get it going again. He continued to run his store until his death. By early 1896, he was also involved in operating with R. R. McBride a "news, literary and stationary depot" in Thibodaux.

Grisamore married Mary Eudora McBride on May 15, 1878. Born January 24, 1845, she was the sister of his business partner at the newsstand. The couple had no children. She died on December 26, 1904, and was buried next to her husband in the cemetery at St. John's Episcopal Church in Thibodaux.

Governor James Madison Wells appointed Grisamore mayor of Thibodaux on July 13, 1865, and he was elected to that post in May, 1866. He had previously served one term in that office in 1860. The town was in bad condition financially, owing a debt of more than $3,000, and existed on what taxes it could draw from an impoverished people. Both the bridge over Bayou Lafourche and the market house, one of the town's main economic enterprises, had been destroyed. With the assistance of the town council, Grisamore improved the town's financial condition through wise money management. Builders had reconstructed both the bridge and the market house by the time he left office on July 3, 1868.

On June 4, 1866, the voters elected Grisamore to the Lafourche Parish Police Jury, and he became its president. He served on that body, with the exception of only a few years, until July, 1892, and acted as its president for all but one term. The parish had a debt of more than $35,000 when Grisamore first took office, but during his service the jury liquidated the debt, made many needed improvements, and turned over to his successors a parish free of debt and with funds on hand to run itself on a cash basis. Grisamore proposed a plan of dividing the parish into districts for the purpose of drainage. The plan resulted in the restoration to cultivation of thousands of acres of land.

Grisamore received appointment as a member of the parish school board in 1876 and served as president or superintendent of that body until September, 1888. He served for many years either as chairman or secretary of the Lafourche Parish Democratic Central Committee.

In 1859, Grisamore acted as one of the organizers of the Thibodaux Fire Company No. 1, and he served, with the exception of the war years, as president or secretary of the organization until his death. He acted as chief of the fire department for one term and sat on that body as a member for several years. As a representative of his fire company, Grisamore officiated for several years as manager of the Thibodaux Opera House.

Grisamore became a member of Excelsior Lodge No. 34, Independent Order of Odd Fellows, located in Thibodaux, in 1853. He withdrew in 1855 to become a charter member of Assumption Lodge No. 43, I.O.O.F., located in Napoleonville. After the war, the two lodges merged into one under the title of Excelsior Lodge No. 34. Grisamore occupied all of the offices of that lodge at various times and served as its secretary until his death. He became a member of the Grand Lodge of Louisiana in 1859 and after 1865 never missed a session of that body except when detained by illness. The membership elected him Grand Warden of the Grand Lodge in 1872, Deputy Grand Master in 1873, Grand Master in 1874, and representative to the Sovereign Grand Lodge from 1875 to 1879.

For thirty years, Grisamore was a member of St. John's Episcopal Church and served as clerk, treasurer, and warden of the church.

In August, 1892, Grisamore assisted in forming a camp of Confederate veterans in Thibodaux. Upon the organization of the Braxton Bragg Camp No. 196, United Confederate Veterans, on September 11, 1892, its members elected him commander. Every year thereafter, the membership reelected him to that position.

Grisamore became coeditor of the bilingual Thibodaux *Sentinel* in February, 1869, assuming charge of the English language department. He held that position until August, 1875, when Duncan S.

Cage, Jr., replaced him. Shortly after Grisamore became coeditor, the Lucy (Louisiana) *Le Meschacebe,* referring back to an episode during the war, wrote: "One day, it was at Texana, we saw Uncle Silas climb on the roof of an old shanty to see what Weitzel was doing. Birds were flying in that region in the shape of Minnie balls. We then had a vague idea that our Uncle delighted in outlandish situations. We are now satisfied that nothing can terrify him. A man may escape Minnie balls; but the Printing Bill never misses a conservative newspaper." To this Grisamore replied in the *Sentinel:* "Uncle S. never feared unbogging a Wagon Train, so long as the ears of the lead mules and the driver's whip were visible, and if his services will be of any avail in drawing the conservative Party out of apathy and listlessness they will be freely tendered."

In January, 1877, Grisamore resumed his position as editor of the English language department of the *Sentinel,* and he worked for the newspaper until July, 1887, when it merged with the Thibodaux *Democrat.* He continued to contribute to the *Sentinel* until his death, his chief stories consisting of a history of the parish police jury down to the 1880s and a column entitled "Fifty Years Ago," which described Louisiana and Lafourche Parish during the 1840s. During the last decade of his life, Grisamore was the local correspondent for the New Orleans *Daily Picayune* and *Times-Democrat* newspapers.

On July 24, 1897, Grisamore died at his home in Thibodaux after a brief illness. He was buried in the St. John's church cemetery.

THE CIVIL WAR REMINISCENCES OF
MAJOR SILAS T. GRISAMORE, C.S.A.

I   THE INITIAL CAMPAIGNS

On the 16th September, 1861, a military company called "The La-fourche Creoles" was mustered into the service of the State of Louisiana by Louis Bush, Captain, in the town of Thibodaux, numbering 108 rank and file.[1] The company had its quarters in the parish school house on Lower Canal Street, now occupied by Captain L. M. Hargis as a school room.

The company remained in those quarters, under military discipline, being regularly drilled by De La Bretonne[2] in ordinary exercises and by Robin[3] in the bayonet exercise, until the 23rd of the same month, when it was removed to New Orleans by way of the Opelousas Railroad.[4] Arriving at the wharf, we were met by one company of the Orleans Guard Battalion and escorted to their headquarters in the old Orleans Theater,[5] where the company was treated to a huge bowl of Champagne Punch. After which we were marched to the St. Charles Hotel,[6] and partook of a bountiful sup-

1. Colonel Valery Vicknair mustered in the company on the corner of Lower Canal and St. Bridget streets (*Weekly Thibodaux Sentinel*, September 26, 1874).

2. Probably Charles de la Bretonne, who later commanded Company H, 30th Louisiana Infantry Regiment (Compiled Service Records of Confederate Soldiers Who Served in Organizations from the State of Louisiana, National Archives Microcopy No. 320, Roll 356, hereinafter cited as CSR).

3. Possibly Napoleon Robin, who later commanded Company K, 29th Louisiana Infantry Regiment (*ibid.*, Roll 352).

4. The New Orleans, Opelousas, and Great Western Railroad, which ran between Algiers and Berwick Bay, opened in May, 1857 (Walter Prichard, ed., "A Forgotten Louisiana Engineer: G. W. R. Bayley and His 'History of the Railroads of Louisiana,'" *Louisiana Historical Quarterly*, XXX [1947], 1148, 1155).

5. The Orleans Theater, built in 1809 at 721 Orleans Street, was the third theater erected in the Crescent City (Federal Writers' Project, *New Orleans City Guide* [Boston, 1938], 124).

6. Located between Common and Gravier streets, the St. Charles Hotel was normally frequented by Americans rather than Creoles. The original structure was erected in 1837, but workmen rebuilt it after a fire destroyed it in 1851 (*ibid.*, 313; Martha Ann Peters, "The St. Charles Hotel: New Orleans Social Center, 1837–1860," *Louisiana History*, I [1960], 191–211).

per.[7] On the 24th, the company was located in Fassman's Cotton Press,[8] near the depot of the Jackson Railroad,[9] where we remained several days in order to procure our equipments, camp equipage, etc. The company was armed with the Mississippi rifle, a weapon then believed to be one of the best in use.[10] At this camp, we had pleasant quarters, a fine drill ground, and the members all enjoyed themselves finely during this portion of their initiation into military duties.

Whilst we were at this place, 500 prisoners captured at Manassas were received by the Jackson Railroad, marched by our quarters to the parish prison, where they were confined.[11] It was here also that I, for the first time, had the honor of meeting Alfred Mouton, then captain, afterwards colonel and brigadier general, who came to visit the captain of our company concerning the organization of a new regiment.[12] On Friday October 4, we took passage on board the Jack-

7. The company apparently spent the night at the St. Charles Hotel, because the next day a newspaper reported: "They are a remarkably fine looking body, and appeared to great advantage in their gray linsey uniforms, trimmed with red, as they drew up this morning in front of the St. Charles Hotel, manifesting that they have been drilled and under fine discipline" (New Orleans *Daily Picayune*, September 24, 1861).

8. Located at Calliope and Locust streets near the Jackson railroad depot (Charles Gardner, comp., *Gardner's New Orleans Directory, for 1861* [New Orleans, 1861], 164, 456).

9. The New Orleans, Jackson, and Great Northern Railroad ran from New Orleans to Canton, Mississippi (Prichard, ed., "A Forgotten Louisiana Engineer," 1133–34).

10. More properly known as the United States Rifle, Model 1841, the Mississippi Rifle was the first general issue army rifle that used the percussion cap system. After the introduction of the minié ball in 1850, the rifle was modified from .54 to .58 caliber. It used a 22½-inch bayonet and weighed 9¾ pounds. Originally called the Jager Rifle because of its effectiveness, the weapon was renamed after 1847 when Colonel Jefferson Davis' 1st Mississippi Regiment made it famous during the Mexican War (Francis A. Lord, *Civil War Collector's Encyclopedia* [New York, 1963], 242–43).

11. These prisoners—principally from Maine, Massachusetts, Vermont, Minnesota, New York, and Ohio—arrived in New Orleans in two groups on September 29 and October 4 (New Orleans *Daily Picayune*, September 29, October 4, 1861).

12. Mouton had served as a captain in the regular Confederate army and commanded the Infantry School of Practice at Baton Rouge and New Orleans. He resigned his commission on July 16 and recruited a volunteer company in his native Lafayette Parish. About September 28, six of the companies that later made up part of the 18th Louisiana (including the Lafourche Creoles) formed themselves into what was called the Creole Battalion and elected Mouton as lieutenant colonel. He continued to try

son Railroad cars and in a few hours were debarked at Camp Moore in the piney woods,[13] where we immediately put up our tents and made ourselves as comfortable as possible. On the first view of the place, we were all delighted with the prospect. The water from the cool, flowing springs was delicious, the drill grounds were ample and well prepared, the surrounding groves dense and shady, whilst the pure and clear waters of the Tangipahoa furnished excellent bathing facilities, impressing upon our minds the idea that we were to have a nice time during our sojourn at this encampment.

Two or three days, however, convinced us that the whole camp was one mass of filth and corruption without any system of decency or propriety having been inaugurated; sickness was prevailing throughout the camp; funeral processions were daily seen, followed by volleys of musketry over the bodies of those who had so early given up their lives; and the question "when are we to be removed?" was seriously asked by all of us.

On the 5th of October, our company was mustered into the service of the Confederate States, and on the same evening the 18th La. Regiment was organized, consisting of seven companies. Alfred Mouton of Lafayette, Colonel; Alfred Roman of St. James, Lieutenant Colonel; and Louis Bush of Lafourche, Major. Company A from St. James, left bank, ——— Druilhet, Captain; Company B from St. Landry, H. L. Garland, Captain; Company C from Natchitoches, Dr. Wood, Captain; Company D from St. Martin and New Orleans, J. D. Hayes, Captain; Company E from St. James, right bank, Mire, Captain; Company F from Lafayette, Wm. Mouton, Captain; and Company G from Lafourche, J. K. Gourdain, Captain.[14]

---

to increase his command to regimental strength (Richard P. Weinert, "The Confederate Regulars in Louisiana," *Louisiana Studies,* VI [1967], 55–56; Lucy [La.] *Le Meschacebe,* September 28, October 5, 1861).

13. Camp Moore was located near Tangipahoa, seventy-eight miles from New Orleans. Established May 12 and named for Governor Thomas O. Moore, the camp was set up because of restricted and unsanitary conditions at Camp Walker in New Orleans (Powell A. Casey, *The Story of Camp Moore* [Baton Rouge, 1985], 6, 11).

14. These companies were the following: A, St. James Rifles, Captain Jules A. Druilhet; B, St. Landry Volunteers, Captain Henry L. Garland; C, Natchitoches Rebels, Captain John D. Wood; D, Hayes Champions, Captain James D. Hayes; E, Chasseurs of St. James, Captain E. Camille Mire; F, Acadian Guards, Captain William Mouton; and G, Lafourche Creoles, Captain J. Kleber Gourdain (Arthur W. Bergeron, Jr., *Guide to Louisiana Confederate Military Units, 1861–1865* [Baton Rouge, 1989], 117).

The muster roll of the "Lafourche Creoles" was as follows, viz.:

J. Kleber Gourdain, Captain.
John A. Collins, 1st Lieutenant.
Joseph P. Tucker, 2nd Lieutenant.
Cleophas Gautreau, Jr. 2nd Lieutenant.
Silas T. Grisamore, 1st Sergeant.
Robert Savoie, 2nd Sergeant.
J. Scuddy Levron, 3rd Sergeant.
Alfred L. St. Martin, 4th Sergeant.
Levi M. Hargis, 5th Sergeant.
Theodule Robichaux, 1st Corporal.
Gustave Abrebat, 2nd Corporal.
J. Emile Naquin, 3rd Corporal.
J. Louis Aucoin, 4th Corporal.

Privates

Abadie, Amadeo H.
Achee, Belisaire
Augeran, Alfred
Aucoin, Franklin
Arceneau, Harris
Aubert, Charles
Ayot, Elphege
Badeaux, Thomassin
Barrios, Prosper
Baille, Onesippe
Bazet, B. Filuean
Beauvais, C. Fergus
Benoit, Claiborne J.
Bourgeois, Ulysses
Boudreaux, Auguste
Bergeron, Emile
Bergeron, Edouard
Besson, Charles
Boudreaux, Louis F.
Boudreaux, Dozelien
Bouvier, Theophile
Bouyan, Augustus J.
Burk, William

Cherami, Augustin
Collins, William F.
Cook, Malcolm B.
Dantin, Magloire
Delaporte, Joseph J.
Delatte, Clerfe
Delaney, James
Elliott, Adolphe
Falgout, Jules B.
Ferret, John
Gaudet, F. Justin
Gauthier, Severin
Gautreaux, Leoni
Gros, Justilien
Guedry, Paul
Giroir, Jules
Guidroz, William
Guillot, Francois
Grubbs, Amos W.
Guillot, J. Baptiste
Hebert, Joseph
Holcombe, Milton S.
Hymel, Ulysse

Jeandron, Olezimon	Parr, Marcelin
Jeandron, Aristide	Paris, Victor
Jeandron, J. Baptiste	Plaisance, Jean
Knoblock, J. Victor	Pitre, Auguste
Laine, Claiborne	Pontiff, Joachim
Lagarde, Pierre	Price, Washington
LeBlanc, Aristide	Ramagossa, Louis F.
LeBlanc, Demophon	Roger, Francois
Ledet, Henri	Robichaux, Leo
Ledet, Marcel	Rouvert, Edmond
Lejeune, Amadeo	Rouye, Florian
Lejeune, Augustin	Savoie, Estival
Leonard, Joseph	Sevin, Onesippe
Leonard, Noel O.	Sevin, Felix P.
Levron, Aurelien	Supke, Herman
Lombas, Augustin	Thibodaux, Paul
McAuliff, William	Theriot, Augustave
McEvers, Douglas L.	Toups, Joseph P.
McDonald, John	Triche, Dorville
Meyronne, Adam	Trahant, Joseph
Molaison, Justilien	Trone, Joseph
Montz, Homer	Vedroz, Antoine
Naquin, Volsi	White, William

Total one field officer, four commissioned officers, five sergeants, four corporals, ninety-four privates, one hundred and eight rank and file.

Of the above list 96 were natives of Louisiana, four of France, three of Ireland, one each of Indiana, Alabama, New York, Germany, and Spain. Thirteen were married men, and a majority were under 25 years of age.

The organization of the regiment was completed by appointing Lieutenant Barthelemy[15] of St. James as Adjutant, Dr. Littlell[16] of St. Landry as Surgeon, Dr. Gourier[17] of Iberville as Assistant Surgeon, Lucius J. Dupre[18] as Quartermaster, Wm. Sanchez of St. James

15. Second Lieutenant Edward C. Barthelemy of Company E (CSR, Roll 290).

16. Dr. R. H. Littlell (*ibid.*, Roll 294).

17. Dr. Alfred Gourrier (*ibid.*, Roll 293).

18. Lucius J. Dupre, Company B, had served as a district judge and a member of the secession convention in January, 1861. Elected to the Confederate Congress from the state's Fourth District, he left the regiment on November 14, 1861 (Lucy [La.] *Le Meschacebe*, October 12, November 5, 1861; CSR, Roll 292; Ezra J. Warner and W. Buck Yearns, *Biographical Register of the Confederate Congress* [Baton Rouge, 1975], 80).

as Sergeant Major, Deluc Etie of New Iberia as Quartermaster Sergeant, and Thadeus Mayo, Hospital Steward.

On the 8th of October 1861, three days after we were mustered into the Confederate service, we received orders to strike tents, and to the great satisfaction of us all, we were embarked on the cars and transported to the rear of Carrollton, 7 miles above New Orleans. On the next day we established a camp on the upper suburbs of that village, which was named "Camp Roman" in honor of the venerable Ex-Governor A. B. Roman, father of our lieutenant colonel.[19] Then commenced a strict system of discipline and a thorough course of company and battalion drills.

October 14th. Our company was ordered to detail two commissioned officers, four non-commissioned officers, and 50 privates to guard the Federal prisoners confined in the parish prison in New Orleans. Lieutenants Collins and Tucker, with Sergeants Savoie and Levron and Corporals Robichaux and Aucoin, were placed in command of the detail.

This detail remained in charge of the prisoners about one month. In the meantime the remainder of us fitted up our camp comfortably. Our tents were large and supplied with flies, and our floors were planked.

Nothing much of importance occurred at this camp during this month. The men were healthy and enjoyed themselves well.

November 11th. George W. Winder of Terrebonne was mustered into service as a member of our company by Col. A. Mouton.

November 16th. Thomas J. Daunis was mustered into service as a member of our company by Col. A. Mouton.

November 25th. The measles made their appearance in the company. They had been in the regiment for some time and had caused several deaths.

December 2nd. Private Onesippe Baille died of measles. I had been on the watch for the appearance of this disease for several days, and upon Private Baille complaining of being unwell, I suspisioned him of being attacked by measles, but he persistently contended

19. Located about a mile and a half above Carrollton, Camp Roman probably received its name because it stood on land owned by Mr. V. Roman, although some sources indicate that it was named either for Lieutenant Colonel Roman or his father (Lucy [La.] *Le Meschacebe*, October 19, 1861; New Orleans *Daily Picayune*, October 15, 1861; Powell A. Casey, *Encyclopedia of Forts, Posts, Named Camps and Other Military Installations in Louisiana, 1700–1981* [Baton Rouge, 1983], 186–87.

that he had had them and not until their appearance were we aware of the nature of his complaint. He was immediately sent to the hospital in Carrollton and nursed by the Sisters of Charity, until death relieved him from his sufferings, and on the next day his body was accompanied to its final resting place in the Catholic grave yard in Thibodaux by his friends O. Sevin and H. Ledet.

During the prevalence of the disease the following members of the company were attacked by it, viz.: Sergeant Hargis and privates Rouvert, N. O. Leonard, Barrios, Aubert, Thibodaux, Bouyan, Arceneau, Demophon LeBlanc, Beauvais, Guedry, Gros, Besson, and F. Aucoin, of whom Aubert and Besson had narrow escapes from death.

About this time another company, commanded by Capt. Henry Huntington, was added to the regiment, making eight companies. This company had been formed in New Orleans.[20]

December 13. Lieutenant Joseph P. Tucker, having forwarded his resignation some time previously, received the notice of its acceptance. Ill health was the cause of this action of the lieutenant. He retired from the company, regretted by us all, as a good and kind friend and accomplished officer, and on bidding him farewell he had our earnest wishes for his speedy restoration to health and prosperity.

December 14. An election held to-day by the remaining officers of the company; Lieutenant Gautreau, 2nd Lieut. Junior, was elected to fill the vacancy occasioned by the resignation of Lieutenant Tucker.

December 17. At an election held to-day Sergeant S. T. Grisamore was chosen 2nd Lieut. Junior, to fill the vacancy occasioned by the promotion of Lieut. Gautreau. This caused the following promotions among the non-commissioned officers:

> J. S. Levron to be 1st Sergeant.
> A. L. St. Martin 3rd Sergeant.
> L. M. Hargis 4th Sergeant.
> T. Robichaux 5th Sergeant.
> J. E. Naquin to be 1st Corporal.
> J. L. Aucoin 3rd Corporal.
> P. Thibodaux 4th Corporal.

20. This company bore the nickname Confederate Guards.

December 18th. Private Herman Supke having obtained a furlough to visit New Orleans forgot to return and the title of "deserted" was appended to his name.

About this time a brigade was formed composed of the 16th Regiment at Camp Moore, the 17th Regiment at Chalmette, the 18th Regiment at Camp Roman, and the 19th Regiment encamped near us back of Carrollton. This brigade was commanded by Brig. Gen. Daniel E. Ruggles.[21]

Christmas week was a very pleasant [one], and our kind friends at home had sent us so many good things that we hardly knew what to do with them.

Christmas eve the boys got up a little exhibition of fire rockets, and were regaled with short speeches from several of the orators in the regiment.[22]

January 1st, 1862. William Ledet was mustered into service in our company by the commanding officer.

And we received orders to remove to a new camp on the Pontchartrain Railroad,[23] to be known as Camp Benjamin.

When, in the autumn of 1861, the 18th La. Regiment was encamped near Carrollton and being disciplined by the gallant Colonel Mouton preparatory to the hardships and trials which future campaigns might develop, it was thought necessary to complete the organization of the regiment to have a band of music. Such an institution was considered of immense importance at dress parades, tattoos, etc., more especially when our lady friends paid a visit to

21. The 16th Regiment was commanded by Colonel Preston Pond, Jr., the 17th by Colonel S. S. Heard, and the 19th by Colonel Benjamin L. Hodge. General Ruggles had received orders to go to New Orleans in October, but he became ill shortly after his arrival and did not return to active duty until November 26. Soon afterwards, Major General Mansfield Lovell placed him in command of the volunteer regiments stationed in the city (*The War of the Rebellion: A Compilation of the Official Records of the Union and Confederate Armies* [Washington, D.C., 1880–1902], Ser. I, Vol. VI, pp. 560–61, 751, 770, and Vol. LIII, p. 747, hereinafter cited as *OR*. Unless otherwise indicated, all citations are to Series I. New Orleans *Daily Picayune*, October 18, November 27, 1861).

22. Colonel Mouton complimented the men on the maintenance of their weapons. The men "received with frantic hurrahs" the speeches of Roman and Bush, both former politicians (Lucy [La.] *Le Meschacebe*, January 4, 1862).

23. Put into operation between New Orleans and Milneburg in April, 1831, the Pontchartrain Railroad became the first railroad west of the Alleghenies (Prichard, ed., "A Forgotten Louisiana Engineer," 1117–18; Federal Writers' Project, *New Orleans City Guide*, 27, 401).

our camps and we desired to impress upon their minds that we were strangers to sadness and melancholy.

Accordingly, a complete corps of performers was detailed, instruments purchased, a set of tents of the peculiar colors that rendered Jacob's cattle famous procured, and a space of ground set apart for their private camp.[24]

Then came the practicing, which was carried on all day long, until the birds in the adjacent woods, astonished at the variety of music that echoed and resounded through the groves in which they only had been accustomed to chant their merry songs, remained mute with wonder.

I remember nothing more productive of kind and sympathetic feelings or better calculated to soothe the angry passions of man than to be in the midst of a newly organized band of musicians whilst each one is practicing his own tune according to his own time and notions, unless it was, in ante bellum times on some well-regulated plantation, the melodious responses of half a hundred hungry mules to the sound of the dinner bell.

Our major, whose musical qualities were so well known, had the pleasure of seeing them fully appreciated by an appointment to take especial charge of the discipline and organization of the band, and he often was noticed in the afternoon to extend himself on the grassy lawn in the shade of a moss-covered oak during the practicing hours of his performance, smoking his cigarette, and amusing himself in the perusal of the illuminated and interesting pages of one of Hardee's best novels.

Among the numerous instruments was an immense drum—the pride of its owner, the pet of the band, and a most complete piece of astonishment to the little boys of Carrollton, whose ecstasies knew no bounds when they saw the big drum stick come down on it with a bang, and when they had succeeded in walking *entirely* around it, they ran home to inform their mamas of the extraordinary feat of pedestrianism which they had accomplished.

However, daily improvement was perceptible, and by [a] diet of hard practice, the band made its appearance at dress parade, played

24. A sergeant in Company E wrote in his diary that a regimental band was being organized and that twelve instruments arrived on January 12, 1862. He stated that "they are going to practice at the old sugar house of Mr. Hopkins." By January 20, the sergeant noted that "our musicians [have] made some progress" (Diary of Elphege LeBoeuf, in possession of Loretta Gilibert of Aurora, Colorado).

retreat, tattoo, etc., and were rapidly acquiring a sonorous reputation among the men in camp.

Everything was progressing finely until Brig. Gen. Ruggles was placed in command over us, who gave an order to have dress parade at 8 o'clock A.M., instead of sunset, as had been our custom. This brought the dew upon our musicians' shoes and grief into their hearts, and it was thenceforth easy to perceive that the pride and ambition that had so nobly borne them up had received a shock from which it would hardly recover. Orders to play at reveille was another source of dissatisfaction to our performers that produced anything but joy in their little camp. However, all their little troubles were forgotten in the excitement occasioned by our movement to Corinth, where for a month the regiment was placed on picket duty near Pittsburg Landing, whilst our musicians had an easy time in camp, but the bloody day of Shiloh arrived, and when the regiment moved forward in line, they held their proper position. No particular attention would have been bestowed upon the band during the day had it not been for the restless and uneasy disposition of the big drum, which was perceptible to everyone.

Twice it had been violently thrown down in front of its owner as a bulwark to protect him from a shell that was supposed to be directed at his devoted head, and this part of the performance being so different from any of the duties previously required of it that it became sullen and barely responded to the pounding of the drumstick. Finally a shell that came whistling through the air and exploded nearby with a thundering noise so enraged our big drum that it broke loose from the owner and, turning around, chased him to the bottom of the ravine with a speed that would have been gratifying to an advocate of pedestrianism as one of the fine arts. But the big drum never caught *him*, and there in the bottom of that ravine were heard the expiring strains of the band of the 18th La. Regiment.

Many spasmodic efforts were made to resuscitate the old, or organize a new, band, but three little drums was the utmost extent ever attained in that direction.

In 1863, on our return from Natchitoches, we were encamped in the piney woods west of Alexandria, at which place the 11th La. Battalion was attached to our brigade. One evening, someone invited me to go over to their dress parade, as they had a band of music. Since our former major had left, I felt it incumbent on myself to pay some attention to the musical department of the army, as my musical abilities were considered by our friends almost equal to those for which he was famous, and accordingly I went.

The battalion was in line in an old cornfield, and not until the command to "beat off" was heard was the band perceived coming out of a fence corner.

The number of performers were three, one 5 feet high had a little drum upon which he rolled his sticks with a most extraordinary rapidity, the music resembling peas poured upon loose clapboards. On his left was a long-legged six footer—the happy owner of a fife. A pig under a gate and a cat with caudal extremity caught in a trap door would give an idea of the sounds of harmony that were blown out of that wonderful instrument. The third, six and a half feet high, carried a half brother to *our* big drum, and the idea I formed of him was that he was a Yankee in disguise, sent into our lines under a contract to smash in the head of every drum in the Confederacy. During the trip to the Lafourche country, this band disappeared, and ever after peace, tranquility and decorum, minus three small drums, reigned triumphantly about the camps of the glorious old 18th Louisiana.

During our service at Camp Roman from October 9th, 1861, to January 3rd, 1862, time passed away pleasantly with us. The weather was generally fine and cool enough to be comfortable. Being near home our kind friends kept us bountifully supplied with things good for the hungry, and our tables were seldom found empty. The sergeants of the company had a mess of their own and generally fared sumptuously every day, and each one made it a point to secure something nice for his messmates. One day the timid and bashful fourth sergeant began to throw out some mysterious innuendoes of something that would cause us all to rejoice, which was to arrive soon, and sure enough one evening after dinner we were notified that the lightening express had arrived with a fine chicken nicely dressed and cooked and proposed that we have a supper in honor of the occasion and proudly preparing to add a few bottles of wine to wash it down, but on investigating the case we found that the lightening express had been six days reaching camp, and it was decided that eating supper would be in violation of our camp discipline, so the participation of the fine present was postponed until breakfast of the next day. Breakfast came—dinner followed, but "nary" chicken, and to this day no one has ever disclosed the fate of the memorable bird.

Our company cook was in the habit of dripping a large pot of coffee at night, warming it in the morning and serving it to the men immediately after roll call. One cool frosty morning as the coffee was being served out according to custom, I noticed that the men did not drink it down as freely as usual, some of them supping it as if they were doubtful whether it was Mocha, Java or common Rio. Others were seen to pour the contents of their cups on the ground making remarks neither polished nor polite. Upon investigating the matter it was ascertained that some one had carefully sweetened the coffee with salt previous to its delivery to the men.

Dinner was one of the daily duties of the soldiers which was taught in three easy lessons without any previous study of Hardee's tactics.[25] It did not require any trumpet to insure prompt and full attendance upon the ground at dinner time. It was a curious scene, that of a 100 men dining in camp. There were more tables than there were in a cabinet shop, made of more different materials, and of more different constructions than ever entered the head of a vendor of second hand furniture, and of more different patterns than ever were conceived by the imaginative genius of a clock peddler or vendor of wooden nutmegs. Candle boxes, pickets, fence rails, barrel heads and soap boxes were impressed into service and made to do duty entirely foreign to the original intentions of their first owners.

Some of the men used a table composed of two legs ingeniously placed close enough to hold a tin plate, and this was one of the tables that seemed to hold out the longest and as the men always had the materials handy to form one, it was more universally used than the other.

Our old friend Sylvain T. Daunis was appointed sutler of the regiment and erected a monster tent in our camp where he dispensed such articles as were required by the members of the command.

Boggins, a member of the Natchitoches Rebels, under Capt. Wood, got a little elevated on Christmas day and became quite jolly. In fact, he found himself in an excellent humor, so much so that he felt it to be his duty as a soldier to deliver his sentiments concerning the 18th La. publicly and explicitly in something after this style.

"This is-hic-fine regiment, a-hic-splendid regiment. I got-hic-gloriously tight—before-hic-breakfast, and I-hic-did not get into the guard house—nary time—I slept it off-hic-and I got bully drunk

25. William J. Hardee's *Rifle and Light Infantry Tactics* (Philadelphia, 1855) served as the standard textbook for training infantrymen.

again—and I'm-hic-not in the guard house yet, hic-hurrah for the hic-18th regiment."

Boggins was a great favorite with the boys and had large audiences and was no doubt rejoiced and surprised that he did not get into the guard house, for such a thing never happened to him before, but Christmas saved him. Poor Boggins! he found things more terrible than the guard house a few months later, became a great strategist, and carried his favorite strategy into practice.

This was the only camp at which the men ever rejoiced to be placed on guard, and premiums were often given for a place on the daily guard.

The reason for this was that all who were on guard, on being relieved in the morning, had permission to go to New Orleans and return by 4 o'clock at battalion drill.

The boys very often missed the cars, and on returning they had the honor of a free admission into the guard house,[26] where they remained until their officers procured their release.

Many of the members of our company will remember one evening when two of their associates came in too late and were taken care of by the guard. It was a heavy blow for them, for the guard house then had terrors that no one cared for in after years, and they presented an appearance anything but amiable and dignified.

The captain had them released after he returned from battalion drill, but it was a sore subject to them ever afterwards, as the men of our company boasted that they had steered clear of that building and the idea of being the first ones caught was anything but agreeable to their feelings.

January 3rd, 1862. This morning we were aroused before day and put on the march to Camp Benjamin on the Pontchartrain Railroad.[27] At this camp we were annoyed a great deal on account of the scarcity of water, which had to be brought from the river on the cars.[28] We were here also introduced to some very wise regulations

26. An old store located on the side of the road near the camp became the guard house at Camp Roman (Lucy [La.] *Le Meschacebe*, October 19, 1861).

27. Camp Benjamin, named for Judah P. Benjamin, was established near Hopkins' plantation on Gentilly Ridge about January 1 to accommodate all of the troops of Ruggles' brigade (New Orleans *Daily Picayune*, December 31, 1861; New Orleans *Daily Delta*, January 1, 11, 1862; Lucy [La.] *Le Meschacebe*, January 11, 1862).

28. A private in Company A wrote home: "This Camp is the D—nist hole on earth[,] mud up to ones kness [sic] when it rains & that is not the only thing[.] there is a great scarcety [sic] of water[.] we have to dig wells & they are salty yet we have

emanating from brigade headquarters. One was that no whiskey should be sold in camp, but every soldier, in going to the cars after water, had to pass by three beer saloons, where they could obtain that article of any strength they might desire. Another was that but one man in a company should leave camp at a time, whilst every man in a company could sling a canteen around his neck and go for water and stay away all day if wished. A few days after our arrival the regiment was increased by the addition of the Orleans Cadets, commanded by Capt. Joseph Collins, which became the senior company of the regiment,[29] and also by the Opelousas Volunteers, commanded by Capt. Louis Lestrappes, completing the ten companies.[30]

In all regiments there is, daily, one commissioned officer selected as "officer of the day." This officer was designated by a red sash, and at first none but captains were thus detailed, but they soon began detailing lieutenants, and the privilege of wearing the red sash and keeping order in camp was an object devoutly to be desired by those gentlemen who were allowed but one or two stripes on their collars. Of course, as officers were strict in carrying out daily instructions, so the men were ingenious in contriving ways and means to outwit them. One day our first lieutenant, who was generally designated by us as Uncle John, was the happy wearer of the coveted insignia and had passed away the day in peace and harmony. About sunset he had come to the conclusion that his duties had been performed to the satisfaction of his superior officers, and experiencing that content of mind which a man feels when conscious of having performed his duty, he entered a tent of one of his associates to indulge in a little game of old sledge during the early hours of the night. But just as he had succeeded in scoring six points and held king and tray for the other point, a noise was heard in Capt. Collins' company which was stationed farthest from the guard house, and the cry "put him in the guard house" was heard all around, and a crowd appeared carrying a

to cook with it[.] we do not drink it[.] There is [sic] five men detached to the City to get River Water" (Frederick R. Taber to Mr. and Mrs. A. F. Trust and Lillie, January 11, 1862, in Frederick R. Taber Papers, 1861–1862, Louisiana and Lower Mississippi Valley Collection, Special Collections, Hill Memorial Library, Louisiana State University, Baton Rouge).

29. The Orleans Cadets had been mustered into service on June 19, 1861. They became Company I of the 18th Louisiana (Napier Bartlett, "The Trans-Mississippi," in *Military Record of Louisiana* [Baton Rouge, 1964], 37).

30. The Opelousas Volunteers became Company K.

man apparently by force in the direction of that little tent kept up for the especial purpose of accommodating obstreperous individuals. Uncle John quit his game and, sash over his shoulder, moved majestically up toward the guard house to give necessary directions for the punishment of the troublesome individual and to maintain the dignity and quiet of the camp. The crowd moved on with the prisoner, being increased from the quarters of every company until they reached the headquarters of the guard. The weather was cool, and the men on duty had built a fire, around which they were standing. As the squad who were transporting the prisoner approached, Uncle John was just about giving instructions to put a stop to such riotous proceedings when the troublesome soldier, instead of being brought to him, was thrown on the fire and was soon wrapped in flames.

Our officer of the day ran to the spot to know what that meant, and soon found that the prisoner was composed principally of rags, and on turning round he perceived that about half of the men in the crowd had continued on outside of the lines and were free for that night.

To express the dismay of the worthy officer would require an abler pen than mine, neither will I attempt to put on record Uncle John's emphatic and classic "cuss" words when he regained possession of his feelings sufficiently to speak his sentiments.

Almost from the organization of our company a feud had been kept up between that portion of the men living above and that portion residing below Thibodaux. Frequent quarrels were occasioned, and abuse of those dwelling "en haut" and "en bas" was heard every day. The officers of the company were getting tired of complaints arising out of this foolish strife, and we concluded that the best way to stop it would be to let them fight it out, and I was ordered to let them know that they could settle their fuss in that way. I told them that at two o'clock, whilst we were at dinner, they could sling canteens over their shoulders and go out on the railroad track and fight it out on that line. At the appointed time nearly every man in the company started for the race track. We ate our dinner, and the crowd still remained but appeared very quiet. Shortly after, they began to scatter, some to camp, others to the water carts, but there had been no fight, nor ever afterwards did we hear anything of "en haut le bayou" or "en bas le bayou" but all, both up and down, let their foolish strife sink into oblivion.

February 5th.   J. S. Levron, our orderly sergeant, who had been in the hospital for six weeks, was honorably discharged from service, much to the regret of the whole company. His jovial qualities as a companion, his kindness and amiability had endeared him to all his associates. He subsequently recovered his health, and in 1862, when the Lafourche country was abandoned by the Confederates, he left with the troops, joined Cornay's battery of artillery, but was detailed as clerk at Gen. Mouton's headquarters until the death of the old hero at Mansfield, and was then transferred to the ordnance department as clerk, in which capacity he remained until the war closed, and is now residing in Greenville, Alabama.[31]

During the time we remained at Camp Benjamin, the weather was generally very wet and disagreeable, and the mud was so deep that it was with difficulty that we could get about for several days at a time. On the 10th of January the whole brigade was paraded for the first time and reviewed by Major General Lovell. Gov. Moore, Gen. Ruggles, Gen. Labuzan, Gen. Lewis, and Gen. Jeff Thompson were on the ground assisting in the proceedings.[32] We were also detailed to conduct the Federal prisoners confined in the parish prison to the Jackson Railroad depot, which took up one day of hard and tiresome marching over the pavements of New Orleans, covered about two inches deep with soft mud, reaching camp about ten o'clock at night.

31. Levron joined Captain Florian O. Cornay's 1st Louisiana Battery (St. Mary Cannoneers) and received his parole as a member of the Ordnance Department, District of West Louisiana and Arkansas (CSR, Roll 47).

32. Brigadier General Charles A. Labuzan, of the 2nd Brigade, 1st Division, Louisiana Militia, commanded Camp Lewis and later Camp Roman. Major General John L. Lewis commanded the 1st Division, Louisiana Militia. Brigadier General M. Jeff Thompson, Missouri State Guards, served temporarily as a volunteer staff officer under General Lewis (New Orleans *Daily Crescent,* January 10, 1862; Special Order No. 64, First Division, Louisiana State Troops, July 6, 1861, Louisiana State Records, in War Department Collection of Confederate Records, National Archives Microcopy No. 359, Roll 24, hereinafter cited as M359; Bartlett, *Military Record of Louisiana,* 243–44; New Orleans *Daily Picayune,* January 10, 1862).

In reporting the review, one newspaper said: "The line had a fine, substantial appearance, though many of the men were rather roughly appareled compared with our neat and showy city troops. They looked, however, as if got up more for effectiveness than display. After being reviewed in line the brigade marched by companies, in review, and evinced, for such new troops, a high state of efficiency and drill" (New Orleans *Daily Delta,* January 11, 1862).

Capt. Mouton's company was detailed to conduct the prisoners to North Carolina.[33] We remained in camp until the 13th February, when we received orders to prepare for our departure to some other point of the Confederacy.[34] During the 14th we were occupied in disposing of surplus baggage and preparing for the active scenes of the war that were soon to arise before our eyes and develop realities that far surpassed anything the imagination had yet conceived.

February 14. The following appointments were made in the company occasioned by the discharge of the orderly sergeant, J. S. Levron. R. Savoie to be 1st Sergeant; A. L. St. Martin 2nd Sergeant; L. M. Hargis 3rd Sergeant; T. Robichaux 4th Sergeant; and J. E. Naquin 5th Sergeant; G. Abrebat to be 1st Corporal; J. L. Aucoin 2nd Corporal; P. Thibodaux 3rd Corporal; and L. Gautreaux 4th Corporal.

Before leaving I might as well relate an incident that occurred at Camp Roman in December. An orderly sergeant who had been in the habit of presenting his pass to the guard when he was going out of the lines was promoted to be a lieutenant, which rank relieved him of the necessity of presenting his papers when inclination or duty carried him out of camp.

Having taken the stripes off his sleeve and placed a bar on his collar, he started off towards the city but was halted by the sentinel and ordered to show his pass. Now the shadow of the stripes on the sleeve was more conspicuous than the little bar on the collar, hidden behind a pair of massive whiskers, which had been carefully combed and brushed in the most killing style, and the trouble the unfortunate lieutenant experienced in bringing said bar within the range of vision of the dull-eyed sentinel afforded considerable amusement to those who happened to witness the scene.

February 15. This morning we were marched to the depot of the New Orleans, Jackson, and Great Northern Railroad and halted in an open plain, where the regiment remained during the day and night in the full enjoyment of a rain which was falling most of the

33. The entire regiment escorted the prisoners to the depot on February 6, and Captain Mouton's company went with them as far as Raleigh (New Orleans *Daily Picayune*, February 7, 1862).

34. Following the fall of Forts Henry and Donelson, the Confederate War Department ordered Major General Mansfield Lovell to send five thousand of his best troops to reinforce General Pierre G. T. Beauregard in west Tennessee (*OR*, VI, 823, 825).

time. I was more fortunate than others, having been detailed as officer of a guard, stationed in the depot, where I was protected from the inclement weather.

February 16. The troops embarked on the cars, and at 10 o'clock P.M., we arrived at Canton, Mississippi, where we changed cars and departing, reached Grand Junction, Tennessee, at 4 o'clock P.M., February 17th, when another change of cars was effected, and at 9 o'clock we arrived at the little village of Pocahontas, where the train stopped. On receiving marching orders at Camp Benjamin, we were supplied with three days' rations, and by this time our food was consumed.

About sunrise, noticing a neat white cottage on the outer limits of the town, I determined to try the effect of a Confederate dollar and good looks to obtain something to allay the cravings of my appetite. Entering, I found the major and Capt. Garland already there on the same errand of mercy. We were bountifully supplied with fried pork, corn cakes, and sassafras tea by the kind-hearted and amiable wife and sullen frowns and sour looks from the vinegar-faced husband.

February 18. At nine we again started and ran as far as Chewawly Station and halted. The men being out of rations were becoming clamorous of something to eat, or at least, to be hurried on to their destination. The conductor pretended that he could not move until the train going west had passed, but a rumor obtaining circulation that he was willfully delaying the train, some of the officers approached him on the subject, which scared the poor fellow so badly that his hair became sufficiently self supporting as to stand alone. However, we finally got away and arrived at Corinth at 10 o'clock P.M.

The night was cold, and the men generally spread their blankets in the depot and passed the night therein.

This Corinth which was considered a very important position in the earlier part of the war is situated in the northeastern county of Mississippi within 4 miles of the Tennessee line and at the junction of the Memphis and Chattanooga Railroad with the Ohio and Mobile Railroad. It was a small place of some 300 or 400 inhabitants, containing several stores and one large hotel.

The surrounding country was poor and thinly settled, and if there ever was a drink of good water in the place none of us had the good fortune to obtain it. Capt. Gourdain ordered a breakfast for our company at the Tishimingo Hotel and by mid-day they had all partaken of a good meal.

During the day we were quartered in a church, the other companies being stationed in different parts of the village.

February 20.   The regiment was moved out about one mile and encamped, but our company being detailed as provost marshal guard returned to Corinth the next morning.

February 21.   Major Bush, Capt. Gourdain and Lieut. Shepherd were ordered out to reconnoitre the advance positions on the Tennessee River, returned on the 23d, and reported Pittsburg Landing as the most eligible position for an advance guard.

February 25.   Corporal Leoni Gautreaux was honorably discharged from service on account of ill health. A good soldier and agreeable companion, an honest and upright man was lost to the company, and he left regretted by all his companions. Having returned to his home, he died shortly afterwards.

February 26.   Struck half of our tents and leaving Company K to guard the remainder, we departed towards Pittsburg Landing, distant about 20 miles.[35]

February 28.   Arrived at Pittsburg Landing on the Tennessee River. This was simply a shipping point. There were but two buildings, one on the bank of the river, and the other about 200 yards back. The road is cut down through the bluffs which are 100 feet above highwater mark. A tract of land about 200 yards wide and a half mile in length along the river was cleared and cultivated; behind was dense woods. Our company, with that of Capt. Druilhet, was stationed in the ravine between the two dwellings, whilst the remaining seven companies were encamped in the woods behind the open field—all being invisible from the river. In the evening I was ordered to take a detail of men and picket the point near the mouth of Owl Creek about one mile and a half down the river.

In posting my sentinels in such position as to best conceal them from view, I stowed them away so snugly that when I undertook to relieve them in the darkness, I hunted around half an hour before I could find one of the posts.

March 1.   Being relieved, I returned to camp and partook of a

35. General Ruggles had ordered the 18th Louisiana, Miles Artillery, and a cavalry detachment (2nd Mississippi Cavalry Battalion?) to Pittsburg Landing to observe and defend the area (*ibid.*, VII, 909).

good breakfast. We had been fairing sumptuously since we reached Corinth as we could obtain anything we wanted at very low prices.

J. V. Knoblock was appointed corporal in place of L. Gautreaux, discharged.

March 1, 1862. Pittsburg Landing, Tennessee River. Miles Artillery, commanded by Capt. Claude Gibson,[36] came in the morning and posted two howitzer pieces on the bank of the river about 100 yards below our camp and four other pieces about 300 yards further up the river on a high and conspicuous bluff.[37]

About 12 o'clock N., the report was circulated that "gun boats were coming," and upon looking down the river two columns of black smoke curling over the tree tops attested the correctness of the statement.[38] As they advanced up the river, apparently unconscious of any enemy, the pieces on the bluff above us opened on them. They made a few shots which were doubtless well aimed but which fell short of their mark some 200 or 300 yards. As soon as the position of the battery w,as exposed, the boats prepared for action. We were immediately called to arms, and whilst the officers were endeavoring to form their companies the shells were whizzing over our heads, causing every one of us to bow down just at the moment we were commanded to "eyes right," to jump backwards at the command of "right dress." Our captain, who seldom lost the equilibrium of his mind, became a little excited on the occasion, but the line was finally formed. It was the first time any of us had ever heard the peculiar music of a bomb shell, and I believe without exception every man thought he was going to be hit just below the ear; at least every fellow first bowed his head and then came down on his knee. Solemn as the affair was likely to be, I know that several of us could not keep from laughing at the sudden and uniform movement of everyone as a shell passed over our heads.

36. The Miles Artillery had left New Orleans for Columbus, Kentucky, on February 8, 1862 (New Orleans *Daily Picayune,* February 9, 1862).

37. Second Lieutenant Charles A. Montaldo commanded the two 12-pounder howitzers of the Miles Artillery, and Junior 1st Lieutenant E. D. Terrebonne had charge of the four 6-pounder rifled pieces located about a thousand yards south of the howitzers (CSR, Roll 395).

38. The two Federal gunboats were the *Tyler,* Lieutenant William Gwin, and the *Lexington,* Lieutenant James W. Shirk (*Official Records of the Union and Confederate Navies in the War of the Rebellion* [Washington, D.C., 1894–1922], Series I, Vol. XXII, p. 643, hereinafter cited as *OR, Navies.* Unless otherwise indicated, all citations are to Series I).

A few well-directed shots from the boats caused the battery above to fall back, whilst the two howitzers, from not being properly prepared, were not fired at all, and all fell back into the woods.[39]

Col. Mouton, who was absent at the beginning, came up and assumed command. Our company was ordered to a rifle pit that was being made on the bank of the river in front of our camp, but not being completed, we were unable to protect the men in it and being too far from the boats to have any effect upon them with our arms and visible to the gunners who were now firing upon us, we were withdrawn to the rear, not however until two or three shots passed so close to us that we could feel the wind raising the hair on our heads. Had one of the shots been a couple of feet lower it would have enfiladed the company and settled up the accounts of a good many of us.

The troops were then all withdrawn to the woods behind the field and concealed. The enemy, after shelling the woods in every direction, sent a detachment of about 100 men on shore.[40] Having never seen but our company and the battery, it is presumed that they imagined the force on land to be small and to have retreated. As soon as they reached the top of the hill, forming into line, they advanced towards the woods, where they were met by the fire of the whole

39. Lieutenant Montaldo withdrew his howitzers without firing a shot after the gunboats opened on his position. During a court-martial in mid-April, he testified that he did not have enough men or the proper implements to work his guns. The rifled section opened with three of its pieces and exchanged rounds with the gunboats for ten to fifteen minutes before withdrawing. Testimony in the court-martial proceedings of Montaldo reflects badly on Captain Gibson's leadership. The court concluded: "It appears from the evidence that the company was not in a state of preparation either as to discipline, numbers, instruction or appliances, thereby not only hazarding the lives of the men entrusted to these officers, but the cause they were engaged in defending." General Pierre G. T. Beauregard's reaction to the proceedings was even stronger: "The evidence in the case manifestly shows a degree of culpability and neglect of duty on part of Captain Gibson which should have caused him to exercise more forebearance toward Lieut Montaldo—To have ordered the Lieut to the front with a mounted stovepipe would have been an absurdity perhaps equal to but not greater than with Howitzers which it was impossible (as shown by the evidence) to discharge." The battery was never again engaged with the enemy and ceased to exist after its consolidation with a Missouri battery on June 30, 1862 (CSR, Roll 395; Bergeron, *Guide to Louisiana Confederate Military Units*, 32).

40. Two boats from each gunboat took ashore portions of two crews and detachments of Companies C and K, 32nd Illinois Infantry Regiment (sharpshooters) (*OR, Navies, XXII*, 644).

regiment. The enemy precipitately rushed to their boats, our men following them closely, and as they were obliged to embark on small crafts, the gun boats not being able to get nearer than 50 yards of the shore, they became good marks for our men, who could fire from the top of the steep banks and step back out of their sight whilst they were reloading their pieces.[41] The gun boats were wooden affairs, and our riflemen silenced their pieces easily.[42] Had the battery been present then we could have sunk them or compelled a surrender. As it was, they floated off down the river and did not use their engines until the current had carried them a mile or more below the scene of action. Our loss was about a dozen killed and wounded.[43] The enemy report 12 killed and 60 odd wounded and missing.[44] The missing with three exceptions were all in the Tennessee River.

Lieutenant Lavery[45] of the Orleans Cadets was shot through the thigh, and Lieut Watt[46] of Capt. Huntington's company was slightly injured by a shell, these being the only officers hurt. The engagement lasted three hours. The shells of the enemy being thrown promiscuously throughout the woods played havoc with the branches of trees, frequently cutting them off over our heads. Once whilst we were posted in the road some distance back, Lieutenant Gautreau remarked that whilst we were doing nothing, he might as well stand behind a tree which was close by, and he accordingly took that position, but no sooner had he posted himself than a shot cut off a limb which came tumbling down at his feet and caused him to so completely change his mind that he was satisfied the open road was the safest place.

41. Later the Federals reported that they had fought two infantry regiments and one cavalry regiment (*ibid.*).

42. Lieutenant Gwin wrote that the *Tyler* was exposed to "a tremendous fire of musketry" and was "perfectly riddled with balls" (*ibid.*).

43. The 18th lost approximately seven men killed and thirteen wounded (New Orleans *Daily Picayune*, March 9, 11, 1862).

44. The Federals reported losing two men killed, six wounded, and three missing (*OR, Navies*, XXII, 645, 646).

45. First Lieutenant John T. Lavery. One account stated that when he was wounded, he refused to leave the field, and "having borrowed a Maynard rifle, he leaned against a sapling, and blazed away as hard as he could" (New Orleans *Daily Picayune*, March 11, 1862).

46. First Lieutenant Andrew J. Watt "was struck with an iron ring of a grape stand, which had glanced from a tree, bruising his leg very severely, but did not prevent him from following up the fight" (*ibid.*).

The major had a servant who was mounted and had directions to watch his master and be near with his horse in case of necessity. It would be difficult to tell how many positions Eugene assumed in order to keep in view of his master and not come in contact with a shell, and how little time it took him to do it.

As we were falling back from the rifle pit, one of the members of our company who was over six feet high stopped behind a tree which was not quite so large as his body, and the way in which he extended his arms over his head so as to make his size as diminutive as the tree was ludicrous in the extreme. When it was ascertained that the shots were all flying over our heads, we could look with wonder and admiration upon the scene, and although it was a small affair to what we subsequently experienced, it was one of intense interest to us all.

Tradition, however, relates that a member of our company, unable to appreciate any of the sublimity of the scene, upon seeing some of the artillery horses going to the rear, mounted one of them, but failing to make him travel fast enough abandoned him and pursued his way on foot, having had the crupper of his saddle and the visor of his kepi knocked off by shells. At least he so reported and he ought to have known all about it.

Pittsburg Landing, March 1st, 1862. After the retreat of the gun boats, Col. Mouton, leaving Companies C and D as a picket guard, marched the remainder of the regiment to Shiloh Church, where we remained over night.

This edifice was a small log building situated on a high piece of land in the woods some three miles from Pittsburg Landing. Adjacent to the church was the cemetery which the citizens of the vicinity used as their burial ground.

March 2. The gun boats returned up the river and shelled our camp for several hours, and afterwards sent a flag of truce on shore to ascertain if their dead of yesterday had been buried.

The regiment was moved out towards the river and kept in line during the forenoon. At midday we returned to the church and stood there two hours, whilst the rain came down in torrents. Towards evening we fell back to Lick Creek and encamped nearby that stream. About dusk the rain changed into snow, and as we had not brought our tents we were exposed to the inclement weather the whole night. Lieutenant Collins and myself obtained permission to go to a neighboring house and started, but no sooner had we left the camp than we found the night so dark that we could not see a foot before us, and we returned to the fires. About midnight the snow ceased falling, and Sergeant Savoie and myself scraped off a piece of ground before the fire, where we lay down, the one next to the blazing pile burning whilst the other was freezing. However, by continually swapping sides, we managed to pass away the night as comfortably as if we had been freezing or burning all the time without the variations. The other men had about as pleasant a night of it as we did.

March 3. This morning I was detailed to go on a picket with Sergeant St. Martin and about 10 men of our company.

The post assigned to us was near a cabin, and, having purchased a side of bacon and a peck of meal, we hired the lady of the house to cook it for us. This was the first time in my life that I ever ate a piece of fat pork with any satisfaction, but hunger, cold and excitement effects wonders in a man's appetite.

For a Confederate five we rented the house, and whilst the owners went off to stay over night with their neighbors, we passed a comfortable watch around the fireside. The next morning we gave up the cabin as we found it. I have often thought that if this family kept up their kindness during the war that their household furniture must have become very limited in quantity.

March 4. This morning our company fell back behind the little village of Monterey and established Camp Bush, where the regiment came in a day or two afterwards.

During our march to Pittsburg Landing, one set of company officers by some means were without a cook, and out of the abundance in our mess we supplied them for several days. In those days provisions were cheap and plentiful, and we thought nothing of the matter at the time.

On the third, Lieutenant Gautreau had been sent back on picket duty near Shiloh Church, and before he was relieved and reached camp this morning, our company was gone. Being hungry, as pickets generally are when they come off duty, he naturally began to look around for something to satisfy the cravings of his appetite.

Seeing a lieutenant,[47] whom we had fed at our table during the march out, quietly sipping a cup of coffee and eating his breakfast, Lieutenant G., out of the fullness of his heart, went to where he was and informed him that his mess had left, that he was just off

47. From succeeding descriptions by Grisamore, the editor has determined that this was Second Lieutenant J. D. Etie of Company D (CSR, Roll 292).

picket, and had had no breakfast. But the lieutenant could not take a hint and continued on in the even tenor of his way without ever saying so much as "have a cup of coffee," which so disgusted Gautreau that he went off and made his situation known to Capt. Wood, who immediately had a breakfast prepared for him.

Poor Gautreau never forgave the treatment he received that morning, and all the eloquence his friends could bring to bear on the subject never convinced him that any man's head could be so thick as not to take such a hint as he gave the lieutenant, and when any of us wished to hear Gautreau use "cuss words," we had only to ask him to invite his friend Lieutenant ——— over to dinner.

Monterey was a village of half a dozen houses about half way from Corinth to Pittsburg Landing. Crossroads led to those two places as well as Farmington, Hamburg and Purdy. Our camp was about one mile from Monterey on the road to Corinth.

As soon as the regiment came up, our tents were brought to us and fitted up; Company K, which had been left in Corinth, came out; and we fixed up ourselves as comfortably as possible. Our duties were onerous and constant. Four or five pickets were kept constantly and nearly every day one or more companies were sent off on a scouting expedition.

The enemy under Gen. Grant was landing and establishing themselves at Pittsburg Landing,[48] and we alone had all the roads to watch, aided by one company of cavalry from Alabama commanded, I believe, by Capt., afterwards Gen., Clanton.[49] The weather was disagreeable, rain or snow falling almost daily.

March 10th. Private John Ferret was honorably discharged from service for disability on account of too advanced age to perform military service.

March 15th. Thomas J. Daunis, who had been left in hospital in New Orleans, was honorably discharged from service on account of ill health. He subsequently served in Capt. Whitaker's company on the Bayou Teche and in the Opelousas country.[50]

---

48. The Federals did not land in force until March 16–17 (*OR*, Vol. X, Pt. 1, p. 25).

49. The 1st Alabama Cavalry Regiment, Colonel James H. Clanton (Willis Brewer, *Alabama: Her History, Resources, War Record, and Public Men* [Montgomery, 1872], 677).

50. Captain William A. Whitaker commanded Company C, 7th Louisiana Cavalry Regiment, and his men performed scouting duty in the areas named during the latter months of the war (Bergeron, *Guide to Louisiana Confederate Military Units*, 50–51).

About this time a pistol in the hands of Capt. Gourdain, which he was examining, accidently discharged itself, the ball passing through the thigh of Private Augustave Theriot. The wound was a flesh one but kept Theriot in hospital until after the battle of Shiloh, when he was sent home with the other wounded to recuperate.[51]

Camp near Monterey, March 1862. One night we were aroused and ordered to prepare rations for three days. The news circulated that the enemy had landed some distance down the river and were marching on Purdy, a small place on the railroad leading to Columbus.[52] At 10 o'clock we were en route. Capt. Collins' [company moved] ahead as pioneers.

After marching some three or four miles until we reached the direct road to Purdy, the rain began to fall in torrents. We were halted in an old field when some of us protected ourselves in some old buildings, whilst others succeeded in starting big fires of fence rails and endeavored to dry themselves as much as they could.

On the cessation of the rain, we were returned to camp,[53] wading through creeks and bottoms in which the water was up almost to our arms. Many of the "short" boys had to transport their guns and cartridge boxes over their heads to protect them from the water. Reaching camp about dusk, we all dried our clothes around the fires and awoke the next morning to find the earth covered with snow. Capt. Collins, whose company had gone further than the remainder of the regiment, did not arrive until late at night, and some of the men did not reach camp until the subsequent day.

A couple of days afterwards Major Bush was ordered on a scout towards Hamburg, a village about six miles above Pittsburg Landing on the Tennessee River, taking with him the companies of Capt.

---

51. Captain Wood was present and quickly took care of the wound (Lucy [La.] *Le Meschacebe*, March 29, 1862).

52. A Union force under Brigadier General Lew Wallace disembarked at Crump's Landing on March 12 with the mission of destroying part of the Mobile and Ohio Railroad near Purdy. Confederate troops began to concentrate at Purdy under Brigadier General Adley H. Gladden, and on March 13 the 18th Louisiana received orders to march toward that town. The regiment left on the morning of the following day (*OR*, Vol. X, Pt. 1, pp. 9–10, and Pt. 2, pp. 319–20; Lucy [La.] *Le Meschacebe*, March 29, 1862).

53. Having destroyed part of the railroad north of Purdy, the Union troops returned to Crump's Landing. Gladden sent Mouton orders to halt his regiment and later ordered the regiment to return to Monterey (*OR*, Vol. X, Pt. 1, pp. 10, 12; Lucy [La.] *Le Meschacebe*, March 29, 1862).

Gourdain and Capt. Hayes. Arriving within three or four miles of Hamburg, we were halted and encamped. Capt. Gourdain was ordered to take 20 men and proceed to Hamburg, enter the town, and obtain all the information possible concerning the movements of the enemy's gun boats, with permission not to enter the town until after dark, should he think it expedient to do so.

Capt. Hayes was sent with the same complement of men to a road which led to the river about half way from Harrisburg to Pittsburg Landing, and to follow the said road to the river and ascertain if the enemy had made any landing in that vicinity. I was then started off with six or seven men to examine the country lying between the two directions taken by the captains as to the probability of troops marching through the woods and over the hills.

I returned before dark and was sent on picket about a half mile on the Hamburg road. Taking six men, I established myself upon a level space of woodland from which a good view of the road could be obtained and, placing two men on their posts, quietly awaited events.

I expected the captain back on that road by ten o'clock, but on his not appearing at that time, I concluded that he had deemed it expedient not to enter the village until dusk and gave him until one o'clock to return.

Time passed away and no news of the captain. At two o'clock I awakened all my men and stationed them so as to command a good view, with instructions to keep a close look out. I was under the impression that the whole detail might have been captured and that the enemy, obtaining the information that a small detachment was in the woods nearby, might make an attempt to capture us. My suspense, however, was soon relieved by the rain and darkness, the one falling in torrents, the other dense enough to be felt. Thunder and lightning accompanied the rain, each flash revealing six men with white blankets around them, resembling ghosts, standing under the trees.

Daylight at length came, and I sent to camp to know if any information had been had of Capt. Gourdain and his men and learned that they had been in camp since 9 o'clock. Excited with his wonderful achievements of marching into a friendly town and then marching out again, he got lost on his return and was piloted to the camp by a citizen, going entirely around my post.

"Uncle John," who was officer of the day, visited all the other posts after Gourdain's return, and when I was going to give him a left handed blessing about neglecting his duty, he tried to smooth it over by insinuating that he "knew I was all right" and "didn't think it worth while." I never yet have been able to discover what right a captain of a company had to get lost when there was a plain, smooth road to conduct him to his destination.

The next day we returned to camp, wading creeks and valleys. A little rain would cause the streams to rise three to six feet in a couple of hours, and we seldom went two miles without wading some of them.

A lot of cavalry had been sent out towards Pittsburg Landing as pickets, the enemy under Grant having landed at that point.[54]

I was on picket duty on the road to Hamburg. About one o'clock A.M., the sentinel on the advanced post halted someone whom I had brought up to me. He proved to be one of the cavalry without any hat, and whilst he was telling of a terrible fight they had been engaged in, another came and finally some half a dozen arrived. Sending them into camp, we had quiet the rest of our watch. It appeared afterwards that our cavalry had encamped near Shiloh Church and that a scouting party of the enemy came along, when the firing commenced. The principal contest appears to have been not who could maintain the ground but who could get away soonest, the Confederates toward Monterey.[55] Being relieved by the 16th La. Regiment, we returned to Corinth about the 20th.

March 25.   Private C. A. Engeron was honorably discharged from service on account of disability to perform military duty.

March 27.   Private Olezimon Jeandron died in the hospital at Corinth and was buried in the cemetery adjoining that town.

Corinth, March 1862.   On our arrival at Corinth, we were informed that a brigade had been formed of which ours was the senior regiment, Col. Mouton thus becoming brigade commander.[56] About

---

54. Brigadier General William T. Sherman's division disembarked at Pittsburg Landing on March 16, and soon most of the Union army joined it there (*OR*, Vol. X, Pt. 1, p. 25).

55. On the night of March 16, a detachment of Federal cavalry under Lieutenant Colonel Thomas T. Hatch skirmished with five companies of Tennessee cavalrymen. The Federals took two men prisoner and had four of their own men wounded (*ibid.*, 25, 28).

56. About March 9, Mouton had been placed in command of the 4th Brigade, I Corps (Ruggles), Second Grand Division, Army of the Mississippi Valley. His brigade consisted of the 18th Louisiana, 4th Louisiana Infantry Regiment, Lieutenant Col-

the 21st, he assumed command and selecting Capt. Sanders,[57] our regimental quartermaster, as his quartermaster, Lieutenant Col. Alfred Roman, commanding our regiment, appointed myself as acting quartermaster for the regiment. But a few days afterwards, owing to the supposed loud talking of other parties, the brigade organizations were changed, and we were placed in a new one commanded by Col. Preston Pond of the 16th La., an unfortunate change it proved to the 18th, as its surviving members well know. On Col. Mouton's resuming command of the regiment, he dispatched Capt. Sanders to New Orleans for funds to pay the troops.

April 1st. Belisaire Achee and F. J. Gaudet were appointed corporals to fill vacancies, and M. S. Holcombe, private, was transferred to Company A of the 17th Alabama Regiment, of which his brother was captain.[58]

There was considerable sickness in the regiment about this period, principally pneumonia. We lost two officers, Lieut. Owings[59] of the Natchitoches Rebels and Lieut. Anselm[60] of the St. Landry Volunteers, and several men.

Dr. E. L. Lashbrook[61] arrived a few days ago, and also Dr. R. O. Butler,[62] who were welcome visitors to our camp. Our brigade was now composed of the 16th La., Col. Pond acting brigade commander; the 17th La., Col. Heard; the 18th, Col. Mouton; the 19th, Col. Hodges; the 38th (I think) Tennessee, Col. Looney; and the Orleans Guard Battalion, Major ———.[63]

onel F. W. Desha's 7th Arkansas Infantry Battalion, and Captain C. P. Gage's Alabama Battery (*OR*, Vol. X, Pt. 2, p. 307; St. Charles *L'Avant-Coureur*, March 22, 1862).

57. Captain R. W. Sanders, formerly of Company D (CSR, Roll 296).

58. Captain Edward P. Holcombe commanded Company A, 17th Alabama Infantry Regiment (Brewer, *Alabama*, 617).

59. First Lieutenant William P. Owings (CSR, Roll 295).

60. Second Lieutenant Jacob Anselm (*ibid.*, Roll 290).

61. Dr. Lashbrook, a native of Maysville, Kentucky, had moved to Thibodaux in 1854. In 1858, he was elected as a representative from Lafourche Parish to the state legislature. He supported John C. Breckinridge for president in 1860. Later in the war, he became surgeon of the 26th Louisiana Infantry Regiment (*Weekly Thibodaux Sentinel*, May 23, 30, 1868; CSR, Roll 336).

62. Dr. Butler, also of Thibodaux, later volunteered for duty in the field hospitals at Shiloh (Eighth Census of the United States, 1860: Population Schedules, Lafourche Parish, National Archives Microcopy No. 653, Roll 413; *OR*, Vol. X, Pt. 1, p. 469).

63. The 38th Tennessee Infantry Regiment was commanded by Colonel R. F. Looney and the Orleans Guard Battalion by Major Leon Queyrouze. The brigade also included Captain William H. Ketchum's Alabama Battery (*OR*, Vol. X, Pt. 1, p. 382).

Louisiana, Mississippi, and Alabama
Map by Bobbie Young

On the morning of the 3rd we took up our march towards the front.[64] Capt. Sanders having just returned from New Orleans acted as aide-de-camp to Col. Mouton, leaving me acting quartermaster. The first day we only moved about four miles and camped, taking but half our baggage and trains.

It was late at night before the wagons reached the camp of the regiment, when Dr. L. and myself spread ourselves under a blanket at the root of a tree and slept away the night.

April 4th. This morning as the troops were getting into line, the rain began to fall and continued to do so long enough to make the roads muddy and disagreeable. Passing through Monterey, we were halted about two miles beyond in an open plain. I never can forget the sensations I experienced while we were standing there and some staff officers came riding by us and, each one displaying a flag, announced, "The battle flag of Gen. Hardee,"[65] "the battle flag of Gen. Polk,"[66] "Gen. Johnston's[67] battle flag," etc., etc. Then the regiments of the brigade were drawn up separately, and the beautiful and dignified address of Gen. Albert Sidney Johnston was read to the soldiers and received with loud and hearty cheers.[68] During the day

64. On April 3, Ruggles received orders to prepare his division to move at 6:00 the next morning. His men were to take "five days' cooked rations (three in haversack, two in wagons) and 100 rounds of ammunition to each man and 200 rounds for each piece of artillery. Two tents will be allowed each company" (*ibid.*, Pt. 2, p. 388).

65. Major General William J. Hardee commanded the III Corps, which consisted of three brigades (*ibid.*, Pt. 1, p. 383).

66. Major General Leonidas Polk commanded the I Corps, which consisted of two divisions of two brigades each (*ibid.*, 382).

67. General Albert Sidney Johnston commanded the Army of the Mississippi.

68. The proclamation read to the soldiers of the army was as follows:

Soldiers of the Army of the Mississippi:
I have put you in motion to offer battle to the invaders of your country. With the resolution and disciplined valor becoming men fighting, as you are, for all worth living or dying for, you can but march to a decisive victory over the agrarian mercenaries sent to subjugate and despoil you of your liberties, property, and honor. Remember the precious stake involved; remember the dependence of your mothers, your wives, your sisters, and your children on the result; remember the fair, broad, abounding land, the happy homes, and the ties that would be desolated by your defeat.
The eyes and hopes of eight millions of people rest upon you. You are expected to show yourselves worthy of your race and lineage; worthy of the women of the South, whose noble devotion in this war has never been exceeded in any time. With such incentives to brave deeds and with the trust

numbers of prisoners were occasionally passed through our column towards the rear, showing that our advance was busily engaged in taking in out of the rain the stray pickets and scouts of the enemy.[69] At night the troops were encamped, but it was again near midnight ere I reached them with my wagons. Being unable to find my own messmates, Capt. Sanders, who was fruitlessly engaged in the same business, and myself got into one of the wagons in which the officers of our company had nicely rolled up their bedding. "Uncle John" had a large oil cloth which we spread over us, but we had hardly got ourselves comfortably arranged before it began to rain. As the wagon was not covered, we obtained all the benefits of the "pluvial drops," and before daylight ourselves and our bedding were nicely dampened. The other officers, tired of waiting, had stowed themselves away with the men as best they could. Daylight at length came. I told my bedfellow that I was in for a glorious blessing from the other officers of my company when they found their bedding all wet, but I was careful to say nothing about it at the time and thus to keep off the evil day as long as possible.

April 5th. This morning it was late ere the troops were put in motion. As we had left with three days cooked rations, our provisions were getting scarce, and a detail was left with the commissary train to cook. The march was slow and tedious, the roads being blocked with wagons and advancing troops. At sunset I reached the camp of our brigade, being in line near the enemy on the left of the road leading from Purdy to Pittsburg Landing. Col. Mouton immediately ordered me back to bring up a wagon with cooked rations. It was with difficulty that I could get back on horseback. The roads were full of the troops of Gen. Polk's Division and the numerous wagon trains. However, I finally got a start, but after striving and working until midnight, I was compelled to halt. It was a beautiful clear night, and when I awoke in the morning I found everything covered with a white frost.

---

that God is with us, your general will lead you confidently to the combat, assured of success (*ibid.*, Pt. 2, p. 389).

69. On April 4, Colonel Clanton's 1st Alabama Cavalry skirmished with the Union pickets and captured Major LeRoy Crockett, 72nd Ohio Infantry Regiment, one lieutenant and one private of the same regiment, and one lieutenant and seven men of the 70th Ohio Infantry Regiment (*ibid.*, Pt. 1, pp. 90, 93; *Le Meschacebe*, April 19, 1862).

The whole army was encamped in line of battle extending from Lick Run to Owl Creek, a distance of four or five miles, and directly in front of the enemy, whose scouts and advance pickets had all been driven in. The appearance of day light was awaited with anxiety and suspense for the bloody work to begin.

Shiloh, April 6th, 1862. The morning broke with a clear and cloudless sky. As soon as the light began to drive away the darkness the report of rifles announced that our skirmishers were moving on the enemy's lines, and by the time the sun appeared, their reports were heard from left to right the whole length of the army.

After vainly endeavoring to reach the company with my wagons, I left them by the road side and proceeded in search of it. During my ride forward I passed the headquarters of Gen. Beauregard,[70] who was nervously engaged in sending off couriers in different directions, and those of Gen. Polk and finally those of Gen. Sidney Johnston. Here I stopped for a moment to obtain a look of the honest and solemn face of the commanding general, then advancing to glory and to death. Being directed always to the left, I hurried onward until stopped by heavy firing in my front, which proved to be an attack upon the enemy by the brigade of the subsequently famous Pat Cleburne,[71] who after a severe and bloody contest of 30 minutes, drove the enemy from his position. Finding myself ahead of Pond's brigade, I went towards the rear, and, finally coming up with our artillery train, I left my horse and was shortly afterwards with the members of my company. We were kept moving forward, being, I think, upon the extreme left, as I never saw any of our troops left of us, and part of the time we were on the banks of Owl Creek. Passing through the first line of the enemy's camp, we reached the second line without any engagement. Here we found ovens full of hot loaves of bread, enough to supply every man in the company with one, and some of the men finding a jar of butter, we all had a good breakfast. Whilst waiting here the officers went into some of the tents and soon fitted up all the men with knives, forks, spoons, canteens, haversacks, etc., besides cigars for all who desired to smoke. Coming up to a sutler's stand, we obtained a quantity of sardines, fruits, and other good things, amply sufficient to scare away all symptoms of hunger.

70. General Pierre G. T. Beauregard served as second-in-command to General Johnston.

71. Brigadier General Patrick R. Cleburne commanded the 2nd Brigade of Hardee's Corps (*OR*, Vol. X, Pt. 1, p. 383).

By this time the battle was raging fearfully on our front and right. There was every appearance of the most complete surprise of the enemy, as we found the pots on the fire with breakfast cooking in them, the wash tubs with clothes in them, and everything topsy turvy throughout his camp. Still advancing at about one o'clock, we came up to a line of the enemy engaged with Hardee's Division. They were in line almost perpendicular to us and as soon as we passed around a thick cluster of woods, Col. Mouton ordered our regiment to charge; the enemy immediately began to retreat and were in the act of surrendering when Hardee's troops, seeing us advance, began firing upon us. Our two right companies were dressed in blue, and we were taken for Yankees. Being obliged to fall back, the enemy effected his escape. By this unfortunate mistake, Capt. Huntington was mortally wounded, and Wm. Burk of our company slightly injured in the leg.[72] We are again moved forward until about 3 o'clock, when we again come upon the enemy.

We were in line in a deep ravine standing almost perpendicular to the enemy; the Orleans Guard Battalion was on our left and the 16th La. on our right but standing so as to front the enemy.

It was rumored along the line that we were to charge the battery, and Col. Pond, coming along, remarked to Col. Mouton that "Gen. Hardee says that we must silence that battery."[73] Immediately Col. Mouton gave the order in his loud and commanding voice, "Battalion left half wheel, march," when the regiment rushed up the side of the ravine and formed itself in an open field about 250 yards from the enemy, who was strongly posted in a line three times our length. Looking in vain on our right for the support of the 16th Regiment and upon our left for the aid of the Orleans Guard Battalion, the 18th rushed forward with a loud cheer to the attack. Before we had gone 50 yards the battery opened upon us, and in our company fell Ama-

72. The 27th Tennessee Infantry Regiment of Cleburne's brigade was the unit that fired on the 18th Louisiana. This fire killed one man and wounded three others, not including Captain Huntington (Alfred Roman, *The Military Operations of General Beauregard* [New York, 1884], I, 302; *OR*, Vol. X, Pt. 1, p. 521).

73. Upon receiving orders that his regiment was to attack the enemy battery, Colonel Mouton sent Captain Druilhet and twelve men of Company A to reconnoiter the Union position. Druilhet reported that three regiments supported the battery. Mouton, anxious about the lives of his men, asked Pond whether the order was final, and the latter replied that it was, having apparently come from General Hardee. Mouton then ordered his men forward (Lucy [La.] *Le Meschacebe*, April 19, 1862; *OR*, Vol. X, Pt. 1, pp. 517, 521–22).

deo Abadie and Victor Paris. Whether any other companies suffered loss by this fire I am not able to say. This, however, did not check our advance, and we proceeded onward to within 100 or 150 yards of the enemy's line, when he opened upon us with a terrific fire of musketry. His line being thrice our length,[74] the effect of his fire immediately checked our men, who halted and returned the fire. Our company was next to the flag of our regiment, and the bullets rang about our ears like bees swarming. Once only I looked behind me to see Col. Mouton's horse falling from under him. In our front I perceived the battery moving away and the lines of the enemy wavering, but as two thirds of his force was receiving no injury but enfilading us with terrible effect, the order to retreat was given.

As we were falling back to our original position, the 16th La. made its appearance on the top of the hill where we had expected to find it to join us in the attack. As soon as we had fallen back into the ravine, the Orleans Guard Battalion was ordered up only to be butchered as we were without effecting anything.[75]

Reaching the ravine, I found Lieutenant Gautreau badly and Capt. Gourdain slightly wounded.

Lieut. Collins and myself gathered together the few men belonging to our company and rendered what assistance we could to the wounded. There I found Col. Mouton actually shedding tears of mortification and sorrow over the loss of the men of whom he was so proud. We were then moved backward, and, after countermarching upon a hill to our rear, we had the sad satisfaction of seeing a brigade of Hardee's troops properly brought up and driving the enemy away. But night coming on, the battleground upon which our men lay was between the two lines.

We were encamped in a narrow ravine, and at dusk a small squad of us went into a neighboring sutler's tent and procured a lot of cakes, upon which we made our supper.

Bags of Irish potatoes and sacks of coffee were lying around, but being forbidden to light fires, we, of course, could make no use of them. Tired and sad we lay down and endeavored to obtain a little rest, but before midnight the rain began to fall, and the agonizing

74. The Union units here were the 8th and 9th Illinois and the 13th Iowa Infantry regiments of Brigadier General John A. McClernand's division and Battery D, 1st Illinois Artillery Regiment (OR, Vol. X, Pt. 1, pp. 118, 124, 125, 132).

75. For a description of the attack by the Orleans Guard Battalion, see Bartlett, "Louisiana Troops in the West," in Military Record of Louisiana, 18–19.

voices of the wounded were heard in distressing cries all night long. Attempts were frequently made to render assistance to our wounded but without success, as they were in the range of the enemy's pickets and even the Chaplain of the Orleans Guard Battalion was fired upon and driven away whilst endeavoring to administer aid and consolation to the dying.[76]

The men sheltered themselves from the rain in various ways. But few of them had any blankets or covering, having thrown everything away except their arms. I remember that myself and Justilien Gros made a stack of guns and extended a blanket over it; we sat underneath the little shelter it afforded. Many others, however, had no protection from the inclement weather. We were so near the river that we could easily distinguish the sound of the engineer's bells on the steamers as they were landing in our front. It was afterwards said, but I do not know with what degree of correctness, that our brigade had encamped a full half mile ahead of any other portion of the troops. At all events, we had to go full that distance to the rear the next morning to find any of them. The Tennessee regiment of our brigade came up that night and was placed in position with us for the first time since the morning. I never learned how it was that this and the Crescent Regiment were never with the remaining portion of the brigade. Such was the fact, however.[77]

Shiloh, April 6th, 1862. The result of the charge made upon the enemy by the 18th Regiment was disastrous, especially to our company. The loss of officers and men killed, wounded, and captured was about 200.[78] Captains Wood of Cloutierville and Lestrappes of Opelousas were killed; and Lieutenant LeBoeuf of St. James was wounded and died subsequently in Louisville; Lieutenant Bullard of Opelousas wounded and died afterwards in St. Louis; Lieutenant Young of New Orleans wounded and captured; and Captains Gourdain of Thibodaux, Collins of New Orleans, and Lieutenants Clou-

76. Father François Isidore Turgis, a native of France and a pastor of St. Anthony's Church. He was almost killed while attending to a mortally wounded enemy officer. A Union soldier, who was aiming his rifle at the priest, was killed by a member of the Orleans Guard (New Orleans *Morning Star and Catholic Messenger*, March 8, 1868; New Orleans *Crescent*, March 5, 1868; Bartlett, "Louisiana Troops in the West," in *Military Record of Louisiana*, 19).

77. Both of these regiments were detached early during the battle to protect the army's left flank on Owl Creek (*OR*, Vol. X, Pt. 1, pp. 516, 523).

78. Colonel Mouton reported that 207 men were killed and wounded in this attack (*ibid.*, 521).

tier of Natchitoches, Prescott of Washington, La., Avery of New Iberia, Hayes of Opelousas, and Gautreau of Thibodaux were wounded, Lieutenant Gautreau being the only one who died from the effects of his injuries.[79]

In our company were killed Amadeo Abadie, Victor Paris, Dr. Douglas McEvers, Edmond Rouvert, Aurelien Levron, Prosper Barrios, and Belisaire Achee. M. A. Dantin, Auguste Boudreaux, Joseph Brogden, Paul Guedry, Jean B. Guillot, and Ulysse Hymel were wounded and fell in the hands of the enemy. Of these, Boudreaux recovered from his wounds but died of disease in prison at Alton, Illinois; Guillot died at Camp Chase, Ohio; Brogden and Hymel, after being exchanged, returned to their company.[80]

The fate of Dantin and Guedry is enveloped in some doubt. I am satisfied that one of them died in New Albany and believe that the other died in Camp Dennison, Ohio.[81]

Florian Rouye was captured without injury and was subsequently exchanged.[82]

Joe Leonard, Augustin Lombas, Jules Giroir, Francois Guillot, Augustin Cherami, Jules B. Falgout, Ulysses Bourgeois, F. J. Gaudet, Thomassin Badeaux, J. Victor Knoblock, Paul Thibodaux, Amadeo Lejeune, William Guidroz, Marcel Ledet, and James Delaney were wounded but got off the field.

Of the three field officers of the 18th, neither was hurt. Col. Mouton's clothes and saddle had a dozen bullet marks, whilst his horse only received a slight wound.

The major had not a scratch, nor do I think that Col. Roman had. Every man in our company save three or four could show bullet

79. Lieutenant Elphege LeBoeuf, Company E, died in a Union hospital in Louisville on April 24 (CSR, Roll 294); First Lieutenant Charles D. Bullard, Company B (ibid., Roll 291); First Lieutenant John M. Young, Company I, was held at St. Louis and Alton, Illinois, before being exchanged at Vicksburg on September 23, 1862 (ibid., Roll 297); Second Lieutenant Emile Cloutier, Jr., Company C (ibid., Roll 291); Lieutenant Aaron Prescott, Jr., Company F (ibid., Roll 296); Lieutenant James G. Hayes, Company B (ibid., Roll 293).

80. Private Auguste Boudreaux died September 6, 1862 (ibid., Roll 290); Private Guillot died some time after April 25 (ibid., Roll 293); Privates Brogden and Hymel were exchanged at Vicksburg on September 23 (ibid., Rolls 291, 293).

81. Private Guedry died at New Albany on May 22. There is no record of Dantin's death (ibid., Rolls 292, 293).

82. After being held at Camp Douglas, Illinois, Private Rouye was exchanged near Vicksburg on September 20 (ibid., Roll 296).

marks upon his clothes, of whom I was one of the lucky. Our position was on the left of the flag, and the bullets whistling around our heads resembled the music of swarming bees. Every one of the flag bearers was killed or wounded, and we never have wondered how our loss could be so great, but how any of us escaped at all is the mystery. When it is remembered that the enemy's lines were nearly three times our length, causing the center of the regiment to be enfiladed from right and left, whilst one half of the enemy were receiving no injury whatever, the fact of our heavy loss can be readily accounted for. Many other companies, in fact all but the two St. James companies who were partially protected by a ravine on our left, suffered equally as bad as we did.[83]

The 16th Regiment lost less men than our single company. The Orleans Guard Battalion lost heavily.[84] I have always been satisfied in my own mind that if the whole brigade had been forwarded at the same time and the splendid battery operating with us had been properly used, that we would have driven the enemy before us with less loss in the whole brigade than our regiment sustained and that by breaking their lines at that moment we could have reached the river above Pittsburg Landing without further opposition.[85]

Shiloh, April 7th, 1862.   We were aroused and put into line at daybreak and removed up to the top of the elevation in front of the ravine in which we had encamped. Simultaneous with this movement, the skirmishers of the enemy appeared in the ravine before us. By order of Col. Mouton we fired upon them, driving them back, but in a few minutes a battery which was in position about 300 or 400 yards in front opened on us, sending their shot through the trees over our heads. We were ordered to fall back, and as we were doing so, Lieutenant Collins told me that McDonald of our company had been killed, but in a half hour afterwards Mc. caught up with us. He had been struck with a fragment of shell and made to turn a somersault but had received no permanent injury.

We kept on towards the rear for nearly a mile before we saw any body of our troops. We were kept marching about the woods until

83. Companies A and E lost two men killed and twenty wounded (Lucy [La.] *Le Meschacebe*, April 19, 1862).

84. During both days, the 16th Louisiana lost fourteen men killed, forty-nine wounded, and twenty-seven missing, and the Orleans Guard Battalion lost seventeen men killed, fifty-five men wounded, and eighteen missing (*OR*, Vol. X, Pt. 1, p. 519).

85. Colonel Mouton's official report contains similar convictions (*ibid.*, 521–22).

about 10 o'clock, when we found ourselves at Shiloh Church. During the morning, H. N. Coulon, Amos Roussel, and Thomas Roussel of the Lafourche Guards[86] fell in with us, having been separated from their own company during the night. As we were marching about we came to a halt in a ravine. The battle had been raging for some time, and in front of us the roaring of musketry and artillery was continuous.

Seeing an inspector of a division close by, I asked him some information of the fight, when he remarked: "That if we could hold our position on the right that we were safe, but if that gave way, we were all gone up; as for me I am entirely give out and too fatigued to do anything." I noticed, however, that he was not too tired to get himself close up behind a big tree and straighten out his horse before him.

Leaving the I. G. and his horse looking each other pitifully in the face, we moved onward and were met by an officer who rode up to Col. Mouton and remarked that Gen. Beauregard wished all the Louisiana troops to report to him on the left.[87] The Col. immediately moved us on, and as we reached the line Gen. Beauregard came up, took our flag, and rode forward.[88] Placing us on the extreme left of the line, we opened on the enemy, but in a short time I saw some

86. H. Nicholas Coulon, L. Amos Roussel, and Thomas Roussel were all privates in Company E, 4th Louisiana Infantry Regiment (CSR, Rolls 130, 135).

87. The 18th Louisiana, Orleans Guard Battalion, and two Tennessee regiments were ordered to support General Braxton Bragg's forces (Roman, *Military Operations of General Beauregard*, I, 317).

88. In describing the scene, Colonel Roman wrote:

General Beauregard rode down to them, addressed a few words of encouragement to the first two [18th Louisiana and Orleans Guard Battalion], and ordered them to move promptly to the support of General Bragg. As they passed by, with a tired, heavy gait, they endeavored to cheer their own favorite commander, but were so hoarse from fatigue and overexertion that they could only utter a husky sound, which grated painfully on General Beauregard's ear. . . . He rode, with his staff, to the leading regiment of Pond's brigade, the 18th Louisiana (Lieutenant Colonel Roman, commanding, Colonel Mouton having been wounded), and, seizing its colors, ordered "his Louisianians" to follow him. They started with an elasticity of step surprising in troops that, a moment before, appeared so jaded and broken down. (*ibid.*)

A member of the Orleans Guard Battalion recalled that Beauregard said, "Forward, fellow soldiers of Louisiana! one more effort and the day is ours" (Bartlett, "Louisiana Troops in the West," in *Military Record of Louisiana*, 20).

confusion in our ranks and, looking back, saw our colonel falling from his horse but soon ascertained that his wound was slight but painful.[89]

Leaving Col. Roman in command, he left the field. The lines of the opposing armies were close, and first one and then the other would advance and retreat. At one time Gen. Bragg came up and rode out through the thickets to within 100 yards of the enemy, saw their movements, came back, ordered Ketchum's Battery to open on them, and, then taking our flag, advanced ahead of us. As we were coming into position, William White of our company took the flag and carried it forward some 50 or 100 yards ahead of our line in spite of our remonstrances and, there planting the flag by his side, began firing upon the enemy and remained there until he was severely wounded. Joe Delaporte, also of our company, was still further forward than White but escaped without injury. I have never learned which one of the members of the 18th that went forward and secured our flag.

The whole line again gave way, and I found that Lieut. Collins had left the field, having been wounded; I was then left in command of our company and that of Co. D, both companies reduced to less than 20 men.

As we were going into the fight in the morning, I had ordered Beauvais and Winder to the rear, they having been on picket all night and were unable to fire off their pieces. Efforts had been ineffectually made to obtain permission, during the morning, to fire their pieces, and as the loads could not be withdrawn from our wretched Mississippi rifles, the only method to unload them was to pick powder in the tubes until they could be emptied. The two Roussels were with us during the engagement. Thomas, having advanced too far into the thicket, disappeared, and his fate was unknown for some time, when we learned that he had been wounded and captured.[90] About two o'clock we were moved to the rear, and after a muddy and tiresome march, we reached a cotton gin, near our former Camp Bush, where we obtained shelter for the night. It had been raining all the evening, wetting us to the skin, and having had nothing to eat all day, our

89. Mouton received a wound in the face that partially damaged his left eye (OR, Vol. X, Pt. 1, p. 522).

90. Roussel was later confined at Camp Douglas and exchanged at Vicksburg during the fall (CSR, Roll 135).

rest was none of the best, as we had not more than two blankets with us.

Fatigue had caused the men to throw everything away; I remember taking off my empty haversack, weighing about eight ounces, and throwing it away under the impression that it weighed fifty pounds. During this day Joseph Leonard, Augustin Lombas, Jules Giroir, Francois Guillot, Augustin Cherami, Jules B. Falgout, Ulysses Bourgeois, wounded the day previous, were captured, and William White was badly wounded and captured. White had a leg afterwards amputated, died on board a steamboat, and was buried at Hawesville, Kentucky. The others were all exchanged and subsequently returned to their company, except Falgout, who remained for some time in St. Louis and then came home.[91] Franklin Aucoin, who had been left in camp unwell, hearing the firing, came to the battlefield on the morning of this day but, unable to find his command, went in with some other troops and was wounded but not severely. Some two or three others were slightly wounded, making the loss in our company in killed, wounded, and captured amount to 41 out of 59 who went on the field.

A. J. Bouyan was captured without injury during the day and, being subsequently exchanged, returned to the company.[92]

April 8th.   This morning I took what few men were left and started to Corinth. The rain had fallen all the night, and we had to wade creeks and bottoms waist deep in various places to reach camp, which we did about midday.

I brought in with me Gros, Delaporte, Delatte, Bouvier, Elliott, Meyronne, Toups, Laine, Besson, McDonald, McAuliff, Winder, Beauvais, St. Martin, and W. F. Collins as the remnant of our company who were unhurt and who had remained together during the whole time.

The wounded kept coming in for two or three days until they all arrived in camp save those who had been captured.[93]

91. These men were all exchanged at Vicksburg in September (*ibid.*, Rolls 290, 291, 293, 294). There is no confirmation of Grisamore's information in the service records of Falgout and White.

92. Augustus J. Bouyan was held at Camp Douglas until exchanged at Vicksburg on September 23 (*ibid.*, Roll 290).

93. The casualties in the 18th for the two days were reported as 13 men killed, 80 wounded, and 118 missing (*OR*, Vol. X, Pt. 1, p. 519). Many of the missing were also wounded. The only listing of the regiment's casualties appears in the New Orleans

Corinth, April 8th, 1862. At this time everything was gloom and sadness about camp. Our wounded were suffering, and we could obtain but a few articles of diet suitable for them. The beef which was issued us was of the poorest kind, having been salted with Avery Island salt,[94] which was so much stronger than the ordinary article that the beef was burned up with it, and by the time we could get it out of the meat it was hardly fit to eat. The luxuries sent to us by our friends at home were nearly all lost on the way.

April 11th. I had made a raise of a big chicken and in order to have two meals out of it, we only cooked one half of it, with which and some rice we flattered ourselves into the prospect of a fair meal.

The major, the captain, Lieutenant Collins, Lieutenant Gautreau, and myself were the lucky individuals before whom this pleasant illusion appeared. Gautreau was too bad off to require much, and all the others and myself were unwell. But as the savory flavor arose out of the pot, Gautreau's evil genius, Lt. ———,[95] scenting the contents of our pot, came over and took a seat near us and entered into conversation. This was about half past eleven. We waited until one in hopes the fellow would take a hint, but it was no use, and finally, in their despair, the major ordered dinner and invited the lieutenant to dine with us, which he did. The consequence was that we all got up from the table hungry and not in the best of humor. Some of us actually made use of language that sounded very much like "cuss words." However, this was the last interference of this officer in our dining arrangements, as he was taken sick soon afterwards and died in a few days.[96]

We were pleased to see many of our friends arrive in camp during the week, among them V. Vicknair, J. D. Fulford, Dr. Scudday, Dr. A. L. Plough, Jr., V. Richard, and Gracien Thibodaux.[97]

Daily Picayune of April 18, 1862. For some unknown reason, the casualty list never became a part of the Compiled Service Records, so many of the men killed at Shiloh disappear from official records prior to the battle.

94. The salt works at Avery Island, Louisiana, served as a major source of salt for Confederate armies in the western theater until Union soldiers captured and destroyed them in April, 1863 (Ella Lonn, *Salt as a Factor in the Confederacy* [New York, 1933], 32–33).

95. Lieutenant J. D. Etie (CSR, Roll 292).

96. Etie died May 9, 1862 (*ibid.*).

97. Valery Vicknair was a fifty-one-year-old farmer in Lafourche Parish and later served as lieutenant colonel of the Lafourche Regiment, Louisiana Militia. In 1860, J. D. Fulford, a native of Virginia, was forty-two years old, and the census gave his

Orders were given to send the wounded home, and preparations were immediately made to carry those orders into effect.

About the 15th of the month, we took all who were considered too badly injured to recover in camp to the depot. Placing them all together on the platform, I stationed a guard among them and went off to endeavor to secure a box car for them so as to get them all into one car, which I finally succeeded in obtaining. Then getting a bale of fodder, Louis Boudreaux and myself rolled it about 150 yards and covered over the bottom of the car, and then placing our wounded in it, we went to the hospital and brought Louis Allain of the Lafourche Guards[98] and put him in with them and had the gratification of seeing them all leave, as comfortably as could be expected, in charge of our friends who were returning home.

The following list comprises those who were sent off: Capt. Gourdain, Lieutenant Gautreau, and privates Badeaux, F. Aucoin, D. Boudreaux, Amadeo Lejeune, Guidroz, M. Ledet, A. Theriot, Burk, Delaney, P. Thibodaux, Knoblock, Meyronne, and Vedroz, all of whom reached their respective homes in safety and recovered from their injuries except Lieut. Gautreau.

April 17th.   There was a great deal of sickness in camp, and the few who were able to do service were almost constantly on duty. Captain Sanders, having been wounded on the 6th, had gone home, leaving me still acting quartermaster, and Lieut. Collins being unwell left me in command of the company.

Today our regiment under Major Bush was sent on picket to Monterey, which place we reached late in the evening. Our commissary made a raise of a beef today, which did us all a great deal of good, having had no fresh meat for several days.

---

occupation as carriage warehouse operator. Dr. James A. Scudday was born in South Carolina, was fifty-six years old in 1860, and lived near Raceland. He had performed two of the earliest cesarean sections in Louisiana in the 1840s. Dr. Azzo Louis Plough, Jr., was born in Connecticut on April 6, 1830, and opened one of Thibodaux's earliest dentist offices in August, 1850. After this visit to Corinth, he saw duty in several capacities in Confederate service. He moved to New Orleans after the war and died there on April 12, 1914. Valerie Richard and C. Gracien Thibodaux were both merchants in Thibodaux (Eighth Census: Lafourche Parish, Roll 413; CSR, Roll 389; John Duffy, ed., *The Rudolph Matas History of Medicine in Louisiana* [Baton Rouge, 1958, 1962], II, 73–74; Application of Marie Louise Andre Plough, Confederate Pension Files, Louisiana State Archives).

98. Corporal Allain was in Company E, 4th Louisiana Infantry Regiment (CSR, Roll 129).

April 18th. Our company sent on picket on the Hamburg road. The day was rainy and the following night dark as it well could be. Whilst visiting the sentinels at night, I got lost in the bushes and came very near remaining lost until morning.

April 19th. Several of the men in the regiment had fresh pork, and some of the men of my company intimated to me that they would have no objection to a ration of the same food. I advised them to go out and kill a hog as there were many of them about the camp. They went out and came back without any, reporting that they could not catch any. By this time I was getting a little hungry for pork myself, and I very emphatically told them that they ought to be ashamed of themselves and ordered them off again with instructions to retrieve their reputation, swearing that I would not command a set of men that "couldn't catch a hog." They left and presently an orderly came to me with an order from the major commanding the regiment transmitting an order emanating from Colonel Marshall J. Smith,[99] commanding post, "That any person found killing hogs should be severely punished" and instructing all commanders of companies "to report the names of any of the men found guilty of such disreputable acts." Putting my name on the back, I gave it to the orderly, remarking to myself, *"en ro la de Courrage,* I have got myself into a scrape now." Towards evening the boys had plenty of fresh pork, and the half of a small "specimen" fell to my share. Of course I told the boys the less they said about their hunting feats would be the more easily mended. Having a nice mess of spare ribs baked for breakfast, I summoned the major to partake of the same, thinking that if I had to tell the truth that that would be the most auspicious season. The major partook liberally of our breakfast and finally remarked that "those ribs are delicious, lieutenant, where did you get them?" "I sent one of the men out yesterday to one of the neighbors and bought a pig."

His mind was too obtuse to take a joke on *that* morning. That was the first order that I ever gave to commit depredation and gave few of the kind subsequently, but I never had a man to come and complain that he was unable to catch a pig after that.

April 20th. Harris Arceneau died in the regimental hospital at Corinth and was buried in the grave yard near that town.

April 21. Severin Gauthier died today and was buried in the cemetery at Corinth.

99. Colonel Marshall J. Smith, Crescent (Louisiana) Regiment.

April 23.   The regiment being relieved returned to the regimental camp at Corinth.

April 28.   We are kept either in camp or working on the trenches.[100] Health improving, some of the men are returning from the hospitals in the rear. Today Emile Bergeron was honorably discharged from service on account of disability and left with his father for home, which I never expected him to reach alive, but my predictions were wrong, and he "still lives."

P. S.   I have neglected to state in the proper place that after our return to Corinth from Pittsburg Landing about the 25th of March Corporal J. Emile Naquin accidently shot himself in the hand and was furloughed to go home.

---

100. The Confederate army, determined to hold Corinth, began digging trenches to defend the town. Polk's corps held the left flank, Bragg's the center, and Hardee's the right. The Reserve Corps remained behind the main lines. When Major General Earl Van Dorn's Army of the West arrived from Arkansas, it took up positions on the right and to the rear of Hardee's line (Nathaniel C. Hughes, *General William J. Hardee: Old Reliable* [Baton Rouge, 1965], 118; Roman, *Military Operations of General Beauregard*, I, 382).

2 Garrison Duty in Mississippi and Alabama

Corinth, May 1st, 1862. Sickness had reduced our regiment to about 225 men fit for duty.

Col. Mouton was at home, wounded and sick; Lieutenant Col. Roman was away on a sick leave of absence; Major Bush, unable to perform service, had been sent to the rear to recuperate.[1] Our surgeon was in camp but confined to his bed, and the assistant surgeon was away on sick leave. Our adjutant had resigned on account of ill health, and so many of the officers were unfit for duty that frequently the regiment was commanded by 2nd lieutenants and generally changed commanders every morning. Dr. Ballard[2] from Assumption was temporarily assigned to duty as surgeon in our regiment, and another physician, from some of the upper parishes, was also sent out to us as surgeon—whose name I have forgotten.[3] Cannonading was heard in our front every day, and the enemy kept constantly approaching our lines.

May 5th. Our regiment was sent out on picket on the Monterey road, Lieutenant Collins commanding our company; I did not go with them, but before they left I took a bottle of brandy and a jar of preserves that had been sent to us by our friends at home and handed them to the surgeon who accompanied the regiment (the one whose name I do not remember), telling him that I wished him to take it along for use in case of actual necessity, otherwise to return it to me as it was private property. This he promised faithfully to do and kept his promise manfully by drinking the one article and eating the other before the regiment reached its destination. This kind of care

1. Perhaps because of the absence of all of the regiment's field officers, Lieutenant Colonel Camille J., Prince de Polignac, attempted to have himself assigned as colonel of the 18th Louisiana about April 23. Polignac was then serving on Beauregard's staff and wished to move up in rank and obtain a field command. Nothing came of his effort ("Polignac's Diary, Part I," *Civil War Times Illustrated*, XIX [August, 1980], 14).

2. Dr. W. H. Ballard was a physician living at Crane's Forge in Assumption Parish (Eighth Census: Assumption Parish, Roll 407).

3. See Grisamore's account of the regimental surgeons in Chapter 5.

and watchfulness over soldiers was frequently met with within surgeons, but I am proud to say no regular surgeon of the 18th ever was guilty of such conduct. When I learned the result of my charitable intentions, you can imagine my "pheelinks" as I would not like to express them in just the same language I did on that morning.

May 7th. Our company had just received a new outfit of hats, shoes, pants, and jackets which were run out of New Orleans previous to its capture.

Lieutenant Etie of New Iberia was buried today.

May 8th. The enemy drove in our pickets this evening, approached within less than one mile of our entrenchments on the Farmington road. We were put into the trenches about three o'clock and remained there until sunset, when we were ordered forward and placed in line of battle just outside of the abatis, inside of an old field on the left of the Farmington road. Orders came to the commanding officer of the 18th to send forward skirmishers, and he detached our company for that duty. Lieutenant Collins and myself advanced the company properly about 150 yards and halted until the skirmishers on our right and left would come up in line. On our left was the 21st Louisiana.[4] By this time it was dark, and the commanding officer of the skirmishers on our left began to instruct his men in the art of skirmishing with a loud voice. By this time orders to forward came again, and we started and moved on about 100 yards, when I halted and told Lieutenant Collins that he might send word back to the commanding officer of the regiment that I was not going to move any further unless he stopped that stump speaker on our left. That if the enemy were ahead of us he was just exposing our position, and that oratory and fighting did not work well together on a dark night anyhow.

I do not know whether he sent back this message or not, but the speech soon ended, and we were summoned back to the main lines. I never have ascertained whether this skirmish line was sent forward expressly to furnish the brilliant orator of the 21st an opportunity to make a speech or whether some other object lesson was the cause.

Once in line all became quiet, and the men lying or sitting down

4. This was probably the 25th Louisiana Infantry Regiment, which was on the right flank of the 1st Brigade of Ruggles' division (*OR*, Vol. X, Pt. 1, p. 816). The 21st Louisiana Infantry Regiment had formed a part of the garrison of Fort Pillow and probably had not arrived at Corinth yet. Confederate forces evacuated Fort Pillow on June 3 (*ibid.*, 902).

were generally dozing and dreaming. Boggins was with us that night. Boggins, after the fight at Pittsburg Landing, had become a firm believer in strategy, but somehow Boggins had not got sick that evening but accompanied this expedition. His company was next to ours, and about 10 yards behind us was a ten rail fence concealed in a heavy growth of briars.

Boggins like the rest of the men was dreaming—dreaming of a brother he had in the interior of Mississippi whom he was anxious to see—or dreaming of the lovely cotton fields of Natchitoches on the banks of Red River, where he had selected a home. On the hill behind us was one of our large field pieces. This piece was to be fired as a signal for us to return to camp, but Boggins didn't know it, none of us knew it. About 11 o'clock the gun was fired with a terrible report. I remember that I thought it was a half a dozen thunderbolts exploding and tried to draw my head and my heels inside of my jacket; finding I could not accomplish that feat, I jumped up and saw that everybody else jumped up and jumped up quick. I heard a yell, an agonizing yell, and looked around and saw Boggins give one leap— one "bully" leap—and light exactly upon the top of the briars and roll over on the other side of the fence.

Strategy got the better of Boggins' judgment again. Poor Boggins! In an hour afterwards we were all snugly stowed away in our beds at camp, to be awakened at 2 o'clock by the long roll and ordered to prepare ourselves forthwith with two day's rations and to be at the breastworks by daylight.[5]

Corinth, Miss., May 9th, 1862. We were this morning in a brigade of Ruggles' Division commanded by Major Gober of the 16th La.[6] Our regiment was commanded by Capt. Mire, the junior captain in camp. Some of the companies had no officers. I, a second lieutenant, commanded two of the companies. At daylight we were put into the trenches, and about 8 o'clock we were moved out by the Farmington Road and upon arriving at that little village we were formed

5. The Confederate forces were attempting to smash the advanced Federal forces at Farmington. Bragg's troops were to attack in front while Major General Earl Van Dorn's Army of the West struck them on the flank (Thomas L. Connelly, *Army of the Heartland: The Army of Tennessee, 1861–1862* [Baton Rouge, 1967], 176).

6. Major Daniel Gober commanded the 2nd Brigade of Ruggles' division, consisting of the 11th, 16th, 18th, 19th Louisiana regiments, and the Orleans Guard Battery. The 19th Louisiana remained in the trenches, so it did no fighting (*OR*, Vol. X, Pt. 1, pp. 811, 821).

in a line of battle in front of the enemy, whom we could distinctly see moving to the rear and taking a position in the edge of a strip of woods some half mile in front of us.

Gen. Bragg, who was in command of the forces on that occasion, rode along our lines whilst we were forming and was heartily cheered by the troops.[7] Our regiment was on the extreme left of the division, and as we were moving forward through an open field, we came near a square of woodland which was being shelled by the Orleans Guard Battery,[8] in position on our left.

The whole command was halted and orders came to extend the line towards the left, and our regiment was moved by the flank into the woods. Some of the men said that there were Yankees ambushed in the timber, but I imagined that the woods had been cleared out by the shelling from the batteries. When the left of the line had extended about 150 yards into the woods, we were suddenly fired upon, and being under the impression that it was done by our own skirmishers who had been sent into the woods from another point, we fell back without returning the fire. At all events, we were not in a position to return the compliment, our line being perpendicular to that of the enemy. The Yankees were well concealed amongst the shrubbery, but although they were not fifty feet from the head of our line, not a man received an injury worth mentioning. We immediately reformed and again entered the woods, but this time the 11th La., which had gone in at another point, had driven the enemy away. The whole line advanced about the same time, and after one or two volleys the enemy left and retreated towards Monterey.[9]

Burning up some bridges and destroying telegraphic wires, the forces returned to Corinth before night had set in.

But few lives were lost. The 18th had but one man killed—a member of one of the St. James companies.[10] There was some of the enemy captured, among whom was a poor devil whose horse had mired in a swamp, and when found he was up to his neck in the

7. On May 6, Bragg assumed command of the Army of the Mississippi (*ibid.*, Pt. 2, p. 500).

8. Two sections (four guns) of this battery, commanded by Captain Henry Ducatel, were attached to Gober's brigade (*ibid.*, Pt. 1, p. 822).

9. Van Dorn's command had moved too slowly, and the Federals escaped the envelopment (Connelly, *Army of the Heartland*, 176).

10. The 18th Louisiana lost one man killed and fourteen wounded (*OR*, Vol. X, Pt. 1, p. 822).

mud and unable to extricate himself. As he was brought in, he presented an appearance that was both ridiculous and amusing.

At the battle of Shiloh, a soldier of the 11th Louisiana had secured one of the breast plates which some of the Yankees wore, and this morning had buckled it around his body and probably imagined that he was secure, at least.

The only man in that regiment who was killed was the wearer of that "life preserver." The enemy was commanded on that occasion by old "Headquarters in the saddle,"[11] and this is supposed to be one of the occasions on which he saw Rebels' backs, as he informed the Army of the Potomac at a subsequent period.[12]

May 10th. Under the law of the Confederate Government retaining all volunteers in service for three years whose term of enlistment did not expire at a stated period and granting them the privilege of reorganizing their companies by a new election of officers,[13] Gen. Beauregard had issued an order for the said elections to take place on the 9th, but the expedition to Farmington did not allow us to carry out the order until this morning.

Capt. J. K. Gourdain was re-elected Captain; S. T. Grisamore, First Lieutenant; Levi M. Hargis and J. L. Aucoin, Second Lieutenants. Lieutenant Collins, our first lieutenant, declined to become a candidate for re-election. As soon as the newly elected officers were examined and assigned to duty, I gave the command of the company to Lieutenant Hargis, my duties as acting quartermaster being such as to require all my time.

It is but just to a worthy and meritorious officer to state that the company was commanded throughout the war by Lieutenant Hargis, with the exception of one or two short periods.

---

11. Major General John Pope, commander of the Union Army of the Mississippi. Shortly after assuming command of the Army of Virginia in June, 1862, Pope was asked by a reporter where his headquarters would be, and he replied that they would be "in the saddle" (Mark M. Boatner, III, *Civil War Dictionary* [New York, 1959], 659).

12. On July 14, 1862, in an address to the Army of Virginia, Pope stated, "I have come to you from the West, where we have always seen the backs of our enemies" (*OR*, Vol. XII, Pt. 3, p. 474).

13. Under the Conscript Act of April 16, 1862, men in service whose enlistments would expire before the end of the war were to be retained in service for three years from the date of their original enlistment. All units organized for twelve months were to be allowed to reorganize within forty days by electing their officers (*ibid.*, Ser. IV, Vol. I, p. 1095).

The reorganization of the regiment was completed by electing Lieutenant Col. Roman as Colonel, Major Bush as Lieutenant Colonel, and Lieutenant Armant[14] of St. James as Major. Colonel Mouton had been promoted to a brigadier general a few days after the battle of Shiloh.[15] Sergeant Major Sanchez became Captain of Company A; Lieutenant Cloutier, Capt. of Company C; Lieutenant Poche, Capt. of Company E; Capt. Mouton remained Captain of Company F; Capt. Gourdain of Company G. Lieutenant Leeds became Captain of Company H. Capt. Collins remained Captain of Company I, and Lieutenant Hayes became Capt. of Company K.[16]

The elected officers of Companies B and D did not pass examination. Lieutenant Shepherd, of Company A, was subsequently appointed captain of Company B, and Lieutenant Story of Company H was appointed captain of Company D.[17]

The field officers were all absent sick. Captain Mouton commanded the regiment; Sergeant St. Martin of our company was acting sergeant major.

Corinth, May 13, 1862.   Much sickness prevailed in the army. Every day long trains of sick soldiers were carried to the different hospitals in the rear. Our regiment was reduced to about 300 men fit for duty, in an aggregate of near 700. The water we had to drink was the most abominable stuff that was ever forced down men's throats. It was obtained from wells and holes about the camps and was of a bluish color and greasy taste, with a good deal of something equivalent to castor oil in it. The beef which we had was so poor and so badly burned up with salt that we were constantly thirsty, and I doubt very much if there were 20 men in the regiment who would have said that they were perfectly well. I was ordered to have some wells prepared, and with a detail of men dug out six in one day, as water could be obtained within 5 or 6 feet of the surface. The next morning three of them were filled with a kind of liquid resembling coal tar, dish water, and soap suds mixed. This night we were placed in the trenches, our company numbering 12 men.

May 14.   Several of our friends from Assumption have been in

14. First Lieutenant Leopold L. Armant of Company E (CSR, Roll 290).

15. Mouton's promotion was dated April 16, 1862 (Ezra J. Warner, *Generals in Gray* [Baton Rouge, 1959], 223).

16. William Sanchez, Emile Cloutier, Jr., Alexander S. Poche, Paul B. Leeds, and James G. Hayes (CSR, Rolls 291, 293, 294, 296).

17. C. M. Shepherd and Benjamin S. Story (*ibid.*, Rolls 296, 297).

camp, among them were Numa Folse, Anatole Lalande, Henry Boatner, Wm. Carver, &c., who enlisted in different batteries belonging to the army.[18]

They were welcome visitors, bringing us some news from our homes, with which we had no postal communications.

May 15. The want of vegetables was seriously felt by the men. I remember being near the railroad depot one morning seeing a car loaded with a variety of vegetables, and after a long struggle I succeeded in forcing my way through the crowd to the door, but by this time everything was gone but lettuce, of which I purchased as much as could be packed into a large handkerchief and went on my way rejoicing. But little else was eaten in my mess for that day.

May 16. Dr. Ballard left us today. Our other doctor, finding the brandy and jelly getting short, has also gone. Dr. Littell, our surgeon, is in camp but too sick to attend to his duties. Dr. Key,[19] a son of the late P. B. Key of this parish, was assigned to duty in our regiment, and a very efficient and attentive physician he proved himself whilst he remained with us.

May 17. Orders have been issued to send all extra baggage of our command to Okolona, which is being effected slowly.

Some of the newly elected officers were slow in being examined, and others were in rear, sick, thus causing the old officers, who had declined becoming candidates for re-election, to remain on duty.

Some of them were very anxious to get away. "Their families were suffering, and all the money they had was in New Orleans," under the watchful eyes of the "Beast," and the nearer the prospect of a battle, the more intense became their love for their wives and children. I have often thought that the most effectual way of restoring a man's love to his wife, when it becomes cool, would be to put him in the army, and in a very short time he would be seeking a furlough, basing his application upon the immense desire he has to look again upon the beloved partner of his bosom. One or two applications would effect a permanent cure, and he would henceforward be a perfect model of gentleness and affection.

18. Anatole Lalande enlisted in the Orleans Guard Battery, and Henry J. Boatner enlisted in the 5th Company, Washington Artillery (CSR, Rolls 56, 62). The editor has found no records on the others.

19. Philip B. Key, whose father was a cousin of Francis Scott Key, had formerly served as an aide-de-camp to Major General John L. Lewis of the Louisiana Militia (Philip B. Key to Major General John L. Lewis, March 28, 1862, in Letters Received, Louisiana State Troops, November 18, 1861–August 26, 1862, M359, Roll 23).

Being kept there with the probability of being at any moment sent into battle was not an extraordinary source of happiness to the victims, but it was one from which a good deal of fun was obtained for those who had no desire of leaving.

There was one lieutenant, who had never been accused of any hankering anxiety to charge a Yankee battery by himself, who was extremely solicitous about his discharge papers. Having to go into Corinth every morning for forage or any supplies that might be obtained, I carried back with me the letters and papers for the regiment. I was met generally at the edge of the camp by this officer with "Lieutenant, have you got my discharge," or "Lieutenant, anything for me." "Nary discharge for you, sir." Each succeeding day brought us nearer a conflict of arms, and proportionately increased the anxiety concerning his discharge. One morning, after the usual questions and answers, I replied, "Lieutenant, it is of no use, your successor is at Jackson sick and can't return to assume his position. The weather is now fair, and Gen. Beauregard, expecting a battle at any moment, is not going to have his men left without officers, so you may as well just make up your mind to stay and see it out." Musing over these words for a few minutes, he answered in a lugubrious tone, "Well, I will stay in the trenches, but I'm not going outside of the fortifications any more." The next morning, being in the Adjutant's office when his discharge arrived, I immediately ordered an ambulance to be prepared, and in two minutes after the papers were sent to him, he came running up bareheaded. "Lieutenant, can you let me have an ambulance to take my trunk to town so that I can leave by the morning train?" "Certainly, Lieutenant, certainly, the ambulance is ready and waiting for you." It didn't wait long.

A private in the St. Landry company took another method of getting his discharge. He feigned paralysis of one side, and so well did he carry it out, by hobbling around on crutches with leg and arm shaking about so completely useless, that he not only fooled everyone who saw him but obtained certificates of the examining surgeons, received his discharge, and got entirely well before he reached home.

Another strapping fellow from Natchitoches, of 180 pounds, feigned sickness, visited the surgeon, swallowed medicine, and went through all the maneuvers of a sick man so completely that his deception became a reality, and in a few days his discharge came, by higher orders than those of Gen. Beauregard, depositing him in the cemetery.

May 18.   Dr. Palmer[20] preached an eloquent sermon in the woods adjoining our camp. In the evening the 18th was ordered out on picket on the Monterey road. The two lines of pickets were near each other; the enemy kept up an almost incessant firing, occasionally letting off whole volleys. We were kept in a state of alarm all night, getting but little, if any, sleep. Considerable cannonading was heard in front of Hardee's division[21] on our right, and the shells would frequently come through the trees over our heads. Our brigade was on the right of our division, and we were the right regiment. Lieutenant Hargis, in command of our company with that of Co. D, which had no officers, was posted on the extreme right in a strip of woods.

May 19.   Major Newman[22] of the 21st Louisiana came over from Hardee's division, reporting a gap between the two divisions, claiming that we were not forward enough. Lieutenant Hargis had notified me the evening before that there was a gap on our right by which we might be flanked and contended that we were in advance of the other division. Capt. Mouton, who was the senior officer of the regiment, sent the writer with Major Newman to examine the position and ascertain the facts. Finding Lieutenant Hargis, he still contended that we were in advance, but failing to satisfy the Major, we three started up a little hill to reconnoitre. There was a large open field some 50 yards right of our line, and as we reached the corner of the fence and were looking through the woods for Hardee's troops, a gun was fired at us from behind the fence 100 yards in rear of us. The shot came from one of our pickets and was fired with a deliberate aim through the cracks of the fence. This shot satisfied me that he was a poor marksman and convinced Major Newman that our pickets were in advance of his.

All of us being therefore satisfied, we didn't fight out on that line any longer but gracefully retired.

Corinth, May 20th.   Being relieved from picket duty, the regi-

20. The Reverend Doctor Benjamin M. Palmer, a prominent Presbyterian minister from New Orleans, served without a commission as a chaplain in the Army of the Mississippi (New Orleans *Daily Picayune*, February 22, 1862; Alcée Fortier, *Louisiana* [Atlanta, 1914], II, 290).

21. Hardee's III Corps had only three brigades, the normal composition of a division.

22. Major John Newman (Bergeron, *Guide to Louisiana Confederate Military Units*, 124; CSR, Roll 316.)

ment returned to camp at 10 o'clock A.M. Our numbers having been too small for a double watch, some of the men had stood guard for 48 hours.

At 2 o'clock orders came to cook two days' rations and be ready to march at 6. Notified the men to cook and go to sleep, which they did.

May 21st. Rain during the night, making us hope for, at least, one day's rest. We were now in Hindman's Division and in a brigade commanded by Colonel Marks of the 11th La.[23]

At 5 o'clock we were moved out on the Farmington road about two miles and bivouacked in line of battle in front of the enemy. The movement appeared to be a general one, and we expected the rising sun on the morrow to be the signal for a bloody and terrible engagement.[24] Capt. W. Mouton commanded the regiment, whilst I was second in command, there not being another captain on duty. The captain and I slept in an open wagon during the night and had a friendly talk about the probable qualities of the bed on which we might be resting the succeeding one.

On the 21st, the sun rose bright and beautiful, but no guns were heard; everything was silent and still—not even a picket gun was fired—the stillness itself was oppressive to one whose mind was in such suspense as ours at that moment. The day advanced and at about 9 o'clock, as we were sitting on the grass around the commanding officer of the brigade, one of the company inquired what "this movement indicated," when the Colonel pulled out of his pocket a copy of the General Orders, and we read "that as soon as Hardee's guns on our right denoted a general engagement, the whole line would move forward and attack the enemy."

Hardee never became engaged, and we lay about in the shade until evening, when the artillery threw a few shells and the troops returned to camp.[25]

23. Major General Thomas C. Hindman was assigned to command Ruggles' division on May 10. Ruggles, a poor field commander, had received orders to go to the rear and take command of various depots and guards (*OR*, Vol. X, Pt. 2, pp. 510, 529). Colonel Samuel F. Marks assumed command of the brigade for a time as senior colonel.

24. Another attempt was to be made to destroy General Pope's forces at Farmington by a concerted attack by Bragg's and Van Dorn's troops. Bad weather on May 20 caused a twenty-four-hour postponement of the movement (*ibid.*, 532, 533).

25. Again the Federals evaded a decisive engagement (Robert G. Hartje, *Van Dorn: The Life and Times of a Confederate General* [Nashville, 1967], 179–80).

May 26.   Orders to remove baggage to the rear—but one tent allowed to 10 men. Our stock all in miserable order, having nothing to feed them but corn, which for want of long food they will not eat.

Orders again to prepare for an attack at sunrise tomorrow. Fifty men of our regiment sent on outpost duty. Lieutenant Aucoin and Privates Pontiff, Plaisance, and Toups of our company went with the detail.

Dr. R. H. New, formerly of this place [Thibodaux] but then chaplain of the 11th La., came over to our camp and presented his credentials as surgeon of the 18th and gave me a bottle of good sherry wine which made me think him a very *sensible* surgeon. He left the same day to get his baggage. We have no field officers—no Adjutant— not a captain fit for duty. Lieutenant Septime Webre[26] of St. James was acting as adjutant. Baggage is being daily sent to the depot and shipped to the rear.[27]

Boggins came to me today and said, "Lieutenant, is it true that we are going to evacuate this place?" "Well, Boggins, it looks very much like it." "Well, Lieutenant, I tell you, Beauregard is the greatest general living, for that will be one of the greatest movements ever made." "Oh yes! but the general is not going to leave here without a battle, and as you were too *sick* to go to Shiloh, you will yet have a chance of seeing a general fight." "Well, Lieutenant, I was at the fight with the gun boats at Pittsburg Landing, and I then saw what a battle is, and I have no desire to see anything 'bigger' than that was." "Well, sir, I am inclined to think that you will see something grander than Shiloh before we leave Corinth."

"Well, I am decidedly in favor of evacuation as a piece of strategy, and I think General Beauregard ought to try that before he gets into another fight."

May 29.   Regiment been working on entrenchments for two days. At noon the men returned to camp, piled up everything that could not be carried, ready for the torch, threw all the pots and old greasy kettles into the wells, and lay down under the trees awaiting further orders.[28] Col Reichard of the 20th La. commanded our bri-

26. Second Lieutenant J. Septime Webre, Company E, had acted as adjutant since May 10 (CSR, Roll 296).

27. The Union army under Major General Henry W. Halleck had approached close enough to the Confederate lines by May 25 to be able to begin an artillery bombardment. General Beauregard had decided that he had to abandon the town and began making preparations to do so (Boatner, *Civil War Dictionary*, 176).

28. Confederate troops would evacuate Corinth on the night of May 29–30 (*ibid.*).

gade,[29] and Lieutenant Leeds[30] was in command of the regiment. Our Commissary, Capt. C. T. Patin of Vermilion, was sick and absent and had requested me to assist his clerks in their duties until his return. I was quite unwell today for the first time since leaving home. The wagons were gone, and we had all cooked up three days' rations. My haversack was as full as it could be stuffed, with bread and beef, having a half box of sardines in the bottom. Dr. New, our surgeon, returned today and asked me if I had anything to eat; I told him to take something out of my haversack, but I did not have any idea that he was going to empty it, and when I got up and found everything gone but the box of sardines, I honestly thought I must have had an *error* of *judgment* a few days previous when he gave me the bottle of Sherry wine. This was the first day that there had been no picket firing for a week. Everything was calm and still. About two o'clock a report, as I thought of guns bursting, was heard in our front, and in a few moments three shells came whizzing almost over our heads, one of them exploding over the cemetery, 100 yards to the right of our camp, and another was said to have gone on to Corinth and fallen near the railroad depot, badly injuring one of the engineers, whilst the third exploded near the headquarters of Gen. Beauregard. After this the same silence as before was continued without interruption.

It was now apparent that the enemy could command our camp and throw his shells over it, but we knew that we were going to leave the approaching night and did not care.

There was nothing just then that made us have desire to remain in that delectable place. I have never yet had the opportunity of visiting any town or section that presented so many inducements to emigrate from as Corinth. The miserable stuff which we had to drink under the name of water would have disgusted anybody. I am a dear lover of good pure water and can hardly conceive how any man would ever wish to drink anything else when he could obtain it, but rather than imbibe the abominable draughts of so-called water at Corinth, I would make up my mind to swallow pine-top whiskey, rum, gin, or anything else in a liquid form.

At dusk we were formed into line and silently departed to the rear, passing by the Seminary, and after having marched about four

29. Colonel Augustus Reichard had assumed command of the brigade on May 27 (CSR, Roll 313). The 20th Louisiana Infantry Regiment had transferred from Brigadier General Lucius M. Walker's brigade of the division.

30. Leeds was now captain of Company H (*ibid.*, Roll 294).

miles we stopped. I and Adjutant Webre, both being quite unwell, rode into the woods and bivouacked under a tree umbrageous enough to keep the dews off our heads, and by pulling off some of the branches we furnished our horses with something to appease their hunger.

May 30th.   Today we only marched about 6 miles.

May 31st.   A long march today, some 18 miles. Riding along I found a couple of hardtack that had been lying on the leaves until the mould had become about an inch thick, and picking them up, Capt. Mouton, St. Martin, Hargis, and myself made a meal off of them and my little box of sardines.

We reached 20 Mile Creek about four o'clock, where we all obtained some good water for the first time for weeks.

The men would fill their cups and canteens and sit down and drink draught after draught until it appeared to me that some of them had imbibed a gallon. This evening we had some fresh beef, but as the wagons were all ahead there was no salt to season it. However, the men boiled it over the coals and ate it anyhow, as many of them had had no food for 48 hours.

June 1st.   I was sent back in charge of a train of 20 wagons to bring up stragglers. Found all of the 18th who were behind.

June 2nd.   Was sent in command of a brigade train for forage over one of the hilliest countries I ever saw. Having found corn after travelling 30 miles, we loaded the wagon and returned, reaching camp on the morning of the 4th.

June 5th.   Remained quietly in camp. Dr. New having been discharged from the service left us today. The health and appearance of the men improving rapidly since we have had abundance of good clear water. Our camp is near the Baldwin Depot of the Mobile and Ohio Railroad.[31]

Camp near Baldwin, Miss., June 2nd, 1862.   The army has been quietly resting on the banks of 20 Mile Creek, recruiting and improving rapidly in health and spirits. I was sent off with the brigade trains in search of forage, and travelled 30 miles before finding any. I thought that I had seen crooked and hilly woods before, but I came to the conclusion that I had been laboring under a delusion in regard

---

31. Baldwin is thirty miles south of Corinth.

   Grisamore ended one installment with this June 5 entry, then began the next installment with an entry dated June 2.

to that matter. I could not fail, however, to admire the genius of the wonderful individual who had made the plan of a road that could be stretched over those hills in such a manner that a wagon could pass with safety.

June 3rd. Washington Price died in the hospital at Jackson, Mississippi.

A few days before leaving Corinth, I had received $40,000 for the purpose of paying off the soldiers, but the bills all being of the amount of $100 each but slow progress was made, and when we were leaving, over $30,000 were still on hand. As I had no trunk to carry it in, I placed the money in a small box and carried it in my haversack which for more than a month never left my neck and served for a pillow at night.

June 6th. Started to the rear, travelled until midnight with the trains.[32]

June 7th. Continued our route, making some 30 miles and encamped.

June 8th. This morning instructions came to me about sunrise to move my trains into the road preparatory to continuing the march. Having done so, whilst awaiting orders to move, a body of some six or eight men came riding up, and one of them, a large, robust, fine looking person dressed in a hunting shirt without any insignia, inquired what "those wagons were doing in the road." I told him. "Well, how long are they going to remain in the road here?" I answered that "I have been awaiting orders for half an hour, but that the commander of the trains was camped just in the edge of those woods." "Well, it's very strange that these trains should be here in the way of my troops." Taking another glance at him, I perceived that I was looking for the first time upon the great orator, statesman, and soldier, John C. Breckinridge,[33] and replied "that if his troops were nearby I would move out of the road." "I would be much obliged if you will," was his answer as he rode on.

During the day we reached our camping ground, some four miles

32. The wagon trains of Bragg's corps were to take the westernmost road from Baldwin to Tupelo, moving "via Birmingham and Tom Williams', north of King's Creek" (*OR*, Vol. X, Pt. 2, p. 583).

33. General Breckinridge had been a United States congressman and vice-president, and he ran unsuccessfully for president in 1860. He now commanded the Reserve Corps (four brigades). His troops were marching behind the trains of his and Bragg's corps (*ibid.*, 550, 583).

from Tupelo, and in the afternoon the troops came up and went into camp. Major Bush, who had been absent for some time, sick, arrived today also, and doubtless he yet remembers the fine dinner we had under the shade of a tree, consisting only of rice, chicken, and coffee.

The Major had been absent for some time, and feeling some delicacy in inviting my superior officer to partake of a homely meal after he had been indulging in the good things of the land, I was astonished when he informed me that it was the best meal he had had since he left Corinth. With all its roughness and hardships, the soldier's life is not the worst one in this wide world.

A long march without food brings a good appetite. On the road from 20 Mile Creek, I had purchased two chickens, and I have no recollection of ever enjoying a more gratifying meal than the one I made with the one of them in an open wheat field on the 7th of June, 1862. And after the meal comes a sleep that no man of business or care ever partakes of.

The soldier never thinks—he awaits orders and obeys—he knows nothing—cares for nothing—and worries about nothing—and if he has a mind to make it so, his life is a happy one—he never growls when it rains—nor swears when the sun burns—nor grumbles when dinner is late. If he can't obtain whiskey, he'll drink water; if he can't get sassafras tea, he'll imbibe coffee; if he is tired of beef, corn bread, and rice, he will eat rice, corn bread, and beef or diversify his meal by partaking of corn bread, beef, and rice; and takes everything as it comes with as much philosophy as a pig fast under a swinging gate.

June 13th. Our regiment was sent off on picket duty, but I did not accompany it. The men who had been sent to the rear were returning daily, but we still had some sickness in camp. The diseases in an army are numerous, but the one that is the most destructive, killing more men than the sword and the rifle, is "home sickness." When this one gets a good hold of a man, it sticks to him tighter than a "grey back" or a leech, and if he unfortunately has anything else the matter, it is very apt to make an end of the victim.

There is but one infallible remedy for the disease, and I never knew it to fail in a single instance, and that is a furlough to go home, or a discharge.

I saw a practical example of the application of this sovereign remedy applied to one of the members of our company and witnessed its wonderful and immediate effect.

Augustin Lejeune, who had been afflicted with rheumatism for some time and who had been unable to perform service, had obtained his discharge this morning. I was going into Tupelo with an ambulance containing Estival Savoie and Aristide Jeandron, who were quite ill, in order to send them to a hospital down the railroad. Auguste Bergeron was also being sent with them, and Frank Roger was to go along and take care of them until they reached the hospital. I told Lejeune that there was no room in the ambulance, as two of the sick men had to lie down, but if he could manage to walk to Tupelo (four miles), I could get him transportation and start him home the same day. He said he thought he could walk that far. So, giving "Fanny" to Bergeron to ride, we started, Roger, Lejeune, and myself on foot. The discharged man, with the aid of a stick, kept up very well for about a mile, when he took the lead and kept it the balance of the route. Arriving at Tupelo, I procured him transportation and saw the sick men placed on the cars, and just before they started, Augustin came out of the cars, hurried to the well, filled up his canteen, left his cane and took a double quick for the cars, and left his rheumatism forever behind.

About the 15th we selected a new camp in the vicinity and removed to it.

By digging some four or five wells about 25 feet deep, we found abundance of good, cool water.

We were formed into a new brigade consisting of the 11th, 16th, 17th, 18th, 19th, 20th La., and 45th Alabama regiments, with Col. A. Reichard of the 20th[34] as commanding officer and put into a regular system of discipline and drill.

Camp near Tupelo, June 15th, 1862. Our excellent commissary, Captain C. T. Patin of Vermilionville, had been sent to the rear sick, and on leaving, I had, in a moment of thoughtless good nature, consented to aid his clerks in procuring rations for the regiment. Recollections of my experience in that department at two or three different periods are not very agreeable, as I invariably got the Dutch in my system heated to a boiling point, which, had it possessed any expansive qualities, would have, very likely, produced an explosion. As we were going into camp at 20 Mile Creek, three days after leaving Corinth, I saw a drove of beeves passing, and, knowing that the soldiers were half crazy for fresh meat, inquiry was made if one of

---

34. Reichard's brigade also included Captain W. E. Burnet's Alabama Battery. The brigade was not really "new" (*ibid.*, Vol. XVII, Pt. 2, p. 632).

them could be obtained for the 18th, and the information given that they were for distribution but could only be transferred to brigade commissaries. Col. Reichard had appointed his regimental commissary, of whose name I was ignorant, to that position, [so] I hastened to brigade headquarters, and, finding the Colonel, I made myself known and inquired the name of his brigade commissary. "Well, hish name ish been read at dresh parade." "Yes, Colonel, but commissaries do not always attend dress parades." "Well, he ish de comishary of my regiment." "I am aware of that, Colonel, but I desire to know his name so that I can find him." "Well, he ish in camps over dar; he ish one big man likes me, mid red hair." By this time the beeves were getting out of sight, and I was getting anxious and replied, "Colonel, there are some beeves over yonder for this brigade, and if you will give me the name of your commissary, we can secure some of them for the troops, and if we are not in a hurry about, they will all be gone." "Well, I tells you every body in my regiment knows him." "Well, Colonel, I don't know *him*, and I don't belong to *your* regiment either, and if you prefer seeing these hungry men go without food to telling the name of your commissary I can't help it." "Why, it's Captain Daniels."[35] That was enough for me, and I left without stopping to express any private opinions, and finding Capt. Daniels, the men had fresh beef for supper, the first time in a month.

Threatening to report the evil doings of one another to superior officers was a method frequently used to scare refractory persons when they didn't behave themselves satisfactorily to the whims of some of their fellow soldiers.

Whilst at this camp I had a little experience of that sort myself.

This Captain Daniels, whose name I had so much difficulty in obtaining at 20 Mile Creek, sent one morning for a wagon to go to Tupelo to transport commissary stores. I sent one, and upon it the Captain had a soldier detailed as a guard over its contents. Business requiring my presence in Tupelo that morning, whilst there I visited the commissary depot and endeavored to purchase a ham but was told to go to my own commissariat, who was authorized to sell to officers a limited amount. As I rode back by the headquarters of our commissary, I inquired if I could not purchase a ham but was in-

---

35. Captain A. Samuel Donald. He had been appointed commissary officer of the 20th Louisiana on February 21. On May 27, he became brigade commisary officer (CSR, Roll 309).

formed that they had none. Going to my own quarters, several officers of the 18th complained that they could not buy anything but
sides from the commissary and asked me if I could not procure some
hams for them. I told them the result of my visit. In a few minutes
Capt. Daniels came over and inquired the name of the teamster who
had driven my wagon to Tupelo that morning. Without giving the
name, I asked him "what the trouble was." "Why, he has stolen
three 'hams' out of the wagon." "He has, eh! Well you can settle that
little matter with the guard whom you had on the wagon." "Yes, but
I *know* the guard; he is a man from my regiment, and he wouldn't
steal anything." "Very well, Captain, and I *know* that you can't hold
my teamsters responsible for anything stolen out of their wagons
unless you bring proof that they are guilty, and as you had a guard
on that wagon you can just regulate that matter with him." "Well,
I'll report him to headquarters, and I want to know his name." "All
right, Captain, my teamsters are not guards. They have their animals to attend to, and they have that to do, and they shall not be
held accountable for losses out of their wagons, which they have no
time to stand watch over."

"Well, what is his name?" "His name is Felix ———, and you can
go and report as soon as you please and be doggoned." (I am not
positive I said doggoned.) The Capt. left, and as he was going away,
the idea occurred that *hams* had been mentioned.

I walked over to the Captain's quarters and inquired "how it was
that he had *hams* stolen, when I was informed half an hour previous
that he had none."

"Oh, they were some I had bought for the officers of the 20th
regiment." "Where did you buy them, Captain?"

"Oh! I purchased them at the depot commissary at Tupelo." "All
right, Captain."

Going back to camp and having the saddle put on "Fanny," I rode
over to Tupelo and found out the facts, and on my return stopped
and told the Capt. that I had been over to see the post commissary,
ascertained how he had obtained that lot of hams for the officers of
the 20th regiment, and as he had threatened to report things to brigade headquarters so glibly that morning, unless the officers of the
18th regiment hereafter received the same privilege as those of the
20th, I should indulge in a little amusement of that kind myself.

"Well, they shall all have some tomorrow."

Tomorrow came, but as we were only allowed a certain number

of rations, many of the officers could not make change, most of the money we had being twenty dollar bills.

Some of the officers proposed to give him a twenty and take his due bill for the balance. However, nothing would do but the change, and finally Captain Lavery picked up a ham and walked off, swearing "he was not going to starve." This settled the matter, the Captain giving a due bill for the change.

After that it was always smooth sailing in that department with us until we separated on leaving Tupelo a month or so later.

Camp near Tupelo, June 20th, 1862. About this time a new army organization occurred. Gen. Beauregard retired on account of ill health, leaving Gen. Bragg in command.[36] We were placed in Gen. Sam Jones' division of Gen. Hardee's corps.[37] Ineffectual attempts were made to merge the 26th La. Regiment, stationed near Vicksburg, with the 18th, which would have been satisfactory to us as we had so many friends in that regiment.[38]

The Crescent was broken up, and the men generally put into the 18th, some thirty of whom were attached to our company.[39]

We were encamped in a beautiful grove, furnished with excellent water obtained from wells, and nearby the spot where Desoto wintered previous to his discovery of the Mississippi and upon which he fought the Chickasaw Indians.

June 25th. Today I started off on what was always an unpleasant business, impressing property, having had orders to collect wagons and mules. Selecting about a dozen teamsters, I started with one

36. Beauregard relinquished command to Bragg on June 17, and the latter became permanent commander of Department No. 2 on June 20 (*OR*, Vol. XVII, Pt. 2, pp. 606, 614).

37. On June 2, Major General Samuel Jones assumed command of Hindman's division, the latter general having been relieved on May 26 to go to Arkansas (*ibid.*, Vol. X, Pt. 2, pp. 547, 575). Hardee had assumed command of Bragg's corps upon the latter's promotion. On June 25, Jones's division was redesignated as the II Corps, Army of the Mississippi, the corps of which were to be redesignated as divisions (*ibid.*, Vol XVII, Pt. 2, pp. 623, 636).

38. The 26th Louisiana Infantry Regiment had two companies from Lafourche Parish and one from Terrebonne. The editor has found no evidence of this plan (Bergeron, *Guide to Louisiana Confederate Military Units*, 134–35).

39. General Bragg disbanded the Crescent Regiment on June 30 and assigned its men to the 18th Louisiana. A primary reason for this order was the fact that approximately three hundred men of the Crescent had been detailed as clerks within the army (CSR, Roll 381; Bartlett, "The Trans-Mississippi," in *Military Record of Louisiana*, 5–6).

wagon and drove near Okolona and encamped for the night. The next morning, after travelling about ten miles and making some inquiries, I rode to a fine looking residence with a nice lot in the front and, dismounting, started into the house.

An ugly looking dog, lying by a tree with a chain around his neck, gave an angry bark, but supposing him to be tied, no attention was paid to his notice, but as I neared the house two other little scamps came out from under the building and, being reinforced with the larger one near the tree, began to show a decisive disposition to out-flank me, but with a few good kicks I kept them at bay for a short time, when one of them inserted his grinders into the calf of my leg, which, not being a patent one, proved anything but agreeable. Choking him loose, I endeavored to use him for a weapon to beat off the other two, but having a block fastened to his neck, I doubt whether he was handled with either skill or grace. A little contraband came out and drove the enemy away, when the one I had hold of dropped very heavily on the ground and left without any further ceremony.

The people were very kind and wrapped ever so many clean rags on my wounds and saturated them with turpentine, felt sorry and—and—told me I ought always to holler at the gate before entering. I was thankful for the information and made up my mind to do so the next time I called at that place.

I was two months recovering from the effects of this morning's exercise, and the blue scars remaining will be useful to show to the rising generation as the effects of grapeshot and canister, some 25 years hence when the frosts of winter begin to whiten the locks that now curl so gracefully over the top of my head. I was absent a week on this business and obtained some six or eight good teams. During this excursion I passed through one of the most beautiful sections of country I ever saw—the Palo Alto Prairie—and have never met with more hospitable or generous people.

I had no difficulty in obtaining the transportation desired, and as long as one team was left on a farm, there was no trouble. Once I rode up to a farm house belonging to a fine looking widow who had a good wagon standing under the shed that was just the thing to finish the complement I was desirous of securing.

Stating the object of my visit, the lady demurred, and after some conversation stepped out and brought me in a glass of blackberry wine and invited me to stay to dinner. This had no effect, however, other than to cause me to offer her twenty-five dollars more for her wagon than I had given anyone else. After unsuccessfully trying to change the subject once or twice, the lady went out of the room and came back with a peach pie and a half dozen of splendid figs. As the latter article was something that I did not expect to see so far north, I was considerably surprised, and whilst the lady gave me an interesting account of her troubles and trials as a lone widow, I quietly enjoyed the luxury of the pie and figs, and after partaking of another glass of blackberry wine, I bade her good morning, without stopping for dinner, and returned to the camp.

This would have been a very pleasant trip for me had it not been for the "doggoned" scrape I got into, and when I reached my quarters my leg was paining me so much that I could scarcely stand upon it or use it. It was during this trip that I obtained some information as to the quantity of buttermilk a soldier could drink.

The second morning out, I stopped at a house and was immediately followed by a half dozen of the men with canteens. The lady of the house was on the gallery, and they inquired if they could get some buttermilk; she said yes and had a large bucketful brought out. They drank that, and she told them to go on the back gallery and fill their canteens.

This they did and emptied the churn. We went about a half mile and the same scene was enacted, and I think that they did not fail to follow me into every house but one and that was because they were afraid of dogs. At least that was the excuse they gave when I laughed at them for their failure in doing so. I made a calculation that night, and my conclusions were that each man had drank three gallons of buttermilk during the day, and I don't think that it was a good day for buttermilk either.

No persons connected with the Confederate armies received so much abuse as the quartermasters, whilst but few, if any, officers performed more arduous and constant duties than did those of the Q. M. Department, especially when engaged in field service. Let forage be plenty or scarce, let the roads be good or bad, let the sun shine or the rain fall, subsistence had to be procured, provisions transported, and the army material moved. Perhaps the simple fact that they had so much to do was the principal reason why so many thought that they ought to do, and be responsible for, everything. Not only did they have to bear the censure due their own shortcomings, but they were supposed to have shoulders broad enough to bear all the abuse that irate individuals were desirous of launching forth.

Being under the necessity of procuring forage animals and means of transportation indispensable to the successful operation of the armies, they were often compelled to take such articles wherever they could be found, without regard to the wishes or desires of the so-called possessors, which was not a very effective method of ingrafting themselves into the good wishes of the people who were often left with short rations of forage and no mules to cultivate their crops. And then those people who had been obliged to give to military power what patriotism would not have yielded began to curse the quartermaster.

Sometimes they would visit the headquarters of the commanding officer and dolefully narrate their troubles, and then the generals would curse the quartermaster for pillaging the country and threaten to have their commission broken, and whilst our citizen would go home rejoicing at the punishment in reserve for the devoted Q. M., the said individual was quietly going about his business with the written orders of that same general for his actions, safely stowed away in his pocket.

When four staff officers and two ornamentals required more wagons to haul their baggage than were allowed to a whole regiment and supplies of forage at headquarters became short for want of transportation, they cursed the quartermasters. When the surgeons, with their three or four clerks, used the ambulances to run about the country begging buttermilk and eggs, and any complaints were made about sick men in the rear, *then they* cursed the quartermaster for not putting the sick on top of their loaded wagons where they could receive the benefit of the sun.

When ordnance officers used one fourth of the ordnance train to carry their *own* private baggage and were found short of ordnance, *they*, in turn, gave the quartermaster fits. When the commissaries got short of supplies and the men came for their rations, *they* expressed their opinions more freely than elegantly because the quartermasters had not brought in their meal before they had it ground.

When a patriotic citizen devoted the best horse he had to the service of the glorious Confederacy and actually rode him to death in travelling from one general's headquarters in effecting a detail of his consumptive son (weight 185 pounds neat, that is after he had washed himself) and wanted the department to let him have horses to carry them home and failing to get those officers to perceive the point, *they*, starting off on foot, cursed the quartermasters. When the boys in camp got short of Confederate money and wanted to play poker, then they unburdened their "pent up powers" and let loose on the quartermasters. When those valiant detailed men, stationed at some village busily engaged in making requisitions for their own clothing, heard that the regiments were to be paid off, marched bravely to the front (provided no enemy was near) with descriptive lists in hand showing that they were already paid far ahead of the soldiers, and had to go back without payment, then they gave the quartermaster particular jesse.

So much favorable attention from all parties was calculated to give those officers a very satisfactory estimate of their own importance, but as they were not vain or egotistical, through patience they bravely bore it all. Who could have been a Q. M. if patience had not been his characteristic virtue?

Not only were they made the recipients of all the wrath that was due to the faults of others, but everybody who had a piece of gold lace on his arm imagined that he had a right to issue orders to the quartermasters. (Some of them changed that opinion before the war closed.) However, the agony was piled on a little too strong sometimes, and the Dutch that lay lurking in the system of those officers would seek for a level. I remember once to have received an order from somebody styling himself "Chief of Staff" to a full general, not more than 1000 miles from Tupelo, instructing the Q. M.'s to keep their wagons greased. I would have been willing to bet high that the author of the order did not know whether it was the body or the wheels of the wagon that needed greasing or whether hog's lard or pumpkin pies would have answered the better for that purpose.

But as just 30 days elapsed before marching orders came, I got bravely over the excitement and trepidation occasioned by such a luminous order.

July 3rd. Many of my wagons needing repair, I left camp this morning with all the blacksmiths and wagon makers I could obtain in search of a shop where the workmen could make the necessary repairs, and finding one about four miles from Okolona, stopped and commenced business. I had to take an ambulance with me, being unable to ride on horseback.

July 4th. The old gentleman and lady whose shop we were using insisted that we should all dine with them, and they gave us an excellent meal, such a one as we were not in the habit of getting. The old man was rather corpulent, and the weather was uncomfortably hot, and the principal burden of his song was to curse the Yankees for not allowing ice to be shipped into the country. He asked the question not less than a dozen times, "What good it did the Northern people to forbid ice to be sent down here."

July 5th. Completing our repairs and loading the wagons with forage, we returned. Everything was quiet about the country, no enemy being near. The discipline of the army was being perfected, the numbers in our regiment were being daily increased by the return of the sick who had been sent to the rear from Corinth, and nothing occurred to disturb my equilibrium except that wonderful order that came down from some chief of staff through all the red tape channels of communication ordering me to "keep my wagons greased."

July 8th. Information reached us that Joseph Clotus Trahant had died at Canton about the 4th July.

Tupelo, July 8th, 1862. Corporal Gustave Abrebat, having been honorably discharged from service on account of disability, left for his home.

July 15. Major Bush, having received the acceptance of his resignation, departed today. The regiment now came under the command, by promotion, of L. Armant of St. James, Colonel; Joseph Collins of New Orleans, Lieutenant Colonel; and Wm. Mouton of Lafayette, Major.

The members of the regiment will remember that there was not any extraordinary affection between the surgeon and assistant surgeon of the 18th. Both had left us at Corinth, being sick, and young Dr. Key was the only physician we had with us during the retreat. Once as I returned from a trip of three or four days, procuring forage, I noticed a Sibley tent[40] pitched near my own, and not being aware of any such tents in our regiment, I walked over to see what it meant and found our assistant surgeon, Dr. Gourrier, snugly ensconced therein, with three or four friends, engaged in a game of what he facetiously styled draw poker, and after the compliments of the morning had been passed in due form and manner, I received a pressing invitation to take a hand. Seeing that the bets consisted princi-

---

40. Henry H. Sibley, later a Confederate brigadier general, had invented the Sibley tent prior to the war. It was a conical tent erected on a tripod, with a single center pole, and could hold twelve men and their equipment (Boatner, *Civil War Dictionary*, 760).

pally of a few grains of corn, I thought that I would be sociable and did so.

Having 20 grains of corn given me, the game proceeded for some time until my ration was gone. Before leaving, however, the information was blandly given me that I was in debt to the firm for the amount of ten dollars. "What for?" "For the 20 grains of corn." "The devil you say; I'll give you half of Fanny's rations for a week for half the money." "That's the rule any how, four bits a grain." "All right," and pulling out a Confederate ten, I passed it over and went to dinner. Ever since that time when I see a lot of men playing with grains of corn, buttons, and such, I take a back seat, thinking I can appreciate the game more fully when a short distance off.

The assistant represented that he had been or was to be appointed surgeon and had fitted himself up accordingly. Three or four days afterwards, the surgeon, Dr. Littlell, returned. Here was a mess now, two surgeons in one regiment would never do. Dr. Littlell was still unwell, and every morning he came to me for an ambulance to go to Tupelo to see Dr. Foard, chief surgeon of the army,[41] about the settlement of the great, absorbing question, "who was surgeon of the 18th?"

As soon as he came into camp, Dr. Gourrier would mount his horse, and over to Tupelo he galloped. This was kept up for several days.

Finally, Dr. Gourrier came and asked transportation for his baggage to Tupelo, having been assigned to duty elsewhere, and in a couple of days Dr. Littlell received the acceptance of his resignation and went home, leaving us without any surgeon, Dr. Key having left as soon as the others returned.

In a day or two, Dr. Bonsall, who was a private in a Mississippi regiment, was assigned to duty in the 18th as assistant surgeon, and an excellent appointment it proved to be for us.[42]

From Corinth, the most of our baggage had been shipped to Okolona, and whilst at this camp I went to that place to endeavor to find it and bring it to camp. That which belonged to our company having been stored in the rear room of a drug store was all complete, but that belonging to the other companies, being stored in some ware-

41. Surgeon A. J. Foard became medical director of Department No. 2 on May 10 (*OR*, Vol. X, Pt. 2, p. 510).

42. Dr. W. B. Bonsall. See Grisamore's sketch of the regimental surgeons in Chapter 5.

house, had all been pillaged, every trunk being broken and not a thing of value left.

July 21. The health of our men was good and improving, our aggregate being 977, of whom 595 were present for duty. Sergeant A. L. St. Martin has been appointed Sergeant Major of the regiment.

The army had been decreasing for some time by the withdrawal of troops. The brigades in our division were now removing every day, and we had made all arrangements for our departure also.[43]

One day our friend Boggins came to me to get his pay. Boggins had a furlough to visit his brother in Alabama, and whilst I am paying him off I will relate an occurrence in which Boggins was a principal actor and for which I am indebted to a friend for reminding me of the circumstance which I had forgotten. It was on the evening of the 28th of February. We had marched several miles and arrived at Pittsburg Landing and encamped.

Now Boggins was possessed of so many amiable qualities that all the messes in his company were at loggerheads about what mess he properly belonged to, and on this day the dispute was so intense that Boggins could not find out what mess really was his. Getting hungry and at a loss for means to obtain a meal, he took a mess chest belonging to Capt. Huntington and went off in the woods to cook his supper. Capt. Huntington's cook was considerably non-plused about preparing supper as his chest was missing. A general search was made, and Boggins found in actual possession and brought before Capt. Huntington. Now Capt. H. was not on very friendly terms with Boggins' commanding officer, Capt. Woods, and did not wish to make any complaint to him and let Boggins go, after expressing his sentiments to him in regard to his conduct.

Sending for his Orderly Sergeant, Captain Huntington informed him of the doings of Boggins and said, "Now, sergeant, you just go and tell Larry McCormick that if Boggins comes into camp some evening with a pair of black eyes, that I'll keep him in tobacco for six months." Larry was what was called in common parlance a "shoulder hitter." The next day we became engaged in battle, and the thing was dropped.

Receiving his pay, he left to see his brother and never after did Boggins return to his command.

43. General Bragg had decided to move his army to Chattanooga and to take the offensive in east Tennessee. This movement began on July 22 (*ibid.*, Vol. XVII, Pt. 2, pp. 655–56, and Vol. LII, Pt. 2, pp. 330–31).

August 4. For three days our division has been leaving. Yesterday one half our brigade left, and this morning the remainder were to go.

We were all up at two o'clock and the wagons loaded, so as to reach Tupelo early in the morning. The wells which had been dug to supply the men with water were about 25 feet deep, with a sugar hogshead in the bottom, the tops being surrounded and covered by rails and pickets. When the reveille was sounded, I gave orders to some of the men to build large fires so as to enable the teamsters to see how to drive through the camps and to assist, by their light, the men in loading their wagons, and in so doing they had taken the coverings of the wells and thrown them on the fire.

After the men had fallen into line and the order to march was given, George Winder and Joe Delaporte of our company, who were perhaps two of the most noted men in the regiment for punctuality in being behind time, came running up to take their places, and not noticing where they were going, the former one tumbled down into one of the wells with gun, knapsack, etc.

Fortunately he fell feet foremost in the center of the hogshead, which, being full of water, saved him from any injury. Obtaining a ladder, he was fished out and caught up with the troops before reaching Tupelo, leaving gun, knapsack, and hat in the well. On returning to the camp, I found everything stripped clean by the citizens of the vicinity, except the bake ovens around which were three or four persons whom I imagined trying to contrive some means of getting them away and another squad in evident despair at their inability to carry off the wells. Remaining over the day, preparations were made for the trains to leave on the succeeding morning for Chattanooga. I shall not soon forget the wretched day it was. The flies, which had collected about the camp, congregated about the few of us who were left, and it was one continual battle all day long until darkness came to our relief by driving the pests away. The troops proceeded down the Mobile and Ohio Railroad towards Mobile.

August 4th. As the train upon which the 18th Regiment was transported was nearing Citronelle Station about sunrise, it stopped to wood, and just as it was starting away and before it got into rapid motion, another train came up behind and, striking ours, smashed up the rear car in which the daily guard was riding. By this collision Aristide Jeandron of our company was killed, his body being torn to pieces, and Wm. Ledet was wounded. Several others of the different companies were wounded more or less.[44] The command passed through Mobile and proceeded to Pollard and encamped on the 6th.[45]

Near Tupelo, August 4, 1862.   This morning the trains of our brigade, under direction of Capt. Henshaw[46] of the 11th La., left at daylight for Chattanooga.[47] The wagons transported only provisions and forage for teamsters and animals, and we made from 20 to 25 miles per day. This night we encamped near Okolona. On the evening of the 6th, we reached Meridian, where for the first time I tasted water of an artesian well flowing out of the earth, from what depth I did not ascertain, but it came far enough to taste distinctly of sulphur.

On the 7th, we passed through Columbus. The country through which we travelled was a magnificent one, being considered the loveliest and wealthiest in Mississippi.

Leaving Columbus eastward, we began to enter hilly countries. The weather was very warm, the roads dusty and disagreeable. On the 9th we encamped on a branch called Fire Coal Creek, which we thought was well named, for it was so hot that a bed of fire coals would not have made the heat much more oppressive.

On the 10th, being ordered ahead, I rode 45 miles to Tuscaloosa, in the hope of securing the blacksmith shops to shoe our horses and mules, many of whose hoofs were wearing out on the stony roads. I found Tuscaloosa one of the most beautiful places I had seen, and on that night I slept in a house for the first time since I had left home. Our men had found an abundance of peaches all along the road, the trees being full of fruit and all ripe.

44. The train that hit that of the 18th Louisiana carried the men of the 19th Louisiana. A member of the latter unit wrote home that the collision killed six men of the 18th and wounded a large number of other men, whereas the 19th had only one man killed (John A. Harris to his wife, August 11, 1862, in John A. Harris Letters, 1861–1864, Louisiana and Lower Mississippi Valley Collection, Special Collections, Hill Memorial Library, Louisiana State University, Baton Rouge).

45. Because some of the infantrymen in garrison at Mobile and Pollard had gone on to Chattanooga, the 18th and 19th Louisiana regiments received orders on July 23 to join the Mobile garrison. Both units joined the garrison at Pollard (*OR*, Vol. XVII, Pt. 2, p. 657).

46. Captain John H. Henshaw, quartermaster of the 11th Louisiana (CSR, Roll 227).

47. The wagon trains of Hardee's command were ordered to move via Aberdeen, Columbus, Tuscaloosa, Will's Valley, and Gadsden to Rome, Georgia, on their way to Chattanooga. The 1st Louisiana Regulars Infantry Regiment accompanied the trains (*OR*, Vol. XVII, Pt. 2, pp. 656–57).

On the 13th, we crossed the Cahawba River; the hills now appeared to be piled upon top of each other, and the teamsters having to get up and down so often to unlock and lock their wagons, their patience became exhausted, and many of them began to show a disposition to use "cuss words" for which they became so famous in subsequent times.

On the 14th, we reached a little place called Montevallo, on a railroad running from Selma to Jacksonville, Alabama.[48] Montevallo was a small place, with one street having houses on each side; the principal inhabitants were a few folks, one drug store, two doctors, a grave yard, and big bridge over the creek.

On the 15th, Fanny being too lame to ride, I took her on the cars and went to the terminus of the railroad at Blue Mountain and awaited the train. Stopping at the hotel, I soon acquired the good graces of the landlady by making pets of a couple of five-year-old girls and was bountifully supplied with peach cobbler every day.

On the 21st, the train came up, and we continued our journey through Jacksonville and took dinner in Georgia. Towards evening we approached a little village called Cave Spring. Stopping at a fine-looking residence in the edge of the town to get a drink of water, a Negro girl came out to the gate who attracted our attention so much that we asked her "how old she was." "Eight years." "How much do you weigh?" "180 pounds." "Have you any more girls like you about here?" "Yes, sir, I have another brother of the same kind."

In the edge of this town a spring flows out of the mountain, furnishing water to make a large creek.

On the 23rd, we reached Rome, a very pleasant village, famous as the home of Bill Arp[49] but continued onward and encamped on the Coosa River.

On the 24th, we passed up Van's Valley with high mountains on either side and reached Ringgold on the 25th and encamped on the banks of the Chickamauga Creek.

On the 26th, starting at daybreak, we ascended a mountain ridge, and as the road extended down on the opposite side it seemed to lose

48. The Alabama and Tennessee Railroad.

49. Under the pen name of Bill Arp, Charles Henry Smith (1826–1903), a private in the Army of Northern Virginia, wrote humorous letters in dialect to the Rome *Southern Confederacy*. These letters were continued after the war for more than twenty-five years in the Atlanta *Constitution* (Max J. Herzberg, *The Reader's Encyclopedia of American Literature* [New York, 1962], 1040).

itself in an immense lake beneath us. I looked around to find some other road without success and started down the hill, soon finding that the supposed lake was nothing but an immense fog filling up the valley below us. A few hours travelling over the hills, affording many splendid and picturesque views, we entered the long looked for Chattanooga, seated upon the banks of the clear and tranquil Tennessee.

Our journey had been one of pleasure and satisfaction. During the whole route rain had fallen upon us but once. The roads were splendid, and the country well watered. I can say one thing for the mountainous regions over which we passed; it is a great place for persimmons. The trees were growing in every fence corner and spontaneously about the woods, and they were as full of fruit as the branches could bear; unfortunately they were not ripe, but Jean Plaisance, who was along with me, would continue to taste them, seeing them appear so luscious, and nothing could stop him until his mouth became so drawn up that he could not get a good sized peach between his lips.

As soon as we reached Chattanooga, I reported to the Division Quartermaster, and by the time I got back to where I left my train, I found them all moving into town. The whole army had crossed the Tennessee and were waiting only for the trains to commence their march into Kentucky. During the night they were ferried over the river, and the next day we moved to the main army, some ten miles north of Chattanooga.

Here my wagons were rapidly distributed to the departing troops, and in such a manner that I could not obtain receipts for anything I had.[50] The chief quartermaster referring me to the regimental officers, and when searching for them I found them on the march or not at all, so that I gave up in disgust and let them go. The quartermasters of all the regiments were left in about the same predicament

50. According to a statement dated August 27, 1862, in Grisamore's service record, his train "was taken possession of by Major (Porter) Chief Quartermaster of Brig. Gen. Anderson's Division, sent forward to the army then in motion, without giving me any receipts for any of the property." The train consisted of twelve wagons, forty-five mules, two horses, and two ambulances (CSR, Roll 293). Brigadier General J. Patton Anderson did not have a Major Porter as a quartermaster on his staff. Grisamore may have been referring to Major James T. Peyton, who did serve Anderson in that capacity for a time (Joseph H. Crute, Jr., *Confederate Staff Officers, 1861–1865* [Powhatan, Va., 1982], 4).

that I was in. As I did not find my own regiment here, I prepared to go to Pollard, Alabama, with the teamsters under my charge. The quartermaster of the 17th La.[51] did the same, as our regiments were left at that station together.

Chattanooga, August 28th, 1862. My transportation having been nearly all taken away from me with so little ceremony that I determined to let those who took it without receipting for it take the responsibility of their act also and began to make arrangements to return to my own command, which was stationed at Pollard, Alabama.

Calling upon Gen. Dan. Adams,[52] who was commanding the Brigade into which my trains were being distributed, I requested him to have the teamsters relieved. He said he "had no authority to do so." That a brigadier general had no power to detail teamsters to drive his wagons was a fact of which, up to that time, I had been profoundly ignorant. Proceeding then to the headquarters of Gen. Anderson, commanding the division,[53] applying to him for the relief of my teamsters, he directed his Adjutant to issue an order to that effect, but whilst the order was being prepared he inquired how I "had come to Chattanooga with these men." Explaining that I had brought my trains over here expecting to meet my own regiment but had ascertained that it had been halted near Mobile, he stopped his Adjutant and peremptorily refused to let them leave.

"Well, General, you are now starting into Kentucky; these men have no descriptive lists and will be unable to draw clothing or pay and will freeze during the winter." "Their descriptive lists must be sent to them." "My colonel gave me strict orders to bring my men all back to the command." "Can't help it, sir, they can't go."

"Good morning, General." When I reached my camping ground I found that several of my teamsters had been relieved already, and, telling the others the bad success I had had, advised them "to make preparations to accompany the army, as I thought it doubtful whether they could get away." However, as some quartermaster

---

51. Grisamore probably meant the quartermaster of the 19th Louisiana, First Lieutenant Jack Hodges (CSR, Roll 303).

52. Brigadier General Daniel Adams had been assigned to Jones's division on August 13. The army was reorganized two days later, and Adams received command of all of the Louisiana troops in the army (OR, Vol. XVI, Pt. 2, pp. 756, 759).

53. Brigadier General J. Patton Anderson had assumed command of the division in July when Jones was relieved (ibid., Vol. XVII, Pt. 2, p. 659).

would come around inquiring for a team, I would inquire whether he had a driver, and if so, I generally had a wagon to suit him. I gave Louis, of my company, a fifty dollar bill and warned him to make it go as far as possible, but shortly after a quartermaster came up and wanted just such a wagon as Louis had. Finding he had a driver, I told Louis to hitch up his wagon quickly and I could get him out of the scrape. I have seen teams harnessed in a hurry frequently but have never witnessed the feat done so admirably and so rapidly as it was that morning. Another team, driven by Felix Vicknair of the St. James companies,[54] I accompanied about 200 yards, and seeing another teamster ready to take it, I told Felix to get back to camp quickly.

It was about 200 yards by the road, but a short cut across an old field, with two fences in the way covered over with a hedge of briars about six feet high, shortened the distance about one half.

Felix took the short cut.

I had now liberated all who were with me but one, an Irishman named Tom Mack,[55] who was driving an ambulance. I told him that the boys were all free now but himself and recommended him to get sick with as little delay as possible. In a few minutes someone came up for an ambulance to take a sick man back to Chattanooga. I told him I had one, but the driver was unwell. Going to the ambulance, poor Tom was rolling on the grass in all the agonies of an imaginary colic, but the quartermaster had no teamster and called for some volunteer to drive it; John Rand,[56] one of my men, who wore No. 15 shoes, volunteered his services, and thus I got rid of all my wagons, thinking that if big feet got himself in a scrape, he might get out of it himself.

Immediately packing up our things and making a pack horse of Fanny, we started back to Chattanooga. Meeting one of my teamsters who had been detained, I gave him a pass to cross the Tennessee River, not knowing whether it would be of any account, and advised him to get to Chattanooga as soon as he could; we went on but it was not 15 minutes before he caught up with us, puffing like a porpoise, stating that he got one of the fatigue men with the train to drive a few minutes for him.

54. Felix Vicknair was a private in Company A (CSR, Roll 297).
55. Thomas Mack was a private in Company D (ibid., Roll 295).
56. John S. Rand was a private in Company F (ibid., Roll 296).

Meeting John Rand, I gave him a pass, and in less than a half hour he had given a fellow $2.50 to drive the ambulance to camp. All were now free but one whom I found at the river, and I was studying up some plan to get him off when the quartermaster of the 17th [sic] Regiment, who was in the same predicament that I was, rode up and told me that he was about to be arrested for endeavoring to get his men off. I began to think it was a good time for me to take a hint, and left off maneuvering and turned my attention to an itinerant peddlar with a nose as flat as a slap-jack, who murdered English without any apparent compunction of conscience, and was selling some merchandise he had in a box cart, bellowing out every few minutes, "Tabac six bits, knife two a half, razor two doll, shoes seven doll," occupying the odd moments cussing his old horse for refusing to pull his cart. Crossing over the river about 4 o'clock with all my men except one, I went through the town and encamped in the woods about one mile from the river and instructed the boys that "the less they showed themselves the better it would be for all hands," a piece of advice which they all followed without much coaxing.

Chattanooga, August 29th, 1862. Having procured rations for the men and forage for the horses, we went to the railroad depot at dark and put our horses and baggage on the cars. We were furnished with a box car at the rear of the trains.

August 30th. At daylight the cars left. About 8 or 9 o'clock, we reached and entered Tunnel Hill and passed through the mountains.

This was the first time that the darkness was so dense that I thought it could be chopped out in square blocks, and I felt very much like trying to get a piece of it any how, but having no axe, I could not do so.

"This Tunnel is 1477 feet long, 18 feet in height and 12 feet in width. It is one of the grandest achievements that grace the annals of the human family. It is in a great measure through solid rock. The lateral walls of rock six feet at base and five feet at top. The approaches to the Tunnel are protected on both sides by massive masonry. It is cut through one of the ridges of the Blue Mountains, extending through the upper portion of Georgia."

As we entered the Tunnel, there were many of the men on top of the cars, not one of whom knew anything about such a passage, and as we came out they could be heard to draw long breaths, and an amusing conversation was struck up in endeavoring to explain to each other how close they laid themselves along the top of the cars and how small they had made themselves during the passage.

We reached Atlanta, changed cars, and proceeded onward to West Point, arriving at 11 P.M. and remaining over until morning.

At Atlanta the passenger trains were filled with soldiers of the Virginia army returning home on furlough. It was a season of melons and fruits of various kinds, and at every depot, numbers of boys and Negroes were waiting with carts, wheelbarrows, and baskets loaded with them for sale. As we were moving off from some station, I noticed a soldier jumping into the cars, pursued by a Negro demanding pay for a melon which the soldier had in his arms. As he mounted the steps, the Negro caught hold of him, causing him to miss his step and fall, but fortunately he dropped into a ditch, where he remained until the train passed over him. As we moved over him I noticed the melon, burst into pieces by the fall and green as a gourd. By the time the cars had passed over, the speed was so great that our unfortunate fellow could not catch up with the train. The last I saw of him he was coming at a double quick, bareheaded and coatless, those articles being on the cars.

August 31st.   This evening at 2 o'clock we reached Montgomery during a thunderstorm. After the rain was over, I rode over the town and to the depot of the Mobile road and had our baggage removed to that depot. At night very foolishly took a bed at the Exchange Hotel and was paid for my trouble by passing a restless and uneasy night instead of one of sound and refreshing sleep I might have had under a tree or on some loose plank.

September 1st.   Embarking on a train of open cars, we started this morning toward Mobile, and after getting off the track once and enjoying a shower bath or two during the day, we arrived at Pollard about sunset and in a half hour were in camp with our friends, from whom we had separated a month previous at Tupelo.

Our journey from Tupelo has been very pleasant, and for me, one of the most agreeable recollections of my campaigns.

During the whole distance I had any abundance of melons, peaches, apples, etc.; the people were kind and hospitable and sold us anything we wished to purchase whilst the scenery among the mountains was often grand and sublime. I found the men all in good health and encamped in a beautiful piney wood grove, with springs of clear, pure water and near two running streams affording splendid bathing facilities.

I found that on my return that Capt. J. K. Gourdain, Corporal J. V. Knoblock, and privates Dozelien Boudreaux, Dorville Triche, William Guidroz, Demophon LeBlanc, William Burk, Amadeo Lejeune, and C. J. Benoit, who had been sent home from Corinth, had been in camp for several days. From them I was enabled to obtain news from home for the first time in 60 days.

Joseph Miller and Joseph Roger were mustered into service in our company this day.

September 10.   J. Franklin Aucoin and J. Emile Naquin, who had been absent wounded, returned from home.

September 25.   Privates Jules Giroir, Joseph Leonard, and Florian Rouye, who had been captured at Shiloh, returned today. They were kept prisoners at Pittsburg Landing for two weeks after the battle and then removed to Camp Douglas, where they were kept until exchanged. Many others of the different companies are also coming back from captivity.

September 29.   Privates Joseph Brogden, A. J. Bouyan, Francois Guillot, and A. Lombas, prisoners at Shiloh, returned today.

Also, Marcel Ledet, sent home from Corinth, returned, bringing with him William Ledet, Marcelin Ledet, and Pierre Autin, who had been mustered into service on the 22nd September at Port Hudson and were attached to our company.

Pollard, Alabama, September 1862.   This is a station on the railroad leading from Mobile to Montgomery and about 75 miles from the former place. At this point also a branch road extends to Pensacola in Florida.[57] There were a few cabins around the depot, half concealed amongst the pine trees. There was no evidence of any cultivation of the soil in the vicinity, the general appearance of the country and the inhabitants thereof indicating that the principal food was composed of pine top whiskey and gophers.

This latter is an enterprising animal, something similar to a turtle, which some folks, when they become hungry, think to be

57. At Pollard, the Mobile and Great Northern Railroad, which ran between that town and Tensas Landing, joined the Alabama and Florida Railroad. The latter provided service between Pensacola, Florida, and Montgomery. Pollard was thus an important link in the Confederacy's transportation system. From May, 1862, until early 1865, the Confederates stationed troops at Pollard to guard the junction, to watch Union forces in Pensacola, and to help protect Mobile from threats in that direction (Robert C. Black, III, *Railroads of the Confederacy* [Chapel Hill, 1952], 51, 75–76; *OR*, VI, 762, 766; Vol. LII, Pt. 2, pp. 164–65; and Ser. IV, Vol. I, p. 732.

good food. I never was hungry whilst we remained at Pollard. They live under the earth and throw up small piles of dirt and sand whenever they wish to increase the dimensions of the subterranean mansions or the increase of family requires more room.[58] I awoke one morning and found about a half barrel of sand piled up at the side of my bed and another in the door of my tent. I had cause to congratulate myself that Mr. Gopher had not come under my cot, for in that case somebody might have been rolled out of his bed and his dreams disturbed.

There is a story of a man who was once riding by a Gopher village and who noticed a boy's feet in the air, with his head and body under the ground. Approaching the youngster, he inquired what he was doing. The reply was that he was hunting a gopher. The traveller remarked that he did not imagine he would catch him. "Catch him," says the boy, "Hell! I'm bound to catch him; we ain't got no meat to home." Whether this took place at Pollard or not, I am unable to say, but I was shown the identical hole out of which the boy finally dragged his gopher.

The boys about camp dug so many holes after these creatures that the woods resembled a graveyard out of which the Ku Klux had just been heavily reinforced. When it rained, those sandy plains became so soft that it was dangerous to leave the beaten road. One day I thought I would ride across the woods just after a heavy shower, but before I had gone 100 yards Fanny's fore feet went down into a hole nearly pitching me over her head, and 10 steps further on both hind feet went down and had I not been pretty active I would have gone down too.

Fearing that I would injure my reputation as a skillful horseman, I got into the road and stayed there.

Any person who read the Mobile papers in 1862 will remember that each of them had a column headed "See what Alabama has done," containing a list of regiments, batteries, etc., which that gallant state had sent to the field. This heading had become a sort of

58. The gopher tortoise (*Gopherus polyphemus*) is found all along the coastal areas of the South from South Carolina to eastern Louisiana. They dig burrows that may reach thirty feet in length and that may go as far as twelve feet deep. A large chamber at the end of the burrow provides the tortoise a sleeping area, protection from high temperatures, and a place for hibernation. The tortoise was eaten by the poorer people of the rural South (Peter C. H. Pritchard, *Encyclopedia of Turtles* [Neptune, N.J., 1979], 426–27, 430–431).

byword with us, and when any of the men came into camp with a gopher or any other peculiar production of that state, he would hold it up and begin yelling at the top of his voice, "See what Alabama has done."

Whilst at Pollard I obtained a lot of clothing, consisting of jackets, pants, shirts, and kepis.

The pants and shirts had been made by the kind-hearted ladies of Alabama, who were thinking of their absent mountaineer husbands and lovers and were consequently much too large for our little Creole troops; the jackets, however, had been made by some tailors on contract and were of a good size for 10-year-old boys; the kepis were made of the same material with leather visors that would either stand straight up in front or turn square down over the eyes. They were all made of a species of gray cotton cloth and had they been made of a proper size they would have been of much service to the men.

There was a little devilish Frenchman in one of the St. James companies named Macon.[59] One day after drill, when the men had all gone into their tents or were dozing in the shade of the trees, this Macon put on one of the biggest pair of pants he could find and by rolling up a yard of each leg succeeded in getting his feet clear; then he put on a shirt that reached to his knees and a jacket that would not button by six inches and extending barely half way to his waist; then he put on a small kepi with the visor down behind; and thus equipped, he issued out of his tent and with both arms extending into the air ran all around the camps yelling at every jump, "See what Alabama has done, see what Alabama has done." Whilst the sleepy boys, being thus summarily aroused from their dreams, raised a whoop the like of which never was heard in those woods before.

Pollard was considered of sufficient importance, in the imagination of the colonel[60] commanding the troops in that vicinity (some four or five regiments),[61] to have a provost marshal, and our Capt.

59. Private J. H. Masson of Company A (CSR, Roll 295).

60. Colonel J. R. F. Tatnall. The troops at Pollard made up a part of the District of the Gulf, headquartered at Mobile, and were variously known as the Detachment of Observation or Eastern Division (OR, XV, 770, 850, 1068).

61. Among the units at Pollard about this time were the 18th and 19th Louisiana, 2nd Alabama Cavalry Regiment, 29th Alabama Infantry Regiment, and a battalion of Florida cavalry (ibid., 850, 1068).

Ben. S. Story was the happy individual upon whose shoulders this dignity was placed. In order that everyone might know the huge fact that Pollard had a provost marshal, Capt. Ben had notices posted upon various pine trees similar to the following: "Hereafter the price of watermelons at this post will be $1.00 for large size, 75 cents for medium, and 50 cents for smaller ones," to which was added the usual warning of confiscation, guardhouse, etc., in case of violation. It made no difference how big or how little the melons might be, there was always the large, medium, and small ones to suit the prices.

Some distance above Pollard is a village called Greenville, where melons and chickens grow spontaneously, and every day large numbers of them were brought into our camps for sale. Pollard was also remarkable for the manufacture of an article facetiously called "Beer."

Over persuaded by the eloquence of one of my friends, I once invested five cents in a mug of that article and drank—part of it. I studied over it awhile and came to the conclusion it was composed of dish water, soap suds, old buttermilk, and rotten potatoes, mixed together in a gopher hole, dipped out with an old shoe, and strained through a saddle blanket.

Whilst we were at Pollard, Lieut. Col. Collins, who had been absent since the battle of Shiloh, returned to the command, mounted on a fine horse whose various evolutions (not laid down in tactics) at the regular drills afforded a good deal of fun to the boys.

Owing to some irregularity in the promotions of field officers in the 18th Regiment, orders came from Richmond ordering a new election to take place forthwith, which resulted in the election of L. L. Armant as Colonel, Joseph Collins as Lieutenant Colonel, and Wm. Mouton as Major.[62] Those were the officers actually serving as such by promotion. Lieut. Sept. Webre of St. James was appointed Adjutant.

The duties of the troops were very light, some little guard duty being all that was required.

The health of the regiment was good, and we had but little to do but amuse ourselves generally as each one saw fit to do.

---

62. The trouble evidently stemmed from the fact that these officers had gained their position by promotion rather than by election as called for by the Conscript Act of April 16, 1862.

Towards the close of the month, rumors began to spread that we were soon to be sent to the Trans-Mississippi, which rumors became fact, and the orders to prepare to march were received and the men notified accordingly.[63]

63. On September 1, 1862, Secretary of War George W. Randolph wrote Brigadier General John H. Forney, commander at Mobile, that the War Department wanted quickly to send troops to Louisiana. There they would form an army for Major General Richard Taylor, who had recently assumed command of the state. Randolph asked if the 18th and 19th Louisiana regiments could be sent, but only the former received orders to go to Louisiana (OR, XV, 804).

Silas T. Grisamore
Courtesy Bettie Wurzlow, and Historic Thibodaux Collection, Allen J. Ellender Archives,
Nicholls State University Library, Thibodaux, La.

Corporal Paul Thibodaux
Courtesy Claude J. Knobloch, Thibodaux, La.

Colonel Alfred Mouton
Courtesy Lucile Mouton Griffin Collection, Southwestern Archives and Manuscripts Collection, University of Southwestern Louisiana, Lafayette, La.

Colonel Alfred Roman

From Thomas M'Caleb, *The Louisiana Book* (New Orleans, 1894)

Major Leopold L. Armant
Courtesy Confederate Memorial Hall, New Orleans

Captain Joseph Collins
Courtesy Louisiana Historical Collection, Manuscripts Section, Howard-Tilton Memorial
Library, Tulane University, New Orleans

Captain John T. Lavery
Courtesy Louisiana Historical Collection, Manuscripts Section, Howard-Tilton Memorial
Library, Tulane University, New Orleans

3 To the Trans-Mississippi Department

Pollard, Alabama, October 2nd, 1862. Today tents were struck, and the 18th Regiment removed to the railroad depot. After waiting all night for a train, we left on the morning of the 3rd towards Mobile, bidding farewell to that land of gophers and pine top whiskey. Captains C. M. Shepherd of St. James and J. T. Lavery of New Orleans were left behind, being detained on a court martial.

At 5 o'clock we reached the Tensas River and immediately embarked on board the steamer *Dick Keys.* Our trip over the beautiful bay of Mobile was exceedingly pleasant and agreeable.

The moon was shining brightly, whilst light winds gently undulated the water, whose waves looked like fringes of silver rolling before us. The tall trees in the dim distance resembled rising clouds, and the glimmering lights in the city twinkled like fiery stars.

Two large mounds, one on either side of our pathway, developed themselves into formidable batteries, whilst two pile drivers were continuously at work from morning till night, from night till the morning, placing obstructions in the channel. Moving slowly along, we had a fine view of two immense gunboats and a monster ram[1] lying quietly at anchor as we approached the Mobile wharf and debarked, transportation being in waiting to remove our baggage to the depot of the Mobile and Ohio Railroad.

At midnight, I lay down upon an open car, in company with Lieutenant Aucoin, and covering myself with a blanket, resigned myself to dreams and slumber.

The troops had been encamped in some cotton presses in the city. As I was sinking away into dreamy oblivion, some steamboat passing along the distant bay began to play her calliope, and as the music softened by the passing waters reached my visionary and half forgetful senses, I fancied the strains such as those which were formerly

---

1. The gunboats were probably the *Alert* and the *Selma,* and the ram was undoubtedly the *Baltic* (William N. Still, Jr., *Iron Afloat: The Story of the Confederate Armorclads* [Nashville, 1971], 80, 188).

sung to the gods in the midnight frolics on the heights of Olympus. The steamer moved gradually away, sweeter and softer became the strains until the last notes were lost in the distance.

The 4th we remained in the city to give the men time to make such purchases as they could. I succeeded in obtaining some quartermaster stores and devoted my leisure moments during the day to the study and consumption of oysters. How many dozen I ate upon that day, I know not, but I remember distinctly to have had them served up in every way imaginable that I could think of and was progressing along through the different styles the third time when we were ordered to embark on the cars, and at 5 o'clock P.M. the whistle sounded, the train moved, and the city of Mobile was soon lost to our view. At daybreak of the 6th, we arrived at Meridian. At this point we met Ulysse Hymel, who had been a prisoner since the battle of Shiloh, accompanied by several other members of the regiment.

After some very sociable words with the railroad agents, who talked about keeping us here all day, we changed cars and left, arriving at Jackson, Miss., during the afternoon, at which city we remained until the 7th.

The battle at Corinth took place about this time,[2] and we came very near being sent up there but were finally ordered towards Vicksburg, which city of hills we reached at ten o'clock P.M.

At this place we were pleased to meet our friends of the 26th Regiment, Lieutenants Navarre, LeBlanc, and others.[3]

The troops were marched on board of a steamboat, but daylight was breaking when I finished removing our baggage from the cars and getting on board. The boat immediately left, and after a pleasant run of 24 hours, we landed at the mouth of Red River on the morning of the 9th.

At this point we met some 300 or 400 conscripts from Assumption on their way to Vicksburg,[4] among whom were many of my former friends. Procuring transportation, I removed our baggage to

2. The Battle of Corinth occurred October 3–4 (Boatner, *Civil War Dictionary*, 428–29).

3. Lieutenant Silvere Navarre, Company D, and Lieutenant L. A. LeBlanc, Company I, 26th Louisiana Infantry (CSR, Roll 336).

4. These conscripts were assigned to units manning the water batteries at Vicksburg (Barnes F. Lathrop, "The Lafourche District in 1862: Confederate Revival," *Louisiana History*, I [1960], 317–18).

the landing on Old River, whilst the men cooked up rations, and at dark, embarking on three small steamers, we started down the Atchafalaya. On the 10th we reached the lakes, and as we were passing through Chicot Pass, the weather presented such a threatening appearance that we tied up until the morning of the 11th. Cutting loose at daybreak, we soon reached the Teche, and proceeding up this stream, we arrived at the village of New Iberia during the night, and on the morning of the 12th, the regiment went into camp in the grove opposite that village. Having been ordered to report to Maj. Gen. Dick Taylor, we had no idea what our next move would be. The Crescent Regiment, which had been merged into the 18th, was here met by Col. McPheeters with orders to reorganize the same.[5] Accordingly, the transfer of the members of that regiment was made by our officers. Here I was pleased to meet many friends from Lafourche, from whom I obtained much information concerning matters and things at home.

The men paid a visit to the village of New Iberia during the afternoon, and many came back to camp with a large supply of rum—in their heads.

October 17.   Having received orders to go to Berwick's Bay, the ladies, previous to our embarkation, came over to our camp and presented us with a wreath of roses for our flag.

October 18.   Debarking at the Bay at sunrise, we pitched our tents on the plain back of the village, and on the 19th marching orders came at 3 o'clock A.M., when we crossed the Bay, took the cars for Terrebonne, at which place Gen. Mouton came on board, and proceeded onward toward Bayou des Allemands. We were pleased to meet our beloved Colonel, whom we had not seen since he left us, wounded, at Corinth, and were delighted to see him with a wreath upon his collar, and were still better satisfied to learn that we were to be retained under his command.[6] On arriving at des Al-

5. The Crescent Regiment had been merged into the 18th Louisiana on June 30 at Tupelo. Captains William C. C. Claiborne, Jr., and Henry B. Stevens had gone to Richmond and obtained an order restoring the Crescent's organization. Colonel George P. McPheeters had entered service as major of the regiment and had been promoted to colonel on July 28, 1862 (Bartlett, "The Trans-Mississippi," in *Military Record of Louisiana*, 5–6; CSR, Roll 381).

6. Mouton was promoted to brigadier general on April 16, 1862, while recovering from his wound. Upon his return to duty, he was assigned by Major General Richard Taylor to command of the Lafourche district (Warner, *Generals in Gray*, 223).

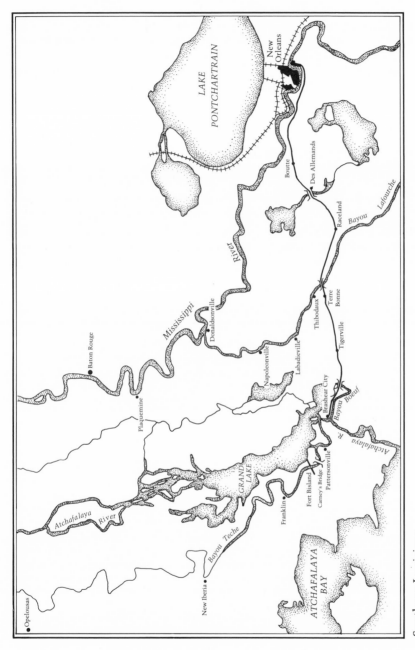

Southern Louisiana
Map by Bobbie Young

lemands, we were drawn up in line of battle in the open space to the left of the railroad beyond the bayou. The Yellow Jacket Battalion of Lieut. Col. Fournet was stationed there, or a portion of it at least. It was said that some mutinous disposition had been shown by some of the officers and men of that Battalion on account of their having been merged with some other battalion so as to form a regiment.[7] Gen. Mouton, having addressed the officers and men and exposed to them the folly and impropriety of attempting to obtain redress of grievances by mutiny, pacified them, and our command was re-embarked, when we returned to the Bay and were snugly in camp at midnight.

Some of the boys thought it pretty severe to pass in sight of the houses containing their fathers, mothers, brothers, and sisters, whom they had not seen for twelve months, without being allowed to stop, but they had to do it notwithstanding.

On the 25th of that month,[8] Thibodaux was a military camp under the command of Brigadier General Alfred Mouton, the first Colonel of the Eighteenth Louisiana Infantry, C. S. A., who had been promoted for gallantry on the battlefield at Shiloh.

About the same date, the Federal forces under General Butler in New Orleans had sent a fleet of gun boats by sea to the mouth of the Atchafalaya River, up which they were to ascend to Brashear, now Morgan, City, and another force, under General Weitzel, by steamboats to be landed at Donaldsonville. With this force they expected to capture the entire Confederate command, whose exit from this section of country was to be stopped at Berwick Bay by the gunboat fleet.[9]

---

7. Lieutenant Colonel Valsin A. Fournet's 10th Louisiana Infantry Battalion was consolidated with Lieutenant Colonel Franklin H. Clack's 12th Louisiana (Confederate Guards Response) Infantry Battalion about October 10 to form the 33rd Louisiana Infantry Regiment. The battalion organizations were restored on November 22 (CSR, Roll 281; Arthur W. Hyatt, Diary, Entries of October 10, November 24, 1862, in Arthur W. Hyatt Papers, 1861–1865, Louisiana and Lower Mississippi Valley Collection, Special Collections, Hill Memorial Library, Louisiana State University, Baton Rouge).

8. Grisamore's account of his regiment's movements from October 25–30 is not included in extant issues of the *Sentinel*. The narrative given here has been reconstructed from two subsequent issues.

9. Major General Benjamin F. Butler, commanding the Union Department of the Gulf, had sent Brigadier General Godfrey Weitzel with five infantry regiments, two field batteries, and four cavalry companies to Donaldsonville to disperse the Confed-

The Confederate troops here consisted of Vincent's Second Louisiana Cavalry, Semmes' Battery, several companies of the state militia, Jumel's cavalry, and some other detached companies.[10]

On October 25, the General commanding immediately issued orders to the commanding officers of the Crescent Regiment stationed at New Iberia and the 18th Louisiana Regiment encamped at Berwick City to report to his headquarters without delay, leaving army trains on the west of that Bay.

Those two commands were greatly reduced in numbers, having been consolidated into one regiment in June and reorganized separately at New Iberia in October 1862. The Crescent did not muster over 100 guns at roll call, whilst the 18th did not produce over 200 men fit for duty.[11] Col. Leopold L. Armant commanded the 18th; Lt. Col. McPheeters commanded the Crescent Regiment.[12]

On their route to Thibodaux, at Bayou Boeuf, they were strengthened by the addition of Ralston's Battery[13] of two guns. The train reached Terrebonne Station about sunset, when the troops debarked and immediately marched to and through Thibodaux and, taking a flatboat, were cordelled up as far as Labadieville. Reporting to Gen. Mouton, they were formed into a brigade with senior Col. Armant in command, leaving the 18th in charge of Lt. Col. Collins. The mounted company of Capt. Jumel was attached to this brigade.

The weather had been turning cold all day; a sharp, stinging, North wind was blowing furiously.

The writer was in charge of the ammunition wagon, all trains being left behind.

Crossing the bridge and proceeding up the bayou, the wind became so powerful that the mules could not withstand its force. Ar-

---

erate forces in the Lafourche district. To cooperate with Weitzel, Lieutenant Commander Thomas M. Buchanan had orders to proceed with five gunboats to Berwick Bay and cut off the Confederate retreat (*OR*, XV, 159; *OR*, *Navies*, XIX, 330).

10. Colonel William G. Vincent's 2nd Louisiana Cavalry Reigment; Captain Oliver J. Semmes' Confederate Regular Battery; companies of the Terrebonne Militia Regiment; Captian Allen Jumel's Company I, 2nd Louisiana Cavalry; and probably some companies of the 33rd Louisiana Infantry (*OR*, XV, 176).

11. General Mouton reported the 18th Louisiana as being 240 men strong and the Crescent as 135 men (*ibid.*).

12. See note 5 above.

13. Battery H, 1st Mississippi Light Artillery Regiment, Captain George Ralston, commanding (*OR*, XV, 169).

riving at Dixie Plantation, the three men in charge of the ammunition unloaded the same in the warehouse, and with two blankets to keep themselves warm, they passed the night. The wind ceased about three o'clock, and on the morning of the 26th the ground was white with frost.

The sun, however, came out, presaging a pleasant day. The command was reached at Wynn's wood, one mile above Thibodaux, on the west side of Bayou Lafourche, in which it awaited events during the day.

From Labadieville upwards for four miles, parallel to and about 200 yards from the bayou, extends an impassable marais. Wynn's wood was about one half mile long, fronting on the bayou and extending rearward into the marais and across it.

At the upper limit of these woods a public road ran from the bayou to the interior settlement of Texana, with a bridge across the marais.

The headquarters of Gen. Mouton were located in the residence of P. Lonsdale Cox[14] at Labadieville, where the gallant officer was suffering so seriously with rheumatism that he was physically unable to go to the front.[15]

On the morning of the 27th the sugar cane was frozen to the ground, but the sun again came out clear and beautiful. The Federal forces under Gen. Weitzel left Napoleonville and moved down Bayou Lafourche on the east side, driving the Confederate forces before them, who offered but little opposition to their progress.[16]

14. P. Lonsdale Cox was a forty-seven-year-old sugar planter and native of Maryland (Eight Census: Assumption Parish, Roll 407).

15. Until the discovery of Grisamore's memoirs, only one other reference to Mouton's illness had been found. An account written at Berwick Bay stated, "The chief officer in command, Gen. Alfred Mouton, is now at this point, but in a bad state of health, so much so as to render his presence on the field an impossibility." This would seem to indicate that the attack of rheumatism incapacitated Mouton for several days, limiting his ability to respond effectively to the Union campaign (Franklin *Attakapas Register*, October 30, 1862, quoted in New Orleans *Daily Picayune*, November 21, 1862). The only author to have cited this source was Barnes F. Lathrop in "The Lafourche District in 1862: Invasion," *Louisiana History*, II (1961), 186n21.

16. This aspect of the battle has proven difficult to document satisfactorily. General Weitzel, in his official report, stated, "I found soon that the enemy on the left [east] bank, after delivering only the fire of its advance guard . . . had disappeared for some unaccountable reason" (*OR*, XV, 168). The Franklin *Attakapas Register* re-

His advance scouts discovered the position of the Confederate forces under Col. Armant. The enemy crossed three regiments[17] over the bayou one mile above, in front of Mallnot's plantation, on a pontoon made out of a flatboat, that stream being at low water mark. Capt. Ralston threw some shells at the enemy, creating some confusion but without arresting their progress.

The Federal commander immediately deployed his three regiments and advanced in echelon against the Confederate line occupying the road leading to the Texana settlement protected by an ordinary picket fence; Ralston's Battery near the bayou on the road, with the Crescent Regiment on its left, and the 18th Regiment on its [Crescent's] left and extending to the marais. This entire force was badly armed with guns of inferior quality.

Capt. Jumel was ordered to pass behind the marais and attack the enemy on the flank by a road some two or three miles above.[18] High weeds and fences obstructed the view of the enemy for a short while. As soon as he became uncovered, the battery opened upon him, and once within infantry range, the rifles began their work, which checked the advance. The Federals lay down in the tall grass, whence the efforts of their officers could not remove them.

For 20 or 30 minutes the fire was rapid from both lines, when the

---

ported on October 30, 1862, that "one of the commands that were in the recent fight on the Lafourche threw way everything they had about them, except their guns, and made back tracks, boasting, as they ran, that they had not fired a gun" (quoted in New Orleans *Daily Picayune*, November 21, 1862). Thomas C. Manning, an aide-de-camp to Governor Thomas O. Moore, wrote to Jefferson Davis on October 31, 1862, saying that the 33rd Louisiana "ran incontinently" to the rear (*OR*, Ser. IV, Vol. II, p. 153). Yet Captain Arthur W. Hyatt, who commanded a company of the 33rd Louisiana on the east side of the bayou, makes no mention in his diary of such conduct; possibly he preferred not to record any cowardice (Hyatt Diary, Entry of October 27, 1862, in Hyatt Papers).

17. Weitzel sent the 12th and 13th Connecticut Infantry regiments and a battery to join the 8th New Hampshire Infantry Regiment, which was already on the west bank (*OR*, XV, 168).

18. A captain of the 12th Connecticut related that shortly after the Confederate main line had been routed, the Confederate cavalry appeared in the Federal rear and skirmished with the baggage train guard. The 8th New Hampshire went to the train guards' aid, and the Confederates "lost heart and hurried off by a circuitous route to Thibodaux" (John W. DeForest, *A Volunteer's Adventures: A Union Captain's Record of the Civil War* [New Haven, 1946], 68).

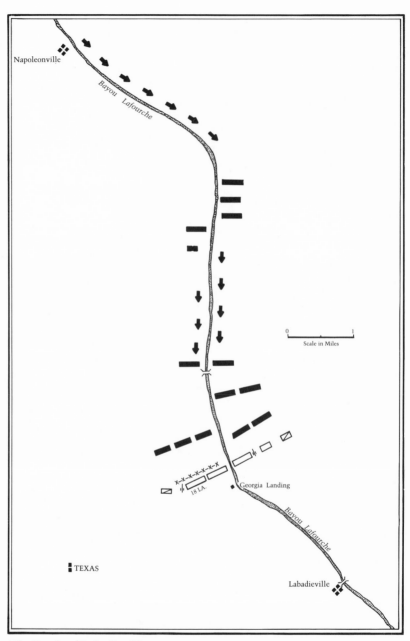

Napoleonville

Bayou Lafourche

Scale in Miles
0   1

18 LA.

Georgia Landing

Bayou Lafourche

TEXAS

Labadieville

The Battle of Labadieville
Map by Bobbie Young

ammunition of the battery was exhausted and a Federal force was discovered approaching under the levee to attack the right flank of the Confederate line.

The order to retreat was given. The scattered Confederates rallied below Labadieville and encamped just above the Tete plantation. The next morning the frost was like a snow and could be raked off of planks by hands full.

The retreat continued to Terrebonne Station, when the railroads transported the troops to Berwick Bay. The next morning another heavy frost was visible on the shores of that bay, and the cane all around was killed, something that had rarely happened. Thus then were four heavy frosts in succession on the last days of October, and one of the most killing freezes ever experienced in Louisiana.[19]

The Federals entered Thibodaux and encamped in the fields of Acadia plantation.

The terror, destruction, and confusion that reigned here at that time can only be described by those who remained to witness it. The cold North wind blew the tides out, and so lowered the Atchafalaya River that the fleet of gun boats could not enter that stream for several days, so that all the Confederate forces had crossed over in safety before their arrival.[20]

Had Weitzel remained quiet at Donaldsonville a few days, the trap so admirably sprung to capture the Confederates would have gathered them all in, but too much haste, in connection with the North wind, interfered with the successful consummation so skillfully prepared.

In the fight at Labadieville, Capt. Gourdain was the only member of the Lafourche Creoles who was hurt, having received a slight wound in the right arm.

Gustave Theriot, Wm. McAuliff, Leo Robichaux, and Homer Montz, of the same company, were captured.

Col. McPheeters, commanding the Crescent, was killed,[21] Capt.

19. Captain Hyatt wrote in his diary: "For the last two days & nights one of the coldest north winds has been blowing that I ever felt. The suffering from cold in the pitts [sic] and on the march was intense" (Hyatt Diary, Entry of October 26, 1862, in Hyatt Papers).

20. The Federal gunboats, plagued by the storm and low water, did not reach Brashear City until November 1 (OR, Navies, XIX, 330).

21. Accounts of McPheeters' death vary, but apparently he was shot through the head (DeForest, A Volunteer's Adventures, 69; John M. Stanyan, A History of the

Ralston of the battery was badly wounded and captured, a few men of the Crescent and the battery were killed,[22] the fire of the enemy being concentrated upon that portion of the line of battle. About 125 men engaged were captured.[23] Ignorant of the nature and depth of the marais, many of them made vain efforts to escape through it.

Gen. Weitzel, on being informed by his prisoners of the weakness of the Confederate force that had held his advance at bay for so great a length of time, could hardly credit the fact and remarked that such soldiers were too gallant to be imprisoned and immediately paroled them all, except the officers, who were sent to New Orleans and confined for some time on a vessel in the river.[24]

Nov. 1, 1862. We left our troops encamped on the plantation of Thomas Bisland, now Judge Baker's, preparing to watch the movements of the enemy and awaiting the tide of events during the winter. All contrived to make themselves comfortable, and our thoughtful captain managed to flank a mule for foraging purposes, but the flanking operation proved unprofitable as there never was a "mool" more disposed to run away, who had the blessing of a pair of good eyes, than was this one who "couldn't see nothing."

In less than a week he was gone and again found some 10 miles off, but in a few days he escaped again and has not been heard of since. We fared well at Camp Bisland. The country supplied us with everything that we wished in the way of food, whilst the orange trees were loaded down with ripe, luscious fruit. The Bayou Teche, upon whose banks we were encamped, furnished us with fish when we were not too lazy to catch them.

Our forces, under the immediate command of Brigadier Gen.

Eight Regiment of New Hampshire Volunteers [Concord, N.H., 1892], 144–45; New Orleans *Daily Picayune,* October 31, 1862).

22. Ralston received a wound in the knee. Mouton reported a loss of five men killed and eight wounded. An officer of the Crescent Regiment wrote that his unit lost four men killed, one wounded, and eleven wounded and captured (*OR,* XV, 178; New Orleans *Daily Picayune,* November 1, 26, 1862).

23. Mouton reported 186 men missing. A list of prisoners appeared in the *Daily Picayune,* and it numbered 195 men. Some of these men may have become prisoners a day or two after the battle (*OR,* XV, 178; New Orleans *Daily Picayune,* November 1, 1862).

24. The Confederates received their paroles on October 29. Mouton stated that the officers were paroled to their homess (*OR,* XV, 178).

Mouton, with Col. Bush as A. A. G.,[25] Gen. Dick Taylor being in command of the District with headquarters at Alexandria, consisted of the 18th La. Regiment, Fournet's Yellow Jacket Battalion, Clack's Battalion, Semmes' Battery of Artillery, and gunboat *Cotton*, under command of Capt. Fuller.[26]

Nov. 4.   Our company was made provost marshal guard, under command of Capt. Gourdain, Provost Marshal.

Nov. 6.   Our first duty was to shoot a Negro condemned to death by a court martial for attempting to pass through our lines to the enemy. The execution was consummated on the banks of the Teche in presence of several hundred Negroes, who were working on the fortifications, near Mrs. Meade's sugar house. Some skirmishing was carried on daily between our advanced pickets and the enemy's boats, the *Cotton* going down occasionally and firing a few shots.

About the 1st of this month, some 25 conscripts were added to our company, most of whom were from the parish of Assumption. They were excellent soldiers and were rather the best men we ever had to send out as advance pickets. Within less than one month, all of them, with the exception of L. E. Baudoin, possessed with a patriotic ambition of learning the exact movements of the enemy, volunteered to go scouting, and for all I know they are scouting yet. At least they never returned to report progress. The 500 distributed among the other companies met with the same ill luck in the attempt to obtain knowledge under difficulties.

Nov. 12.   Armant Aucoin, E. Portier, Francois Gros, and Trasimond Aycock, volunteers, were mustered into our company.

Chas. Aubert, Edward Bergeron, Chas. Besson, Clerfe Deslatte, J. J. Delaporte, Francois Guillot, Demophon LeBlanc, Marcelin

---

25. Bush received assignment as Mouton's assistant adjutant general with the rank of captain shortly after the general assumed command in south Louisiana (Compiled Service Records of Confederate General and Staff Officers and Nonregimental Enlisted Men, National Archives Microcopy No. 331, Roll 42, hereinafter cited as M331).

26. Mouton's command also included the Crescent Regiment. Semmes' Battery had been raised primarily in Louisiana and had served with distinction at the Battle of Baton Rouge on August 5, 1862 (Bartlett, "The Trans-Mississippi," in *Military Record of Louisiana*, 57–58). The gunboat *J. A. Cotton* was a converted river steamer. Captain E. W. Fuller's St. Martin Rangers, a volunteer company, manned her (Richard Taylor, *Destruction and Reconstruction: Personal Experiences of the Late War*, ed. Richard B. Harwell [New York, 1955], 142).

Ledet, Adam Meyronne, Jos. Trone, Justilien Molaison were discharged by order to Brig. Gen. Mouton, being under 18 years of age, at the expiration of the year for which they had enlisted.

About this date our company was sent to Franklin as provost guard but returned the next day. Capt. Gourdain was ordered to New Iberia as provost marshal, commander of the post. It is proper to state that henceforth I wrote generally from memory, as the records of the company's movements after this time were lost at the surrender.

About the middle of November, I was taken sick and was absent from the command a considerable portion of the time until the 1st of January 1863. We remained quietly in camp for two months with but little to do.

Occasional details were sent out over the lakes to watch the movements of the Federals. McDonald, Aug. Pitre, and others of our company occasionally were in those scouting expeditions.

Brig. Gen. Sibley arrived from Texas with a brigade of cavalry and assumed command of the forces in front. Col. Tom Green commanded a regiment in this brigade.[27] Sibley's headquarters were in Franklin.[28]

Dec. 20.   Our regiment was ordered to Fausse Point, some seven miles above New Iberia, on the Teche. Gen. Mouton removed his headquarters to New Iberia, and the 28th La., commanded by Col. H. Gray, arrived and were sent on to Camp Bisland.[29]

27. Colonel Thomas Green led the 5th Texas Cavalry Regiment in Sibley's brigade. He later commanded the brigade and was promoted to the rank of brigadier general on May 20, 1863 (Warner, *Generals in Gray*, 117).

28. Brigadier General Henry H. Sibley's brigade of Texas cavalry had conducted the ill-fated expedition into New Mexico in early 1862. It was ordered to Louisiana but did not arrive until early April, 1863. Sibley reached Louisiana about December 25, 1862, and Taylor sent him to Rosedale to organize a force to defend the approaches to the Atchafalaya Basin via Bayou Plaquemine. On February 12, 1863, Taylor ordered Sibley back to the Bayou Teche, where he assumed command of all forces south of Red River (*OR*, Vol. XV, pp. 191, 819, 901, 910–11, 968–70, 1003, and Vol. XXIV, Pt. 1, p. 339; Jerry D. Thompson, *Henry Hopkins Sibley: Confederate General of the West* [Natchitoches, 1987], 306, 309, 311, 314; Special Order No. 45, Headquarters District of Western Louisiana, February 12, 1863, in Joseph L. Brent Papers, 1862–1865, Louisiana Adjutant General's Library, Jackson Barracks, New Orleans).

29. The 28th Louisiana Infantry Regiment, Colonel Henry Gray, was organized in north Louisiana in April, 1862, and had remained in northeastern Louisiana until December, when General Taylor ordered it to south Louisiana (Bergeron, *Guide to Louisiana Confederate Military Units*, 138–39).

Arriving at Fausse Point, a camp was established under the name of "Qui Vive," Col. Armant in command. A detachment under charge of Major Mouton was sent about eight miles to Dautrive's plantation on the lakes to picket that point, forming Camp Dautrive. Corporal J. V. Knoblock was detailed as blacksmith and sent to the workshops at Shreveport. Private W. F. Collins was detailed as courier at Gen. Mouton's headquarters.[30]

Jan. 6, 1863. Our company was sent to Camp Dautrive, returning on the 15th, when the regiment was ordered to Camp Bisland.

At this camp the enemy made an attempt to drive away our forces. But little fighting was done, however. The Texas troops lost a few men; the 18th had no one injured. The gunboat *Cotton* was burned, and her commander, Commodore Stevens, and a few men were killed. The enemy lost their Commodore, Buchanan, and some men also, when they retired to the Bay.[31]

The weather was rainy and cold, and the men suffered severely in this expedition from exposure and want of food, having been one whole night without shelter, fire, or food in the cold, freezing rain.

The regiment returned to Camp "Qui Vive" on the 17th.

The month of February 1863 was passed without any movement of troops. We remained at Camp "Qui Vive" and "Dautrive," having plenty subsistence and forage, but the weather was generally disagreeable and unpleasant. About the 20th of this month I received from the Confederate government at Richmond my commission as assistant quartermaster of the Confederate States Army and was assigned to duty in the 18th La. Regiment. This was sent, as I after-

30. Corporal J. Victor Knoblock was detailed as a blacksmith in December, 1862. Private William F. Collins was detailed as a courier on November 9, 1862 (CSR, Rolls 291, 294).

31. On January 14, 1863, a combined expedition of Union gunboats, infantry, and artillery attacked the *Cotton* near Pattersonville. Her crew burned her and sank her across Bayou Teche as an obstruction. The 18th Louisiana, Captain Thomas A. Faries' Pelican (Louisiana) Light Battery, 2nd Louisiana Cavalry, and 13th Texas Cavalry Battalion all fought in support of the *Cotton.* Lieutenant Henry K. Stevens, who commanded the *Cotton,* was killed. He had arrived in Louisiana in December, 1862, and Taylor had placed him in charge of naval forces on Bayou Teche. Captain Fuller took over the gunboat after Stevens' death, and he received wounds in both arms. Lieutenant Commander Thomas M. Buchanan had command of the Federal vessels. He was shot in the head by one of the Confederate riflemen (*OR, Navies,* XIX, 517, 522–25; *OR,* XV, 234–35, 1089; Cynthia Elizabeth Moseley, "The Naval Career of Henry Kennedy Stevens as Revealed in His Letters, 1839–1863" [M.A. thesis, University of North Carolina, 1951], 325–31).

wards learned, in response to an application made by Col. L. L. Armant without my knowledge. Two of my kind friends, one of whom lost his life on the bloody plains of Mansfield, volunteered to go on my bonds, which were forwarded to the Secretary of War. This promotion made the office of first lieutenant vacant in our company and was followed on the 21st February by the promotion of 2nd Lieut. L. M. Hargis to be 1st Lieut. and that of 2nd Lieut. Jr. J. L. Aucoin to be 2nd Lieut.

About the 10th of this month I was ordered to Alexandria in search of quartermaster funds and also with the hopes of recovering some portion of my health, which had been so bad as to require me to be relieved from duty.

I left New Iberia at midnight in the stage, being accompanied by Capt. Gourdain, who was going to visit his family at Opelousas, and some three or four more passengers. We arrived at Vermilionville about daybreak and went into a hotel, warmed ourselves, and ordered breakfast. Laying our blankets on a table, we went across the street to a coffee stand and got some hot coffee. Returning and partaking of our breakfast, the stage horn blew, and we prepared to get aboard. This was a simple process for all but myself, who suddenly discovered that he had no blanket.

The house was kept by a big, pot belly Frenchman, who ran about the house like a kitten on a hot stove, pretending to be terribly mortified to think that a blanket should be missing in his hotel. He jabbered French, butchered English, and so on, but no blanket came. The stage was ready, the driver up, some of the passengers on board, but I was standing there with a good chance of leaving a blanket behind or of being left behind myself. There were two horns to this dilemma, neither of which were particularly agreeable to me on a frosty morning, so I told fatty I wanted my blanket and intended to have it.

Just then another chap poked his head out of another door and began making signals to the driver to move off, which motion happened to be seen by one of the passengers inside the coach, who put his head out of the stage window and notified Mr. Coachman that it would not be healthy for him to drive away until that unfortunate blanket was produced.

Our enterprising landlord, seeing the turn things were taking, soon produced it, saying the coachman who had brought us that far had taken it into his cabin, all of which I believed, of course. After leaving Vermilionville, we discussed the incident among ourselves and concluded that keeping a hotel where they change drivers would be a nice business for a couple of enterprising gentlemen and were about forming a partnership for that purpose when the stage upset itself and all our calculations.

With the exception of walking five miles across the Ville Platte Prairie and carrying rails on our shoulder to pry up the empty stage when it stuck in the mud, we arrived safely at Alexandria.

Here I had transferred to me $110,000, which I put in my carpet bag (there were no Carpetbaggers in those days), and finding my friend C. M. Gillis[32] about leaving for Opelousas in a buggy, we put his servant on the stage, sending him on to Opelousas, and drove leisurely through the mud to that place afterwards, where remaining a day or two, I returned to New Iberia.

March 1st. The regiment was ordered to Charenton, and on the 8th I received orders to move the baggage and camp equipage to Camp Bisland. Doing so, I reached that camp on the 12th and found the troops on their old camping ground.

Camp Bisland, March 12th, 1863. Ulysses Bourgeois, who had been wounded and captured at Shiloh, returned to the command.

March 14. F. Aucoin and Corporal Paul Thibodaux, wounded at Shiloh, returned today.

March 20. C. Laine and Corporal McAuliff, H. Montz, O. Sevin, A. J. Bouyan, J. Plaisance, W. Ledet, J. Leonard, A. Legendre, M. B. Cook, and John McDonald, missing since the battle of Texana, returned today.

March 23. Ulysses Bourgeois was honorably discharged from service on account of disability to perform duty occasioned by a wound at Shiloh. Our duties at Bisland were not very burdensome; the principal occupation of all parties was to get enough to eat.

Our beef at this season of the year, having been driven from Texas across the dry prairies, was very poor and unpalatable, and all sorts of shifts were resorted to in order to supply ourselves with something more palatable. I remember to have gone to New Iberia once and bought three barrels of eggs and selling them out before breakfast at six bits a dozen, having the broken ones for the profits on my speculation.

32. Charles M. Gillis, a thirty-four-year-old native of Pennsylvania, operated a farm in Lafourche Parish (Eighth Census: Lafourche Parish, Roll 413).

Gray's 28th La. Regiment was stationed near us, and not having been used to our blue beef, hit upon a very quaint expedient to remedy the defect. The men complained to the officers and the officers to a Board of Inspection ordered, which after due and solemn deliberation and consultation condemned the beef, and the result of the board of inspection was forwarded through the regular channels to headquarters.

This settled the matter exactly. The men had no meat that day and were served up with similar rations on the morrow. I believe that was the last board of inspection I ever heard of in our campaigns.

On the 29th March a heavy firing was heard down towards Pattersonville, which was presumed to be occasioned by some of the enemy's gunboats amusing themselves, firing on our pickets, but soon an express came galloping up the road with the information that our troops had captured a gunboat near Pattersonville. In an hour afterwards our regiment was ordered down to the scene of action. Upon reaching the mouth of the Bayou Teche, we found the gunboat *Diana* in our possession, with about 12 men dead and several wounded.[33] This boat had just been relieved from picket duty in the lakes, and instead of returning through the lakes to Berwick City, passed down the Atchafalaya River. Waller's Battalion[34] and a section of the Valverde Battery[35] had been sent down towards the Bay the same morning and were returning just as the boat approached the mouth of the Teche.

The Valverde Battery was immediately put in position, and ere the enemy were aware of danger, fire was opened upon them in short range, whilst Waller's Battalion, under command of Maj. Boone,[36] attacked with such vigor that every man who showed his face was

33. The *Diana*, armed with five heavy guns, lost thirty men killed and seriously wounded. One hundred twenty officers and enlisted men were captured aboard her (*OR, Navies*, XX, 111, 112; *OR*, XV, 290–91).

34. Major Ed Waller, Jr.'s, 13th Texas Cavalry Battalion (Charles Spurlin, comp. and ed., *West of the Mississippi with Waller's 13th Texas Cavalry Battalion, CSA* [Hillsboro, Tex., 1971], 45–46).

35. Captain Joseph D. Sayers' Valverde (Texas) Battery consisted of six guns captured from Union forces at the Battle of Valverde, New Mexico, on February 21, 1862, and had been organized on May 14, 1862 (P. D. Browne, "Captain T. D. Nettles and the Valverde Battery," *Texana*, II [1964], 6–7).

36. Major Hamilton Boone (Compiled Service Records of Confederte Soldiers Who Served in Organizations from the State of Texas, National Archives Microcopy No. 323, Roll 215).

immediately shot. The boat drifted down for some distance, when the enemy, seeing no possible chance of using their guns and having lost their Captain,[37] hoisted a white flag and surrendered with about 100 prisoners. The men had huddled themselves in the engine room, which was casemated, and thus saved themselves. The cabin was literally torn to pieces, not a chair or table but what had been smashed.

The *Diana* was fitted up by our authorities and put in charge of Capt. Semmes, son of Admiral Semmes.[38]

From this period up to the 10th April, everything was quiet in camp—nothing unusual or interesting occurring.

Camp Bisland, April 12, 1863. During our encampment here and at Fausse Point, we were furnished with a lot of Confederate grey cloth, which was distributed among the different camps.[39] Col. Armant ordered me to go to St. Martinsville to a tailor who was represented as a proficient in his art. I was told to go up to that prosperous little village, and on the corner of two streets whose euphonic names have passed forever out of memory, I would find the personage desired. I did so and found my man. A bargain was made, the tailor came to our camp at Fausse Point and took the measure of the men very minutely, and, in the course of human events and rainy weather, we got some of the coats. They proved to be in the very height of fashion, and the man who was lucky enough to be off duty and had time to promenade around the camp with his new coat was universally admired by everyone who saw him. The coats were admirable fits, but somehow or other the men had forgotten how to put on fashionable clothes since they had been campaigning—and

37. Acting Master Thomas L. Peterson, commanding the *Diana*, was killed instantly by a bullet through his heart (*OR, Navies*, XX, 111; *OR*, XV, 290).

38. Captain Semmes, the son of Admiral Raphael Semmes, famous commander of the raider *Alabama*, had left West Point when Alabama seceded from the Union. After serving as an instructor at Fort Morgan at the mouth of Mobile Bay, he went to New Orleans. There he was appointed captain of the 1st Confederate Regular Battery (Thomas M. Owen, *History of Alabama and Dictionary of Alabama Biography* [Spartanburg, S.C., 1978], IV, 1525–26; Joseph Wheeler, "Alabama," in *Confederate Military History*, ed. Clement A. Evans [1899; rpr. Wilmington, N.C., 1987], VIII, 794–95).

39. In late October or early November, 1862, General Taylor confiscated from a shipment intended for east of the Mississippi enough cloth to outfit approximately six thousand men. The cloth was then distributed to the men in the field (*OR*, XV, 867).

ran their arms through their sleeves up to the elbow and pulled the garment so high up behind the neck that the buttons were right between the shoulders, and the buttons were real shining brass beauties that fairly glistened when the sun dared to shine on them.

And the tails were drawn up so high that the new patches and flags of truce in the rear were very conspicuous, forming an admirable contrast with those brass buttons.

One of the men who had not had any clean clothes since he left home was bashful, and feeling a little ashamed of himself in such a neat fitting coat, refused to appear in public with it on, but a threat of the guardhouse soon made a fashionable young man of him.

Never since our friend Macon of St. James turned himself loose at Pollard, hollering "See what Alabama has done," did our boys have such a jolly time in showing what our Parisian tailor of St. Martinsville had accomplished. Our experience with tailors during the war was very refreshing all the way through. Before leaving Thibodaux, we had a suit of jackets cut out by a tailor and made up under his supervision, and out of 110, there were not more than three fits; the jackets of the large men did tolerably well for the small ones.

Just before the fall of New Orleans, we had a uniform sent to our company, of which none would fit the large-sized man. But we never had such a beautiful and fashionable turnout as was furnished by the St. Martinsville tailor, with the shining brass buttons between the shoulders, the wristbands trimmed with black drawn up to or above the elbows, and the side pockets close up under the arm. If there is ever any more wars or rumors of wars, I am going to steer clear of tailors who make uniforms under contract.

This closed our business with tailors, and after discussing the question for many sittings around the camp fires "why those fashionable gentlemen never succeeded in never cutting one single garment too large" we came to the conclusion that we had best make our own clothing in the future, and many of the officers and men who had never threaded a needle soon succeeded in cutting and making fine suits for themselves. There was at the close of our campaign no less than two dozen men who could have beaten all the professional tailors with whom we ever came in contact in fitting up a suit for utility and comfort, although they might be a little deficient in *fashion*.

Most of us learned that something useful in the way of clothing was more to be desired than anything gotten up "a la mode," and if the sleeves of a coat extended down to the wrist, the buttons were shining some distance below the shoulders, and the tails concealed any little flags that might be waving in the rear, the men were not disposed to make any fuss about it.

Camp Bisland, April 12, 1863. For several days the news had been circulating in our camps that the enemy were transporting large bodies of troops into the Lafourche country and concentrating them on the line of the Opelousas Railroad, with the evident design of making an attempt upon our lines on the Teche, and yesterday it was ascertained that a heavy force had been crossed over Berwick's Bay in our front. Gen. Banks himself was in command of the advancing hosts, whilst ours, not over one third in number, was under the direct command of Gen. Dick Taylor.[40] During the afternoon we were warned of the advance of the hostile forces, and for the first time his banners were seen floating over the sugar fields of the Attakapas. The advance reached Pattersonville and encamped in that vicinity so as to command the mouth of the Bayou Teche.

This morning at four o'clock our forces were moved out to their entrenchments and placed in position. Brig. Gen. Sibley commanded the advance lines, having his position on the west of the Teche,[41] whilst those left of that bayou were under the immediate command of Brig. Gen. Mouton.[42] The Louisiana troops and a portion of Col. Bagby's cavalry, dismounted, composed his forces. At daylight a dense fog hung for several hours over the earth until the sun, meanwhile appearing like a ball of fire in the heavens, succeeded in clearing away the mists and revealed the two armies, with flying banners and glistening bayonets, drawn up in front of each other, their lines extending from the lakes on the east to the sea marshes on the west. Not a sound was heard save the occasional report of a gun fired by some picket in order to clear his piece preparatory to the struggle about to commence.

The camps were deserted save by a few who were on the sick list.

40. The Federals hoped to destroy or disperse Taylor's army before marching for an attack on Port Hudson. This latter attack would come in conjunction with Major General Ulysses S. Grant's campaign against Vicksburg. Major General Nathaniel P. Banks's army numbered some fifteen thousand men, while Taylor had less than four thousand men at Camp Bisland (*ibid.*, 296, 391).

41. The Confederate forces on the west side of the Teche consisted of the 5th Texas Cavalry Regiment, 13th Texas Cavalry Battalion, 28th Louisiana, Valverde Battery, Semmes' Confederate Battery, and the St. Mary's Cannoneers (*ibid.*, 388–89).

42. On the east side of Bayou Teche, the Confederates had the 18th and Crescent Louisiana regiments, 10th Louisiana Battalion, 7th Texas Cavalry Regiment (Colonel Arthur P. Bagby), and Pelican Battery (*ibid.*, 389).

I was left in our quarters by Col. Armant, in charge of the baggage and train. Nine, ten o'clock passed, and still the same silence prevailed and became oppressive. No pen can describe, nor tongue express, the suspense and anxiety filling men's breasts whilst standing quietly awaiting an attack. The roar of a cannon at such a moment is a welcome sound, for it proclaims the commencement of a struggle in which excitement overwhelms thought and the terrible reality drowns all suspense. At 7 minutes past eleven, the distant report of a few cannon is heard and again the same ominous stillness is upon us. A few shells of the enemy simply to feel our strength or scatter our pickets.

Two o'clock. Rumor placed the gunboats of the enemy in the lakes on our left, and long lines of black smoke curling upward in the air above the tree tops confirmed the report. The banners of the enemy were advanced slowly as our skirmishers fell back towards the entrenchments. The space between the two forces was an open plain, and all the movements of the two lines were visible to both armies. Four o'clock, a few shots are heard and all becomes still. Suddenly, as by magic, the artillery on our right and left opened furiously upon the advancing troops. Cornay with the St. Mary's Artillery, maddened at the sight of the enemy standing upon his own homestead with their batteries planted upon the playground of his children, sent forth shell after shell, filling the air with their peculiar and indescribable music.[43] Semmes, ever ready to play the game of Death, opened his guns, long the terror of the invader, whilst the *Diana* moved gallantly down the peaceful bosom of the Teche and hurled her messages of destruction to her former owners, and in a short time the advance fell back to their lines.

April 13.   The sun rose again in a misty atmosphere. At 6 : 40 two reports of cannon announce that our artillerists were awake, and at 7 : 15 the *Diana* sent her morning greeting, and soon the crack of the rifle began to be heard.

At 10 o'clock, heavy firing was heard all along the lines, indicating that the skirmishers were becoming actively engaged. The *Diana* was struck by a 30-lb. Parrott shot which pierced her case-

---

43. The Cornay plantation was about two thousand yards south of the Confederate lines at Fort Bisland. Its main house stood on the west bank of the bayou and was used by Banks as his headquarters during the battle (R. Christopher Goodwin *et al.,* *The Battle of Fort Bisland: Historical Research and Development of an Archaeological Research Design* [New Orleans, 1988], 96, 107).

mates, exploded in the engine room, killing and wounding five or six men and disabling her steampipes.[44]

The enemy made a charge on our right and were repulsed by the gallant Texans, headed by the brave and impetuous Green. In the woods on our left the dismounted cavalry of Col. Bagby were attacked several times, but always maintained their position.

At 12, I rode out to the lines to see the progress of the battle. As I was standing near Gen. Mouton, Col. Bush, and his aides, a minnie ball came whizzing over us and, passing between two soldiers' heads, who were eating from the same plate, buried itself in a post at their side. Gen. Mouton was standing patiently, scrutinizing with his glass every movement in the front. As I returned to camp, I saw Gen. Sibley sitting under the corn shed of Judge Palfrey's sugar house, nearly a mile behind the lines, and as the firing increased toward evening, I noticed him riding still further back towards his quarters, one mile farther to the rear, and the contrast I made between him and that of our gallant Mouton will be left to the imagination of the reader. Late in the evening the firing became heavy, and Co. H of the 18th La., sent to the aid of Bagby, who was badly pressed on our left, was surrounded and captured, save Lieutenant Becnel and 5 or 6 men.[45]

Our commissary being absent, I obtained and had cooked during the day a lot of provisions which was sent to the men of our regiment about sunset, and in the meantime I loaded up my wagons with the officers' baggage and such other property as they could carry and sent most of the other things on one of the transports nearby.

At midnight an aide of Gen. Sibley rode up and ordered me to load up and remove back to New Iberia as rapidly as possible. Having my train already loaded, I was soon on the march and passed through Franklin at daylight. It was then that I learned that the enemy had affected a landing some few miles above Franklin and thus flanked our position at Bisland, necessitating our retreat, and had they marched directly across to the road leading from Franklin to New Iberia, we would all have been captured, but as they preferred to

44. The *Diana* lost two men killed and five wounded and was forced to fall back upstream (*OR, XV*, 390).

45. In addition to the left wing of the 18th Louisiana, detachments of the 10th Louisiana Battalion and 13th Texas Cavalry Battalion were sent by Mouton to Bagby's support. Colonel Bagby received a slight wound in the arm (*ibid.*, 391, 397–98).

make a circuit of six or seven miles to a short-cut of one mile, our forces passed out of the trap and left.[46]

The trains were turned out by the Cypremort Prairie, and thus were placed out of reach of the enemy's grasp.

The infantry following up became engaged with the enemy about 8 o'clock on the morning of the 14th and had a brisk little fight a short distance above the town of Franklin, causing considerable loss on both sides. The 2nd La. Cavalry, Reily's Texas Cavalry, Gray's 28th La., and Cornay's Battery were engaged.[47] Col. Vincent of the 2nd La. was badly wounded, Col. Reily was killed, and Cornay lost his flag and one of his pieces. Two transports were burned to prevent their falling into the hands of the enemy, and one loaded with sick was captured.

The *Diana* was blown up by Captain Semmes, her commander, who was subsequently with most of his men captured. I reached New Iberia with my trains about 4 o'clock, having driven about 50 miles without unhitching. The troops bivouacked in the prairies near Jeanerette. The next day we were collected at Camp Pratt, six miles above New Iberia.

Our regiment lost heavily by desertion and fatigue. Many of the men had but little to eat, had been up for two nights, and were unable to travel.

In our company, privates F. Aucoin, T. Austin, M. B. Cook, F. Roger, G. W. Winder, C. Benoit, Jos. Brogden, E. L. Boudoin, Jos. Hebert, E. Parr, J. B. Jeandron, and P. Lagarde were captured, as well as the few remaining conscripts which had been assigned to our company.

Camp Pratt, April 15th, 1863. Our infantry and trains united at this point some six miles above New Iberia, in the edge of the vast prairie that extends westwards for hundreds of miles and over whose surface is scattered little farms and large plantations, inhabited by a thrifty, frugal and patriotic people, noted for genial hospitality and those social qualities which make life among the Southern people so agreeable and pleasant, whilst the rich pastures afford nourish-

---

46. On the night of April 13, Brigadier General Cuvier Grover's division, which had proceeded on gunboats and transports up Grand Lake, landed in Taylor's rear at McWilliams' plantation and marched to Mrs. Porter's plantation on Irish Bend near Franklin (*ibid.*, 358–59).

47. The 12th Louisiana Battalion, which had just arrived from New Iberia, was also engaged (*ibid.*, 391; Hyatt Diary, Entry of April 14, 1863, in Hyatt Papers).

ment to immense herds of cattle, whose produce pours wealth into the hands of the proprietors of those magnificent plains.

Camp Pratt had been established by the state authorities and was the organizing point of the conscript troops for all southwestern Louisiana.[48]

Today several changes were made in our little army by order of Major Gen. Taylor. Gen. Sibley was displaced from all command,[49] and Gen. Mouton put in his place, and Colonel Gray of the 28th La. became commander of our brigade by order of seniority. Our troops were much fatigued with their long march from Camp Bisland, and many of them had caught ponies and transformed themselves into cavalrymen.

At 9 P.M. I was ordered off with my trains and moved out some eight miles towards Vermilionville and encamped.

On the morning of the 18th we moved onward to Vermilion Bayou and camped in a beautiful grove near the bridge over that stream—and awaited the infantry, who came up during the day.

Remaining here over night, we left at the break of day and passed through Lafayette about sunrise, finding the excited inhabitants in great confusion and consternation at the near approach of the enemy. Towards evening the hostile force arrived near Vermilion Bayou, and a brisk cannonade was heard for a half hour, without effecting much damage. Our troops retired and camped on Bayou Carencro, and proceeded the next day towards Opelousas. The march was continued until we reached Lecompte, about 20 miles from Alexandria, where the troops went into camp in the woods opposite the Mathews place. There was a couple of incidents that were rather amusing which occurred at this place. We found a cer-

48. Camp Pratt was named for Brigadier General John G. Pratt, commander of the militia forces in south Louisiana. Governor Moore established the camp after the fall of New Orleans, and when Taylor arrived in Louisiana in August, 1862, he designated the camp as the camp of instruction for conscripts in south Louisiana (*OR*, XV, 919; Bartlett, *Military Record of Louisiana*, 255, 256).

49. Taylor removed Sibley from command for disobedience of orders and unofficer-like conduct during the engagements near Bisland. A court-martial held in September, 1863, acquitted Sibley, but the members of the court considered that he had not acted properly or wisely in every case (*OR*, XV, 1093–95). Sibley's most recent biographer has called him "one of the worst generals to serve the southern Confederacy" and concluded that "Sibley undoubtedly was seriously ill, but his unexplainable behavior during the retreat hints at inebriation" (Thompson, *Henry Hopkins Sibley*, xix, 329).

tain Brigadier General[50] in command of the Post of Lecompte who wore a conspicuous black feather about 16 inches in length on his hat. As our hats were not much noted for plumes, we dubbed this commander, who was unknown to all of us, as the "knight of the black plume." On our arrival, Capt. Madden[51] of the 28th, who was senior quartermaster, placed his trains in a bend of Bayou Boeuf opposite the camps of the infantry. The next day Capt. Madden was sent for, and the order given that we must move into the rear of the infantry and that there was a fine lake just behind the camp where we could park our trains.

Capt. Madden, Capt. Airey[52] of the Crescent, and myself rode over to select a camping ground, but as soon as we crossed the bayou, we found ourselves in the piney woods amongst a succession of hills without the least resemblance to a country in which a lake might be found. After riding all around the vicinity without finding water, we returned to the headquarters of the "Knight of the Black Plume" and reported our want of success. "Yes, but I tell you there *is a lake* over there, for one of the Negroes on this plantation told me so." "Well, we can't find it, and we do not see how anybody could make a lake stick to the top of one of those hills," and then we returned to our wagons. The next morning Capt. Madden summoned us again and pointed out the intelligent contraband who could show us the wonderful lake upon whose peaceful banks we were to find repose. Riding over the bayou and following our guide some distance into the woods, he pointed down into a ravine and said that "that was the only lake he knew anything about." We descended and found about enough water for a duck to perform her morning ablutions in.[53]

We had a consultation and came to a unanimous conclusion that the "Knight of the Black Plume" was a funny fellow.

There was a young lieutenant, who was Inspector General of this same officer, who came in one day and reported to the "Knight of the Black Plume" that "he had made a thorough examination of the

50. Probably Albert G. Blanchard, former commander of northern Louisiana. Some reports of the engagements just fought are dated "Camp Blanchard, near Lecompte" (*OR*, LIII, 465).
51. Captain Albert Madden (CSR, Roll 354).
52. Captain Thomas L. Airey (*ibid.*, Roll 381).
53. Having grown up in this area, the editor knows of several shallow-water lakes near Lecompte that fit Grisamore's description.

vicinity and had the honor to report that it would take 20,000 men to defend the place as the enemy could easily flank the position."

As there was not a solitary obstruction to an advancing army on the east nearer than Red River, some 20 miles off, or the swamps of Calcasieu, some hundred miles west of us, we thought that the young gentleman had arrived at a very safe conclusion.

We remained quietly here for three or four days collecting the scattered troops and resting the men who were wearied down with their long marches. Many of them were barefooted, and some of them almost naked. I had found a lot of clothing along the road in a broken down wagon which I had saved and distributed to the men who were the most needy.

Lecompte, La., April 25th, 1863.   This little town is located on Bayou Boeuf, about 25 miles from Alexandria by the road, but there is or was a railroad connecting the two places, shortening the distance some 8 or 10 miles. The cars were drawn by a locomotive which was not in the habit of travelling fast enough to run over anything.[54]

We were ordered ahead with our trains, and I did not see the regiment and brigade until we reached Natchitoches. We moved up the Boeuf towards Alexandria, and thence across to Bayou Rapides, passing through one of the most beautiful countries on the face of the earth. Thousands of acres of corn, just peeping out of the ground, were to be seen at any time, the planters turning their whole attention to the cultivation of that grain and such vegetables as were suitable for food and which could be made available for the support of the armies. Arriving at McNutt's Hill, some 18 miles above Alexandria, we parked our trains and remained quiet for several days. In this vicinity I became acquainted with a gentleman, in whose house I ever found the kindest hospitality and whose amiable and excellent wife tore up her window curtains to make Capt. Airey and myself some clothing, of which we were woefully destitute. The troops had

---

54. The Ralph S. Smith Railroad had been constructed in 1833 to connect Alexandria with Lecompte and Cheneyville (Prichard, ed., "A Forgotten Louisiana Engineer," 1127). A Texas infantry officer wrote in his diary of the railroad: "One would think from the appearance of the locomotive and other stock of this road that its manufacture dated back very near the time of Fulton's application of steam power, as it is the slowest and most ancient and odd constructed apparatus of the kind that I have ever met up with" (Cooper K. Ragan, ed., "The Diary of Captain George W. O'Brien, 1863," *The Southwestern Historical Quarterly,* LXVII [January, 1964], 432).

remained in the neighborhood of Lecompte for several days, and finally the 18th Regiment was sent off into the piney woods near Michael Paul's residence[55] on the old Natchitoches and Opelousas road.

The enemy had advanced as far as Cheneyville and halted, but about the 6th of May an advance was made, causing our forces to continue their retreat.[56]

In obedience to orders, we left our encampment and proceeded up the Rapides and Cotile bayous across the piney woods to Monett's Ferry on Cane River, which stream we crossed in flatboats and moved onward by the village of Cloutierville to 24 Mile Ferry, where boats were again brought into requisition to cross Cane River a second time. Proceeding onward, we arrived on a beautiful Sunday evening in sight of the old town of Natchitoches, delightfully situated on the banks of the Cane River, about four miles from Red River proper. Formerly Cane River was the Red River, but the cut off known as the "Rigolets de Bon Dieu" had been made across the country leaving the old stream some distance to the west, both reuniting a few miles below Monett's Ferry.

Since leaving Alexandria, we had seen no sugar plantations, but the Cane River country was a very beautiful and wealthy district in which the inhabitants were engaged in the culture of cotton, corn, potatoes, etc., and which presented every appearance of a prosperous and happy people.

Passing through the village, we went into camp about a mile in the rear, in a pleasant grove, and next day, May 12th, the troops came up, wearied with long and tiresome marches—almost naked and half starved.

Although but little has been said or written concerning the retreat from Camp Bisland, yet it will live in the memory of those participating in it for many a long day in the future. The troops had marched 300 miles in less than 30 days, of which some 12 or 16 days they had remained quiet. Nearly every day's march had reached 20 miles, and the men had lost their clothing, their tents, their shoes had worn out, many had no pants, others no shirts, some were bare-

55. Paul's residence was near present-day Hineston.
56. Banks's advance forces left Washington on May 4 and reached Alexandria on the afternoon of May 7 (OR, XV, 313). Taylor's men had reached Paul's on May 6 and continued their march toward Cane River on May 8 (Hyatt Diary, Entries of May 6, 8, 1863, in Hyatt Papers).

headed, and nearly all were footsore; much of the time they had been happy in securing one meal per day and scarcely a night had passed in which large details had not been made for picket and guard duty.[57]

Whilst remaining at Natchitoches, I was successful in obtaining clothing sufficient to satisfy the most needy of the soldiers of our regiment.

Our brigade was composed now of the 18th, Gray's 28th, the Crescent, and the 11th Battalion, under command of Col. Henry Gray of the 28th.[58] It was here that I first became acquainted with the little colonel and his tall and gallant adjutant, Lieut. Blackman.[59] Talking over the incidents of the retreat around our campfires, I remember one that Lieut. Blackman related of the Colonel.

It was well known to all his friends that if Col. Gray hated anything in this world worse than a Yankee it was a new suit of fashionable clothes. At Bisland, in all kindness of heart and without any malice aforethought, his friends had persuaded the Colonel to get a new uniform, and one was made to order, with gold lace on the sleeves and gold stars on the collar. The Colonel put it on one day long enough to see if it was a good fit and received the congratulations of his well meaning friends on the elegant accession to his wardrobe, and then hung coat, vest, and pants in one corner of the room he was occupying in Bisland's house. The Federals came, and in the hurry of the retreat, the new uniform was forgotten and not

57. Captain Hyatt described the retreat in a similar fashion: "Feet sore, dust intolerable and not allowed to ride a horse which belongs to me. Completely broken down, and secretly envious of my colored cook who rides my horse for me. When we halt, we squat ourselves down, no matter where—in the sand, in the mud, anywhere—and our only hope is that the halt will last fifteen minutes. At night you fall down too tired to be careful of selections, and go to sleep with one blanket, without taking off clothes, shoes or cap" (Hyatt Diary, Entry of May 8, 1863, in Hyatt Papers).

58. The brigade also included the 12th Louisiana Battalion. The 11th Battalion, Lieutenant Colonel James H. Beard, had been stationed in and near Fort DeRussy and was attached to the brigade when that post was evacuated (CSR, Roll 230). When Taylor's forces retreated from Opelousas, he detached Fournet's 10th Louisiana Battalion to the area of Hineston and ordered it temporarily mounted (John Dimitry, "Louisiana," in Confederate Military History, ed. Clement A. Evans [Atlanta, 1899], X, 582). Colonel Gray, as senior colonel, assumed command of the brigade when Mouton received command of the forces south of Red River on April 15, 1863 (OR, XV, 399).

59. Wilbur F. Blackman, adjutant of the 28th Louisiana Infantry, received an appointment as brigade adjutant on May 14, 1863 (CSR, Roll 347).

until several miles had been travelled was it remembered. The Colonel and staff were riding slowly along in silence, musing over the sad condition of things, when the old man spoke up. "Well, Black, there is one thing in this infernal retreat that relieves my mind of a great weight." "What's that, Colonel, I'd like to know, for I'll swear I can see no good in it, for us or our cause." "Why, I left my new uniform at Bisland's, and now I won't be bothered with the gold lace fixings any more, and I'm confounded glad of it."

During this retreat, Capt. Gourdain returned and assumed command of his company.

Natchitoches, May 20th, 1863. This day we were again started on the march, but to the satisfaction of everyone, the direction was southward.

We travelled slowly, and on the 26th went into camp in the piney woods back of Wm. Polk's plantation on Bayou Boeuf. In the midst of the groves near a stream of excellent water, we remained until the 6th of June.[60]

The weather was so hot that the soldiers were seldom required to drill or perform any duty.

We learned that the enemy had crossed the Atchafalaya at Simmesport and gone to besiege Port Hudson. An aide of Gen. Mouton came into our camp and notified us that the road to Berwick's Bay was clear and that we would soon move in that direction.[61]

60. William Polk's plantation, Ashton, was located near the juncture of Bayou Boeuf and Bayou Lamourie. Confederate troops camped on Bayou Claire (Clear) near the plantation on several occasions. Polk took his family to Texas during the war, and Union troops burned his mansion during the Red River Campaign of 1864 (Sue Eakin, *Rapides Parish: An Illustrated History* [Northridge, Calif., 1987], 35; Sue Lyles Eakin and Patsy K. Barber, eds., *Lecompte: Plantation Town in Transition* [Baton Rouge, 1982], 18, 37; Raney Greene Diary, Entries of May 1–3, 26–29, 1863, in Raney Greene Papers, Eugene C. Barker Texas History Center, University of Texas, Austin).

61. Following the Confederate retreat from Opelousas, Mouton received orders to take Green's cavalry brigade to the prairies west of Opelousas and to harass the flanks and rear of the Federal army as it marched northward. A lack of supplies forced Mouton to fall back to Niblett's Bluff on the Sabine River. Reinforced there, he was ordered back to the area of Opelousas after Banks's army had moved against Port Hudson. The few Union troops left in the vicinity fled to Brashear City with large amounts of confiscated property. Mouton failed to press them with his forces, thus allowing the enemy to escape. Taylor confided to Kirby Smith on June 11 that the reports he had received from Mouton "are exceedingly unsatisfactory, and indicate that no movement commensurate with the forces under his command have been

It was at this point that our ears were first delighted with the music of the wonderful band of the 11th La. Battalion, consisting of a fife and two drums.[62]

One of the drummers was about six and a half feet in height, the other about five feet four, whilst the fifer was about mid-way between the two. They never kept step together nor with the music, and it was the opinion of most of us that the tall one was working out a contract to burst in the head of all the drums in the Confederacy.

Whether he succeeded or not, I am unable to say, but the musical entertainment of this band shortly after ceased.

On the 6th of June we packed up and moved off, arriving after a long march at Lecompte, and thence passing down the Bayous Boeuf, Huffpower, and DeGlaize, we encamped near Marksville on Lake Cypress. Here we found a regiment of Texas dismounted cavalry under command of Col. Speight[63] watching the long bridge over the swamps between the DeGlaize and Marksville prairie. These troops remained with us afterwards.

On the 13th we arrived at Simmesport, and thence proceeded down the Atchafalaya River, arriving at Morgan's Ferry on the night of the 14th.

The trains remained at that point, but the infantry were crossed over the river and advanced some few miles towards the Mississippi River, where they remained until the 18th and returned back to Morgan's Ferry.

---

made, and that little activity has been displayed by that officer. While an excellent officer on the field, of great gallantry and fair qualifications, he is, I fear, unequal to the task of handling and disposing of any large body of troops, and I shall, therefore, at the earliest practicable moment, give my personal supervision to that command" (*OR*, XV, 394, and Vol. XXVI, Pt. 2, pp. 4, 32, 461).

62. Grisamore may have mistaken the number of this battalion. Captain Hyatt recorded in his diary that the 12th Battalion had the only brass band in the Trans-Mississippi Department. The 11th Battalion was, however, attached to the brigade about this time (Hyatt Diary, Entry of March 10, 1863, in Hyatt Papers).

63. This was Colonel Joseph W. Speight's brigade, which consisted at this time of the 15th Texas Infantry and 31st Texas Dismounted Cavalry regiments. The brigade had arrived at Simsport from northern Texas on May 30. Lieutenant General Edmund Kirby Smith, commander of the Trans-Mississippi Department, had retained two of Speight's regiments, the 22nd and 34th Texas Dismounted Cavalry, at Shreveport for drilling and discipline (Alwyn Barr, *Polignac's Texas Brigade* [Houston, 1964], 19, 21).

Gen. Major's Texas brigade had preceded us and were ordered into the Lafourche country by way of the river roads.[64]

On the 19th our command resumed the march and encamped on Bayou Rouge.

On the 20th we ferried that stream and moved on towards Opelousas, and passing through that town on the 22nd, we proceeded down the Bayou Teche road, encamping on the 22nd on Dr. Walker's plantation, on the 23rd at Colonel DeClouet's, on the 25th passing through St. Martinsville and New Iberia, we bivouacked near S. O. Nelson's place, on the 26th Charpentier's plantation, and on the 27th crossed Berwick's Bay and bivouacked at Bayou Ramos.[65]

For the last two days we had passed over the various battle-grounds at the commencement of the retreat from Bisland. Along the road near Bisland, we noticed the remains of several of the Yankee dead, who had been thrown between two cane rows and covered up, but the rains had washed off the little covering over them. I have often read finely rounded sentences about vultures and buzzards following up armies, ready to feed and fatten upon the slain, but those who came down the Teche two months and fifteen days after the Bisland fights will remember that horses, cattle, and men who were killed in those contests were lying in the same condition as they

64. Colonel James P. Major's brigade consisted of the 1st Texas Partisan Rangers, 3rd Regiment Arizona Brigade, 2nd Texas Mounted Rifles (Cavalry), and 2nd Texas Partisan Rangers regiments. With Gray's, Speight's, and Major's troops, Taylor hoped to attack the Federal forces stationed across the Mississippi River from the Confederate stronghold at Port Hudson. He planned to cross cattle and other supplies to the beleaguered garrison if the attack succeeded. The Union forces were stronger than expected, so Taylor could not carry out the assault. He then ordered Major's brigade to march by way of the Grosse Tete, Plaquemines, and Lafourche bayous to the rear of the Federal post at Brashear (Morgan) City and to act in conjunction with an attack on that place (*OR*, Vol. XXVI, Pt. 1, pp. 218–19, and Pt. 2, p. 53; Taylor, *Destruction and Reconstruction*, 167–68).

65. Alexander DeClouet's plantation, Lizima (now called St. John), was on the east bank of Bayou Teche about two miles north of St. Martinville (Paul F. Stahls, Jr., *Plantation Homes of the Teche Country* [Gretna, La., 1979], 64). New Orleans businessman S. O. Nelson owned a plantation about two miles north of New Iberia on the west bank of Bayou Teche (*OR*, Vol. XXVI, Pt. 1, p. 291). Joseph M. Charpentier's plantation was on the west bank of the Teche about three miles north of Pattersonville. Union troops burned his house in April, 1863 (Eighth Census: St. Mary Parish, Roll 425; Edwin C. Bearss, ed., *A Louisiana Confederate: Diary of Felix Pierre Poche* [Natchitoches, 1972], 6). Dr. Walker has not been identified, but his plantation was about twenty-one miles north of DeClouet's (Greene Diary, Entry of June 21, 1863, in Greene Papers).

fell, except that the bodies were partly dried up, and that not even a bird of the kind mentioned was ever seen flying in the air during the whole intervening space.

Several of the men of Bagby's command, who were killed in the swamp on our left at the Bisland fight, were found lying just as they fell on that day and were then buried by their comrades.

At the Bay a few mornings previous to this date, some 200 Confederates had crossed through the lakes to the rear of the enemy's camp and captured about 1000 Yankees, as many Negroes, and several depots full of stores.[66] I reached Bayou Ramos at midnight, and after hunting round awhile found a place to spread my blanket, and upon awakening the next morning I found myself in the midst of a graveyard. Passing into a sugar house nearby, I saw one of the most horrible sights I ever witnessed. There were about 50 Negro men and women lying around, some of them dead, others dying, some of them being eaten by worms before life was extinct, the whole scene presenting a panorama of filth, destitution and misery that it is to be hoped will seldom be seen again in any country.[67] The roads from Franklin to Tigerville[68] were lined with Negroes half starved, almost destitute of clothing, sick and unable to help themselves; the only question of the poor wretches, who had been two months experiencing Federal sympathy and charity, was the inquiry if their master was coming after them. Hundreds of them were taken back to their old homes and their lives thus saved by their former owners. On the 27th we reached Tigerville, where my good old friend Moody

66. On June 23, 325 volunteers under Major Sherod Hunter, 2nd Regiment Arizona Brigade, made their way to the rear of Brashear City in various types of boats. After a feint attack from across Berwick Bay by Green's cavalry, Hunter's men surprised the Federal garrison and forced its surrender. The Confederates captured eleven heavy artillery pieces, thousands of rifles, a great deal of ammunition of all sorts, and more than $2 million worth of commissary and quartermaster stores (*OR*, Vol. XXVI, Pt. 1, pp. 210, 211–12, 215–16, 223–24, 225–26).

67. For similar descriptions of the conditions of slaves abandoned in this area by the Federals, see *Official Report Relative to the Conduct of Federal Troops in Western Louisiana, During the Invasions of 1863 and 1864* (1865; rpr. Baton Rouge, 1939), 53–55.

68. Tigerville is now called Gibson. In 1848, Grisamore had described Tigerville as a village that contained "one tavern, one Doctor, one store, one widow, one warehouse, one young lady who complains of being Dyspeptic, and one Post Office" (Silas T. Grisamore Diary, Entry of November 3, 1848, in William Littlejohn [Litt] Martin Collection, Manuscript Collection, Nicholls State University Library, Thibodaux, La.).

and wife[69] insisted that I should sleep in a bed, which I did for the first time in many weeks. They both told me many rich things that had happened to them, but what appeared to give the good lady the most pleasure was to relate how the Federal officers had ransacked the house in search of Confederate flags without success, whilst at the very time they were threatening vengeance they were standing on the coveted flags concealed under the carpets.

Tigerville, June 28th, 1863. On arriving at Berwick's Bay, I was ordered to leave a portion of the brigade trains encamped at Berwick City and bring forward only the commissary and ammunition wagons. Leaving Capt. C. M. Shepherd in charge at that place, I selected the teamsters, who resided in the Lafourche country, to bring such wagons as were ordered to follow the troops. On this morning the troops started, following the railroad track, and arrived in Thibodaux at mid-day and went into camp in the grove in front of Ridgefield plantation, but the trains having to come much further, did not arrive until two o'clock. The weather was excessively hot, the dust flying in every direction, and it was with difficulty that I could restrain my teamsters from killing their mules in their anxiety to see their homes again. Entering into Thibodaux and riding up Jackson Street, I met with a quantity of friends who literally pulled me off my horse and carried me about a square and made me eat, as near as I can remember, some six or seven dinners before I could get away to the spot where the troops were bivouacking. A jolly time we had that day, and during the afternoon I had to exercise all the ingenuity of which I was capable to prevent getting too much of the extract of corn into my head, a liberal quantity of which had been left by a fellow by the name of Ross, who kept a store in the house now occupied by Moore and Stewart. Some of the boys did not succeed so well as I did and didn't get home until some hours after retreat had been sounded.

There were others who actually mistook the excitement into which I had been carried as the effect of Benzine, but they were mistaken as to the cause. If their own heads had been perfectly level whilst we were up in the old Philharmonic Hall, they might have noticed many a drink of good whiskey or brandy passing over my

69. The 1860 census for Terrebonne Parish gave forty-year-old W. M. Moody's occupation in Tigerville as railroad agent. He was born in Virginia, and his wife, Anna, was born in England (Eighth Census: Terrebonne Parish, Roll 425).

shoulders, which they imagined disappearing in another direction. I recollect very well that in trying to send one good horn of brandy over my shoulder, the glass struck the collar of my coat, sending the contents down my back. Well, we had not met for a long spell, and we could not resist the temptation for a little glory over our return, and we had a good time on the evening of the 28th June, 1863.

June 30.   Capt. Gourdain was appointed Provost Marshal of Thibodaux, and I was appointed Commissary of the post at this place.

July 4.   Many new recruits were mustered into the different companies about this time. To our company Joachim Triche, Joseph Guyot, Jos. Lagarde, Oneziphe Guedry, Donatien Guedry, and several others were assigned, whilst J. E. Naquin, Ulysse Hymel, Thomasin Badeaux, T. Bouvier, Leo Robichaux, J. B. Jeandron, G. G. Winder, and A. Vedroz, who had been left in the rear, either wounded or as prisoners, returned to their commands. Joseph Trone, formerly a member of our company, discharged in 1862 being under 18 years of age, rejoined and was mustered into service again.

On this day, the 18th was removed to Labadieville and bivouacked on the plantation of P. L. Cox, Esq.[70]

July 14.   The 18th having been ordered towards Berwick's Bay arrived at and encamped on Bayou Boeuf.

July 21st.   Whilst bivouacking at Bayou Boeuf, orders came to remove to Berwick's Bay, but on the morning of the removal some 25 of the men mistook the direction of the line of march and got lost in the Tigerville swamps, and before they could extricate themselves from their bewilderment, the Yankees came upon them. The balance of the command went by steamer to the vicinity of New Iberia and encamped, removing on the 22nd to Camp Pratt, and thence to Vermilionville on the 23rd.

About the 20th I was ordered to rejoin my command. Vicksburg and Port Hudson had fallen, rendering our position untenable with the force of our little army. At my departure, Rich. Frost of Thibodaux and Charley Barker of Houma accompanied me, and on arriving at Vermilionville were mustered into service in our company.

Our visit to Lafourche personally had been gratifying to the members of our company, having afforded us all an opportunity to see our

70. General Taylor had stationed his small infantry force at Labadieville to support Green's cavalry, which attacked a Union force at Koch's plantation near Donaldsonville on July 13. Following Green's rout of the Federals, Taylor ordered his army back to Berwick's Bay (Taylor, *Destruction and Reconstruction*, 173–74).

friends and enabled most of the men to get a new outfit of clothing, which was very acceptable. We had lived well during our stay, having been fed principally by the commissary establishments of Gen. Banks, whose liberal supplies established for the Confederate army were notorious in several instances. We wish that he would show as obliging a disposition towards us in time of peace as he did during the war.

Camp Taylor, near Vermilionville, July 23rd, 1863. At this camp we were reminded of the gloomy and dismal days around Corinth in 1862. Fevers were prevalent, and our camp exhibited the appearance of a hospital rather than that of a warlike body.

The health became so bad that orders were issued to grant neither furloughs nor leaves of absence to anyone, except upon recommendations of surgeons. We could obtain but little to eat except meal and beef, and in a country where the prairies were covered with thousand of cattle, we considered ourselves fortunate to obtain occasionally a cup of milk, whilst a pound of butter was a thing to be talked of only. My own health became bad, and I was finally obliged to cease performing active duty, and about the 1st of September turned over my property to Capt. C. M. Shepherd, who acted as quartermaster until the 1st of January following.

On the 23rd of August, the regiment was ordered to Abbeville, at which place it remained until the 29th, when it was ordered back to Camp Taylor, and on the 31st it was marched near New Iberia, moving on the next two days into the neighborhood of Franklin, where it remained until the eighth of September.

On that day it moved to Jeanerette, on the 9th to Camp Pratt, and on the 10th again reached this camp. Not over half the regiment went on this excursion, the balance being in hospital. In our single company there were on the sick list at this time Lieut. J. L. Aucoin, D. Boudreaux, Jos. Roger, W. Leonard, D. Guidroz, A. Lejeune, Jos. Guizot, Joachim Triche, A. J. Bouzan, F. J. Gaudet, U. Hymel, and C. J. Barker, besides others who had been sent away to hospitals.

Our encampment near Vermilionville has no pleasant recollections for any of us, save that it gave those who did not get sick a month's rest after our long marches during the previous four months.

The command left Camp Taylor on the 17th September and removed to Bayou Carencro, encamped near Washington on the 18th, bivouacked at Bayou Mallet on the 19th, and reached Chicot on the 20th.

On the 21st, under countermarching orders, the troops encamped on Bayou Mallet, and on the 22nd went into camp on Bayou Crocodile [Cocodrie] near Moundville. On the 25th, left Moundville and bivouacked on Bayou Rouge, and on the 26th at Morgan's Ferry on the Atchafalaya. On the 29th the command advanced on Bayou Fordoche and were close by, but not actually engaged, during the fight and capture of the Yankee troops on that day, returning to Morgan's Ferry the same evening.[71] This day's work was a fatiguing one, as the rain fell nearly the whole day, putting the roads in a terrible condition.

On the 1st October the regiment was ordered up the Atchafalaya, reaching Simmesport on the 2nd, proceeding up Bayou de Glaize, thence down Bayou Rouge and Bayou Cane, after some countermarching reached Evergreen on the 10th and Marksville on the 14th.

When the regiment was ordered towards Franklin on the last day of August, I accompanied it as far as New Iberia, with the expectation of proceeding to Houston, Texas, but the orders being changed, I was sent to Alexandria to obtain funds to pay the soldiers. Taking the stage, I travelled as far as Opelousas, where I remained a couple of days with kind friends and proceeded to Alexandria by stage, expecting to rest a couple of days in that place, but when I arrived in that town I found a report current that the Yankees were out on Little River, twenty miles distant.[72] As Alexandria had been the headquarters of our army and was very much populated with soldiers who never heard many guns go off, the excitement was terrible. Cannons were planted along the levee ready to batter the poor little town of Pineville into a vast number of very small atoms if the said Pineville ever allowed Yankees to show themselves in her streets; the patriotic soldiers and warlike citizens were busily engaged in drinking up all the rum to prevent it from falling into the possession of

71. Green's and Major's brigades of cavalry and detachments of Mouton's and Speight's brigades of infantry attacked a force of 500 Federals at Mrs. Sterling's plantation. Mouton's brigade, except for Clack's 12th Battalion, remained in reserve. Green captured 450 of the Union troops and recrossed the Atchafalaya River before Federals from Morganza could intercept him (OR, Vol. XXVI, Pt. 1, pp. 321–22, 325, 329–31; Hyatt Diary, Entry of September 29, 1863, in Hyatt Papers; Cooper K. Ragan, ed., "O'Brien's Diary," The Southwestern Historical Quarterly, LXVII, No. 2 [October, 1963], 237).

72. A Union expedition under Brigadier General Marcellus M. Crocker left Natchez on September 1 and captured Fort Beauregard at Harrisonburg on September 4. Colonel Horace Randal's brigade of Texas infantry marched from Alexandria to the support of Fort Beauregard's garrison but arrived too late (OR, Vol. XVII, Pt. 1, pp. 273, 274, 280).

the enemy, and a whole regiment of troops were crossed over Red River to go out behind Pineville as an army of observation. I had to accomplish the object of my visit in a hurry so as to leave by the returning stage, instead of lying over for the next as I intended, having been politely informed by the short, chubby, red-faced agent that after that evening "no more would the rumbling wheels of his big coaches ever be heard on the sandy streets of Alexandria," after which speech he entered my name on his book, wiped the dew from his eye, and sought consolation in a bottle of rum, that great friend of distressed humanity.

I received $2,000 from Major Lasere,[73] which I calculated on boxing up, but having no time to get a box, I struck it in the bottom of my carpet bag and then stuffed over it a dirty shirt, of which I generally had a small supply, tied the handles together, and pitched it into the box of the stage.

By this time the red-faced proprietor informed me others had engaged seats before me and I could not go. I rather guessed I would, and whilst the gentleman was taking another drink of rum, I procured an order for my passage, which convinced him that unless I was given a seat in that stage he would be placed in a position that would utterly prevent him from serving the Confederacy by depriving the enemy of the benefit that would naturally be derived from drinking our rum.

Having an outside seat, I rolled myself up in a blanket and lay on top of the stage all night long, as comfortably as a dog tossed in a blanket. The next morning I was taken very ill and passed a miserable day, reaching Washington at night, barely able to stand. The next day I went to Opelousas, where I remained for several days, too unwell to go on to our camp.

The enemy began to advance towards Opelousas,[74] and about the 20th of October I left and proceeded to Tyler in Texas, where I re-

73. Major Emile Lasere, former quartermaster of the 10th Louisiana Infantry Regiment, served as Taylor's chief quartermaster. He resigned shortly after Grisamore visited him (Opelousas *Courier*, October 25, 1862; CSR, Roll 220; Jefferson Davis to Maj. Emile Lasere, September 5, 1863, in *Jefferson Davis, Constitutionalist: His Letters, Papers and Speeches*, ed. Dunbar Rowland [Jackson, Miss., 1923], VI, 22).

74. The Union forces of Major General William B. Franklin left Bisland on October 1 and reached Vermilion Bayou on October 9. They remained near Vermilion and Carrion Crow bayous until October 21, when they occupied Opelousas (*OR*, Vol. XXVI, Pt. 1, pp. 369, 389).

mained about one month, endeavoring to recover my health so as to return to duty.

Simmesport, Dec. 1863. On my return from Texas, I met the division of Gen. Mouton[75] near this place. I learned that they had been perambulating for the last two months in the Big Cane section of country between Opelousas and the Atchafalaya River. The 18th Regiment and Fournet's Yellow Jacket Battalion had been consolidated into one regiment, still maintaining the name of the 18th. The old regiment had been formed into six companies and the battalion into four companies.[76]

By this consolidation the following officers were left out, viz.: Captains Cloutier and J. G. Hayes, and Lieutenants Pollingue, Mayo, Shakleford, Lambre, Bourque, Bernard, and Beauvais,[77] and perhaps two or three others, all of whom were assigned to other duties on reporting to Gen. Taylor, except Lieut. Beauvais, who reported to the City of New Orleans and turned up shortly after as a member of the Convention which formed the Constitution of 1864, said to have been the representative of seven voters from St. James Parish.

Our old company was in command of Capt. L. M. Hargis and Lieutenant Dan. Peters, who had been transferred from the Crescent

75. About October 18, the brigades of Brigadier General Camille Jules Marie, Prince de Polignac, and Colonel Joseph W. Speight were merged under the former officer. Polignac had received command of the 17th, 22nd, and 34th Texas Dismounted Cavalry regiments, the latter two of which belonged originally to Speight's brigade, the previous July. A portion of the 11th Texas Infantry Battalion had been operating with Speight's brigade since August 1, but the men were detached and returned to Texas in late December. Polignac's brigade was united with Gray's to form a division to be commanded by Mouton (Barr, *Polignac's Texas Brigade,* 21–22, 23, 29, 34; Ragan, ed., "O'Brien's Diary," 420–21).

76. The 18th Louisiana and 10th Louisiana Battalion were consolidated on November 14, 1863 (Hyatt Diary, Entry of November 14, 1863, in Hyatt Papers). The company commanders of the new 18th Louisiana Consolidated Infantry were Captain Louis Becnel, Company A; Captain S. Alexander Poche, Company B; Captain William Sanchez, Company C; Captain Arthur W. Hyatt, Company D; Captain Benjamin S. Story, Company E; Captain C. M. Shepherd, Company F; Captain Henry B. Stevens, Company G; Captain John T. Lavery, Company H; Captain A. Pope Bailey, Company I; and Captain Arthur F. Simon, Company K (CSR, Roll 298). Company G of the 18th was assigned to Company F of the consolidated unit.

77. Emile Cloutier, Company C; J. G. Hayes, Company K; First Lieutenant Maurice Pollingue, Company B; Second Lieutenant Claudius Mayo, Company B; First Lieutenant T. B. Shakleford, Company C; Second Lieutenant Jules Lambre, Company C; Second Lieutenant Valery S. Bourque, Company C; Third Lieutenant A. Bernard, Company K; and Second Lieutenant Raphael Beauvais, Company A (CSR, Roll 290).

Regiment. Capt. Gourdain had been promoted to be Major, and Lieut. J. L. Aucoin was transferred into one of the Yellow Jacket companies.

On the next day the troops proceeded onward by way of Marksville and Mansura to the crossing of Red River. Passing through Mansura, I met with my friend Dr. Bordis, who, with the chief surgeon Dr. Martin,[78] was quartered in a building of that village, and upon his invitation I remained over night.

That evening a party consisting of Gen. Polignac and staff came to the doctor's headquarters, and we had a lively time until about midnight. It was the first time I had had the pleasure of meeting the gallant little French general, who was soon sufficiently mellow to be entertaining and enlivened the house by singing every few minutes a verse of a song which had reference to one "Madam Gregoire" whoever she may have been. Capt. Cucullu[79] fabricated a bowl of delicious egg nog, which with the proper ingredients soon brought out the musical abilities and loquacious qualities of the company. As I was forbidden to drink anything stronger than water by my physician, I had only to sit quietly and breathe out silent "maledictions" on the head of a doctor that had no more sense than to forbid a man from imbibing egg nog. Finally, about midnight, the general with his staff left, and the rest of us secured a little repose during the balance of the night.

The next morning I overtook our command at Red River, and by night they had all crossed over and encamped about a mile above the Ferry.[80] The next morning as we were preparing to move, the rain began to fall slowly, and by ten o'clock it was pouring down in torrents, which continued for three hours. Capt. Shepherd had just gotten his train across a muddy bottom when the rain stopped everything and in a short time the Crescent wagons were all standing in water three or four feet deep, where most of them remained over night.

78. Dr. Charles Bordis, born in France and from Assumption Parish, and Dr. Ed Martin, Chief Surgeon of Mouton's division (Eighth Census: Assumption Parish, Roll 407; CSR, M331, Roll 164).

79. Captain J. Earnest Cucullu, Acting Inspector General on General Polignac's staff, or Captain Sainville Cucullu, aide-de-camp to Polignac (CSR, M331, Roll 67; OR, Vol. XXXIV, Pt. 1, p. 156).

80. Voorhies' Ferry crossed Red River seven miles from Marksville (Walter Prichard, ed., "A Tourist's Description of Louisiana in 1860," Louisiana Historical Quarterly, XXI [1938], 1151).

In our train we had one of those rolling monuments of human folly and inhumanity known as a three-mule cart, which stuck in a deep hole. Finding the mules could not pull it out, Capt. Shepherd ordered it to be unloaded, and noticing that the driver was rather slow in his movements, he had to repeat the command, when the first thing that was tumbled out was a fat hog that would have weighed about 200. Nobody knew how it had gotten into the wagon, but "Goss" was connected with that train for that day, and we each formed our own opinions. The general impression was, however, that hogs were good jumpers in that section of the country and that this one had leaped into this cart. At sundown we reached a creek from which the bridge had been carried away after the troops and commissary trains had passed over. The men with the provisions were five miles ahead, and we had the utensils and nothing to cook, but nature often provides where man fails in that important particular.

As we were getting out some pots to cook up what few things we could scrape together, we found that two more 200 pounders had jumped into another one of our wagons, the effort having been so great as to have cleaned themselves nicely by the operation. Out of this bountiful provisions of jumping hogs, which Nature had grown in these woods, we procured a good supper. Some remarks were overheard by some of the soldiers the next evening, when we reached camp, about the quantity of "grease" they had lost, but whether it had anything to do with our supper of the previous night, I never learned.

The whole of the next day was consumed in rebuilding the bridge, getting up the wagons in the rear, and removing to the camp, at which we arrived about ten o'clock at night.

The next day the general made the wagons precede the troops, which was another evidence of the value of experience. On the 18th day of December 1863, we encamped in the woods opposite Alexandria, when we were informed that our orders were to proceed to Monroe, La.[81]

Alexandria, December 19th, 1863. Under marching orders, we left this place and proceeded through the piney woods towards Winnfield in the parish of Winn. The day we approached this little

---

81. Mouton's division was orderd to Monroe to cover the crossing of arms across the Mississippi River (*OR*, Vol. XXII, Pt. 2, pp. 1110–11; Taylor, *Destruction and Reconstruction*, 185).

village, I rode on ahead of the troops in order to see about procuring forage. Arriving in town, we noticed a few persons collected about the court house, among them a smiling youth of about 17 years of age, dressed in white linen, coat and pants, which were doubtless clean as they had apparently been through the washtub some two or three dozen times. The young fellow appeared to be a little nervous and was anxiously inquiring for Squire Walker, who was officiating as Clerk of the Court, Justice of the Peace, and Post Quartermaster.[82] A lady of about 35 was sitting on the steps of the court house in plain habiliments and watching with some interest the movements of the young man. The Squire having been discovered delivering corn to myself and the other quartermasters and the difficulty in the way of the young gentleman being explained, we all adjourned over to the court house and became witnesses of the ceremony that united threadbare linen to homespun flannel. The blushing bride remarked that "one year would have to glide away into the unknown dimness of the future before the conscript law would catch her darling boy," which we thought a very philosophical view of the matter. An hour afterwards we noticed the gallant groom and the happy bride going out of town, both mounted on the same grey horse which had brought them 20 miles that morning. We heard that this was one of the first effects of woman's rights movement in Louisiana and that the boy, with his white linen garments, had been run away from home by the gay lady in homespun.

As we left Winnfield that afternoon, we passed by a house about a half mile from the village, on the gallery of which the bride was coolly sitting on a stool, smoking a pipe. The weather was cool enough for pleasant marching during our trip, and on the evening of the 26th we encamped near Trenton, La. As our journey had been through the piney woods, and the nights cool enough to require fires, the men had thrown up each night huge heaps of pine knots and, firing them, sat around them until they were smoked into a color that would have enabled them to pass for a colored regiment in any civilized country.

82. John L. Walker, a native of South Carolina, was editor of the *Southern Sentinel* in Winnfield when the war began. On January 5, 1864, he was appointed clerk of court for Winn Parish and justice of the peace for Ward 1 of that parish. Because of Walker's date of appointment, this incident may have actually occurred when the brigade marched through Winnfield in February, 1864 (Eighth Census: Winn Parish, Roll 426; Secretary of State's Register of Appointments, 1856–1865, pp. 23, 118, in Louisiana State Archives, Baton Rouge).

On the 28th, we ferried over the Ouachita River at Trenton and moved down about one mile below Monroe and pitched our tents in a grove on the river banks.

The last days of the year were rainy and disagreeable, and on the last night of 1863, the rain ceased, the wind blew almost a hurricane, turning the air most bitterly cold. On the morning of the 1st January 1864, everything was frozen hard, with a sharp wind sweeping down the river from the North. About sunrise, Col. Armant sent for me (as I had entered upon my duties as quartermaster again on that day) and notified me as we stood shivering with cold by his burning log heap that we had orders to march and that I must be ready to move directly. Comfortable information, I thought. All the gearing, having been wet, were frozen stiff; the men had to thaw every bridle, collar, and piece of gearing before they could get it upon their mules, and we were fully two hours hitching up. The day before I had given some money to "Paul," who had gone down the river in search of fodder, to purchase some eggs for me. This morning the whole lot were frozen as hard as brick bats, and knowing that I could not use them myself, I gave them to the men to cook up before leaving. It was rather amusing to listen to the comments of the boys and hear their exclamations of wonder and amazement as they saw the first frozen egg. Such a thing had never entered their philosophy, and the "nom de Dieu's," "tonnerres," and "sacres" were heard all about the camp.

There is not a man of the 18th who forgets the march on that New Year's day, up the river and through Monroe. The wind came directly in their faces for an uninterrupted space of two miles, blowing almost a hurricane and freezing so rapidly that the earth was frozen hard enough to bear up our heavy loaded wagons in ten hours after the freeze commenced. Many of the men had their fingers and feet frozen, but when we passed Monroe, we turned to the right, through the woods, and the wind slackening up, the afternoon was not so chilly as the morning had been. Our men knew but little about ice, and many of them were practising the act of sliding on the little frozen ponds along the roadside. One of them, a low, heavy-set chap from Calcasieu, came to a little pond 25 feet in diameter, walked carefully over it to test its capability, and then backing out about 10 yards like a ram going to war, he ran and jumped upon the ice, expecting to slide across, but as soon as his shoes struck the smooth surface, his heels went up like a pair of rockets and his head went down like a pumpkin. Sitting up and casting his eyes around to see if anybody had seen him, and being convinced that not less than 50 men were laughing at him, he scratched his "knowledge box," crawled to firm ground, got up, and giving one long, lingering look of unutterable disgust upon the treacherous pond, he went on his way, but he did not practice skating any more on that trip.

We encamped about ten miles above Monroe, where the men went to work to build tents and cabins for protection against the severity of the weather.

Camp near Calvary Church, January 3rd, 1864. Under instructions from our officers, the men began to erect huts and cabins for their protection against the severity of the weather. There were not over two dozen tents in the brigade, those articles having been left behind at Alexandria.

The ground was frozen hard, many of the men were barefooted, some were without blankets, and others almost destitute of clothing.[83] I remember one morning that one of the men in our company came to me and showed me the only remnant of a blanket that was remaining to him. I think that there were ten holes in it about the size of a man's hand. The troops were not long in making a considerable clearing for the owners of the land upon which we were encamped, and all day and all night immense log heaps were kept burning with the men standing around them, roasting pork and potatoes, of which we had as much as we wanted. The country on the Ouachita was a wealthy section, consisting of large cotton plantations, where the planters made nearly all their own provisions of pork, corn, potatoes, &c.

On the 9th, we were ordered to march again, and leaving our sick and barefooted behind at Calvary Church, the command moved up towards Arkansas. On the 11th we passed through Bastrop and, proceeding a few miles above, went into camp on the ragged banks of Bayou Bartholomew.

On the trip to this place, as I was passing near a little dwelling house, I saw the lady of the house run out with a broomstick in hand towards some bee hives and was laughing at the idea of seeing her rap some of the men over the head, but when she reached the hive

83. On October 5, 1863, a member of Walker's Texas Infantry Division recorded in his diary that the Texans had met Mouton's brigade at Moreauville. The Louisianians "were nearly all dressed in Federal uniforms that they had captured at Brashear City" (J. P. Blessington, *The Campaigns of Walker's Texas Division* [1875; rpr. Austin, 1968], 133).

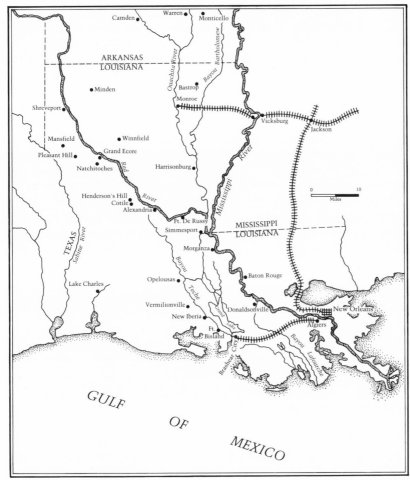

Louisiana and Arkansas
Map by Bobbie Young

and saw that the contents were all gone, her weapon dropped, and raising both hands into the air, she put on one of the most comical looks of despair and horror I ever witnessed on a human face. I ordered the men off in as savage a tone as my desire to laugh at the comedy would allow and saved one hive for the poor woman, but when we came back a few days afterwards, I noticed that it had subsequently met the same fate as the first one.

A few hundred yards onward, the wagons were halted for some purpose, when the irrepressible "Goss" came up and offered me a quarter section of honey as a peace offering. Giving him a moral lecture on the sin of taking things that did not belong to him, I ate the honey and rode onward in peace. On the 13th we were ordered to return, and as the ground had just thawed enough to let wagons through, the roads were horrible. I had not proceeded over a mile before every wagon I had was stuck fast in the mud. We had to pass through a lane about a quarter of a mile long, and by throwing both fences across the road, we corduroyed the whole distance, no doubt to the extreme disgust of the owner of the fencing. Arriving at Calvary Church, we remained one day, when the troops were removed about two miles nearer Monroe and again encamped where we remained for several days.

The weather moderated, and the men had some relief from the sufferings endured by the extreme cold of the previous 20 days.

This was the severest season our troops experienced during their four years' service. On the march to Bartholomew Bayou, the blood from the feet of the men was frequently to be seen upon the frozen ground, owing to the want of proper clothing, the suffering was great. I paid off the men some of the wages due, and they roamed the country for miles around picking up chickens at $2 a head, $2 for a [illegible], 50 cents for a pound of pork, [illegible] for a section of gingerbread, [illegible] for a grab into a bee gum.

Camp near Monroe, January 30th, 1864. The soldiers used to amuse themselves catching squirrels, and if one of those little animals ever showed his head, they got him, certain. Whilst in this camp, one of the little creatures was discovered, and the boys went to work and cut down 15 trees averaging two feet in diameter before they caught him. The amount of hollering and yelling during the time must be left to the vivid imagination of the reader. How much yelling a regiment of troops can do without injuring their lungs will always remain a mystery to my mind. Did ever an unfortunate dog venture into their quarters, such a yell was raised as to terrify the poor brute out of his wits and often make him sit down trembling, not knowing what to do.

This morning I was awakened about 1 o'clock with orders to proceed immediately to Monroe and report myself to Gen. Mouton. On so doing, I was placed in charge of the brigade trains and ordered to cross them over the Ouachita River at Trenton. On the 31st the crossing was effected, and the next morning the line of march was taken up for Alexandria by a more northern route than the one by which we had gone.[84]

Our route passed through Forksville, Vernon, and Lewisville. The 28th Louisiana Regiment had been raised in this portion of the state, and as we pursued our journey, their wives, sisters, and sweethearts came on horse back and in wagons to see them, often following for two or three days.

The number of women became so great as to cause one of Capt. Patin's Irishmen to exclaim in the fullness of his heart that "Be Jabers, and the 28th must all have three or four wives a pice." An old lady on horseback, who perhaps had several sons in the command, accompanied us for several days, generally riding in the advance. Upon reaching the top of a high hill, presenting a good view of the line of advancing troops for a long distance in the rear, she halted her horse and, gazing back upon the road filled with men as far as she could see, remarked, "Well, well, there's a heap of sons, and it took a heap of mothers to raise all them sons."

Leaving Lewisville, we had to cross the swamps of the Dugdemona, which the people up there facetiously called a river. In some places the road was several feet underground, and such a cracking of whips was never heard outside of an army train, nor such a swearing ever heard since the disbandment of the army in Flanders. We reached Winnfield at 10 o'clock P.M. with only six wagons broke down.

The 10th day's march brought us to Pineville, behind which, on the pine hills, we went into camp upon a stream of a fine running

---

84. On January 27, Taylor ordered Mouton to move one of his brigades to Alexandria, while the other was to remain in the vicinity of the Ouachita River (OR, Vol. XXXIV, Pt. 2, p. 919).

water. Here we met with many of our friends in the 26th Regiment,[85] who had lately come out of the lines from Thibodaux, and with whom we passed away many pleasant hours in conversing about our friends at home and learning how things were being conducted in the dominions of the enemy.

Our command was so destitute of clothing that it was known as the ragged brigade—only the members of the 28th, whose homes were nearby, had anything like a decent outfit.

The beef which we were getting as rations was almost worthless, the men having to depend upon bread and such food as they could gather up. Along the march they did very well, but in camp it was otherwise, as everything was gathered up for 50 miles around. The boys used to say that the commissaries laid down a fence rail and drove the beeves over it, and only butchered those that fell down in the attempt to step over the rail.

Alexandria, Feb. 1864. During the war, especially after the fall of New Orleans, there were a goodly number of patriotic men who were compelled to remain at home within the limits of the enemy's lines. Generally, they were not lacking in war-like ardor, neither were they deficient in military genius; most of them took the enmity oath against Uncle Sam's government, and there were no citizens in the whole Southern country who were better qualified to criticize the Confederate movements and to point out the military errors committed by our Southern generals. But the Confederacy, very unfortunately, everybody will admit, was deprived of the advantages which might have been obtained by the aid of this genius and ardor which circumstances prevented those patriotic individuals from turning to the good of the "Lost Cause."

Some of them had married wives, and they had to be protected; others were men troubled in mind lest some of their cattle might fall into a ditch; many were the reasons given, all of which were satisfactory and conclusive that they were justifiable in remaining behind.

These men, as the war progressed, began to imagine themselves terribly persecuted by the Federals. That the spies and informers of

85. The 26th Louisiana occupied a camp for paroled prisoners of war near Pineville. It and several other regiments that had been surrendered at Vicksburg were awaiting exchange (Winchester Hall, *The Story of the 26th Louisiana Infantry in the Service of the Confederate States,* ed. Edwin C. Bearss [1890s?; rpr. Gaithersburg, Md., 1984], 122).

Butler and Banks were always on their trail, watching every movement, reporting every word, and detailing every action; finally, many of them came to the conclusion that the whole object and aim of the Federal government in keeping an army of 50,000 men in and around Southern Louisiana was simply to watch them and that the sole occupation of the commanding officers, with their staffs, was simply to contrive some means to get a halter around their necks.

Once having arrived at this conclusion, they determined to make an exit from the Federal quarters and escape into some part of the country where the pure atmosphere of the Southern Confederacy might tranquillize their perturbed spirits and relieve their fears of dancing a jig in the air without anything to rest their weary feet upon.

Many and terrific were the dangers through which they passed in making their exits—the hair-breath escapes would have astonished Othello himself; some had to pass days and weeks in the swamps with no companions but mosquitoes, bull frogs, and alligators. Others traversed Lake Pontchartrain on logs, having been beaten about by the waves and winds for many a long day and many a weary night; some swam every bayou and waded every swamp from Algiers to New Iberia; others more smart managed to obtain the name of some poor prisoner who had died and got himself exchanged in the name of the departed hero.

About this time, many of these persecuted exiles came into our camps, and we were necessarily compelled to listen with extended ears to the relation of those wonderful stories, in the hope that at the end of the narrative we might learn something that we wished to know. These patriots generally were not famous marksmen and were very willing to perform military duty, provided they did not have to handle a gun.

The boys used to tell a story after this wise, and it was a fair sample of what they all had to say and to require.

One day one of the soldiers of a regiment approached his colonel. "Bon jour, Colonel—Colonel, my broder Jean Pierre has come. He jist out o' New Orleans, he had to run away and swim Lake Pontchartrain to keep old Butler from hanging him. Jean Pierre one brave man, he fight one, two, four duels—one time he get his finger shot off." (Colonel, aside to himself—"Wish he'd gotten his cowardly head shot off.") "My broder, he one brave *garcon*, he no afraid of Butler, he nevaire took de oaf. My broder he took the oaf of henmity—my broder he come to get his revenge—he ain't afraid to fight." "Well," says the colonel, "and I am glad to hear it. I suppose he's going to join the army, and I can have him mustered into service at any time." "Oh, yes, Colonel. My broder he very mad at the way the Yankees made him go away—he come purpose to get one revenge. He goin' to join right away." "All right," says the colonel, "that's the kind of man we want."

"Well, Colonel, my broder he not very strong. 'Spose you got no one place in the *commissaire* for he?"

Our stay at Pineville, which some of the boys named Pinetown, was pleasant and afforded us an agreeable rest after our winter's marching.

We were fortunate to receive some clothing which was distributed to the most needy. But our stay did not last long. Orders preparatory to march were transmitted to the command, and we were soon ready for motion.

4 THE FINAL CAMPAIGNS

Alexandria, March 1864.   Our quiet in camp in the rear of "Pine-town" was interrupted about the beginning of this month with orders to remove over Red River and proceed towards Lecompte, some 25 miles on the road to Opelousas.[1] Gen. Walker's Division[2] had wintered on Yellow Bayou near Simmesport, and as rumor had the enemy advancing in that direction, the two divisions of Walker and Mouton would thus be in supporting distance of one another.

Crossing Red River, I was ordered to put our baggage on cars of the Lecompte Railroad and retain the transportation at Alexandria except a few commissary and headquarters wagons. I urged Col. Armant to allow me to go on with the baggage, contending that I could haul it down and return with the trains before that burlesque of a railroad could transport it. But he had it unloaded, and it was nearly a week ere it reached Lecompte. The troops were kept maneuvering around considerably in the neighborhood of Marksville, Mansura, and Cheneyville, but I was quietly encamped with the trains just above Alexandria. News at length arrived that Fort DeRussy had been captured and that Walker was retreating before the advance of Banks' army.[3] Upon receiving this information, I went down to Alexandria to the headquarters of Gen. Taylor and saw Major Levy[4] and asked permission to go and bring the baggage of our brigade away from Lecompte, as there was no transportation with the command to save it in case of the enemy's advance.

Major Levy, who was chief of Gen. Taylor's staff, endeavored to

1. Gray's brigade left for Lecompte on March 8 (*OR*, Vol. XXXIV, Pt. 1, p. 574).
2. Major General John G. Walker commanded a division consisting of three brigades of Texas infantry (Blessington, *The Campaigns of Walker's Texas Division*).
3. On March 14, troops of the XVI Corps, Brigadier General Andrew J. Smith commanding, captured Fort DeRussy. Smith's men acted in cooperation with Banks's army in its invasion of the Red River Valley (*OR*, Vol. XXXIV, Pt. 1, p. 578).
4. Major William M. Levy, adjutant and inspector general on Taylor's staff. Levy had formerly served as colonel of the 2nd Louisiana Infantry (*ibid.*, 569; CSR, Roll 107; Taylor, *Destruction and Reconstruction*, 145).

persuade me that the enemy would not reach Cheneyville; I was not satisfied and insisted upon going after the baggage. Finally, consulting with Gen. Taylor, he gave me permission to exercise my own judgment. In one hour all my wagons were on the road, and before we had gone ten miles, the black smoke curling over the tree tops announced the advance of the gunboats up Red River, and at sundown they were anchored in front of the town. After driving hard all day and working most of the night, we secured the baggage, all of which would have been lost in less than 24 hours.

The next day the division moved forward through the piney woods, having taken the road from Cheneyville to Natchitoches. We had a long and weary march and encamped within a few miles of Carroll Jones' on the road from Alexandria to Sabine Town. There we remained for a few days. The trains were kept several miles ahead of the army, and we could only draw one ration at a time. The consequence was that we were, three-fourths of the time, living on parched corn and what the boys called "mud larks." These creatures resembled hogs very much, except that all those they brought into camp had no skins on them. Those caught in this region were so miserably poor that we could scarcely eat them. Parched corn did very well for food for about three or four days, when it began to burn the stomach and produce rather unpleasant sensations. We managed to get along on it for about two weeks, with a change of meal during 3 or 4 days. The troops did not do much better, and during night a guard had to be kept over the corn for the horses to keep the men from taking it all for themselves. I had three or four chickens when we left Alexandria, but on our retreat Mr. R. D. Jordan, of the Virginia army,[5] came up with us and spent some days in our company. One day my last chicken was cooked, and after making our dinner upon it, he put on his hat and remembered that he would have to call upon somebody near Natchitoches and, bidding me goodbye, deliberately walked off. This was about as cool an exhibition of misplaced confidence as I ever witnessed.

I sent off my wagons down on the Cotile after forage, and about the middle of the afternoon, they came back in a hurry without anything and Scroggins' wagon minus a bed, reporting that they had been chased by Yankees and narrowly escaped. About this time the

5. Private Richard D. Jordan, Company F, 14th Louisiana Infantry, was absent from his regiment on recruiting duty (CSR, Roll 258).

La. Cavalry was captured on Henderson's Hill, after being surprised by the enemy.[6]

Camp near Carroll Jones', March 23, 1864.   We were ordered onward towards Natchitoches; as we were moving along slowly, the trains were stopped. Gen. Gray and staff came galloping towards the rear, reports innumerable spread with rapidity along the lines, everybody said that the enemy were attacking our rear, &c. We afterwards learned that the enemy were encamped 40 miles behind us. On the 24th, our division was moved out towards Cloutierville on Cane River, where they remained a couple of days. On the 26th, I received orders to remove my trains to Pleasant Hill, store all the baggage, and return to the command with commissary stores. On the evening of the 26th, we passed by the remains of Fort Jesup, one of the frontier forts of the olden time. It was situated on the road leading from Natchitoches, La., to Nacogdoches, Texas, the one claiming to be the oldest town in Louisiana, the other having the same pretentions in Texas. General Zachary Taylor, in his early career, was stationed for some time at this post, which is now almost one entire mass of ruins.

On the 28th, we reached Pleasant Hill, stored our baggage in one of the unfinished buildings intended for a college,[7] loaded with meal and bacon, and started back towards the command, and encamped on the 29th near Fort Jesup.

Learning that Gen. Mouton's Division was nearby, I rode over and reported that my train of commissaries was nearby. Finding the general encamping in the woods, he ordered me to return towards Pleasant Hill at daylight.

I was also ordered to send into camp a load of bacon, and as I left the general called to me, "Captain, don't forget to send me some corn to feed my horse tonight," which was the last order I ever received from him, and it was also the last time that I ever looked upon his noble and loved form.

The general was very explicit in his orders about having all government stores guarded, and any officer who did not have a guard over the public property in his charge was held to a strict accounta-

6. On the night of March 21, Union troops marching out of Alexandria surrounded and captured the 2nd Louisiana Cavalry and Captain William Edgar's Texas Battery (*OR*, Vol. XXXIV, Pt. 1, p. 562).

7. The Pierce and Payne College for men was being built at Pleasant Hill by the Methodist Episcopal Church (Prichard, ed., "A Tourist's Description," 1172).

bility for such negligence. This was a very good system at the beginning of the war, but I had begun to lose faith in the purity of these guards, especially when placed to watch over anything that might be worn or eaten.

When I left Pleasant Hill, there was not a person with my train except the teamsters and wagon master. At night I gave them all a double ration of bacon and notified them that I wanted nothing touched by any of them. I have always thought that my orders were obeyed, but the next night, knowing the general's views about guards, I requested him to send me one, which he did. As my responsibility ceased then, I did not notice very closely what was going on, but Major Mouton complained that there was a woeful deficiency in the weight of *that* bacon. Generally afterwards, when I wanted nothing stolen, I kept clear of guards, but I was once subsequently induced to get a guard over some blankets for which I repented in sackcloth and ashes until the end of the war. The trains again reached Pleasant Hill on the 31st.

April 2nd. The division came up and went into camp, near the camp meeting quarters about one mile from Pleasant Hill on the Natchitoches road. Today I was lucky enough to buy two chickens for $5 and a dozen eggs for $3, and as a couple of friends from Cornay's Battery paid me a visit, we dined sumptuously on them, with a sprinkling of bacon and biscuits.

The troops came over to the wagon train, and such a general changing of clothes had not been seen for many a day, as they had not seen their knapsacks for more than three weeks. Some of them, who had like Flora McFlimsey no changes, pulled off those they had on and put them on again, being carried away from strict rules of propriety by the examples around them.

April 3rd. During the afternoon rumors were current that we were to continue our retreat, but it was not until 10 o'clock at night that I had any orders, when the chief of artillery[8] rode up and directed me to move forthwith. Some of my forage wagons were off towards Red River, and my mules were without supper. Ordering a courier to proceed after the foraging party and unloading my wagons of their commissaries, they were loaded with baggage, and before midnight we were beyond Pleasant Hill.

8. Major Joseph L. Brent served as Taylor's chief of artillery, while Major Thomas A. Faries held the same post in Mouton's division. This was probably Brent (CSR, M331, Rolls 32, 90).

The next day we passed through Mansfield, and on the 5th reached Keatchie, stored our baggage, loaded up with corn, and started back. On the 7th, the trains reached the command about 4 miles from Mansfield on the lower road to Shreveport. I called in the afternoon at the headquarters of Col. Armant, and after conversing awhile with him, I arose to return to my own quarters. The colonel remarked to me, "Captain, there are several months' wages due me, I am owing certain sums," which he specified, "and I want you to see them paid if anything happens to me." Promising that I would do so, I bade him good evening, little imagining that in a few hours that gallant and heroic young form would be silent in death. Under orders, I removed my trains over on the middle Shreveport road on the morning of the 8th, whilst the infantry filed back through Mansfield and on the road to Pleasant Hill.

Mansfield, April 8th, 1864. This morning the infantry divisions commanded by Major Gen. Walker and Brig. Gen. Mouton were drawn up in line of battle four miles below Mansfield, across the direct road leading to Pleasant Hill. The division of Gen. Mouton being on the left of the road, with the cavalry division of Gen. Tom Green[9] on their left; Churchill's division of Missouri and Arkansas troops were ordered from Keatchie, but did not arrive on the ground until night.[10] Gen. Dick Taylor was present in command of the whole force.

There was a large open field in front of Mouton's brigade, commanded by Col. Henry Gray of the 28th La. Regiment. At noon skirmishing began; the line of skirmishers were continually strengthened until about 3 o'clock.[11] Gen. Mouton had been suggesting an attack on the enemy since midday, and at this moment he sent word to his brigade commanders "that his suggestions had become an or-

9. This was Brigadier General James P. Major's division of two brigades, which was later reinforced by one regiment from Brigadier General Hamilton P. Bee's division. General Green exercised immediate command over this cavalry force (*OR*, Vol. XXXIV, Pt. 1, pp. 563, 564).

10. Brigadier General Thomas J. Churchill commanded his own Arkansas division and Brigadier General Mosby M. Parsons' Missouri division, both from the District of Arkansas. These divisions received orders to march from Keatchie to Mansfield on the morning of April 8. Churchill's division, commanded temporarily by Brigadier General James C. Tappan, reached Mansfield at 3:30 P.M. and was directed to the Gravelly Point road to prevent any flanking movement by the enemy from that direction. Parsons' division did not reach Mansfield until 6 P.M. (*ibid.*, 602, 604).

11. Taylor's official report stated that the attack began at 4 P.M. (*ibid.*, 564).

der," when the command from his manly and powerful voice echoed along the lines. "Throw down that fence, my boys, and charge across that field and drive the enemy away." The charge was instantly made.

The skirmishers of the enemy were driven from the open field, but the line of the Federals, protected by a high fence, disputed possession of the ground with earnestness and valor but were finally compelled to retreat and take to the woods. The severest fire of the enemy was concentrated upon our brigade, and our loss was heavy. The gallant Col. Beard[12] of Shreveport, of the Crescent Regiment, seeing his men wavering, took the regimental flag, and leading his men forward was killed, when Major Canfield[13] of Alexandria seized and carried it until he met the same fate of his colonel; Captain Martin[14] of Monroe, serving on the staff of Col. Gray, then seized the flag and carried it until he fell mortally wounded. It was then taken by Sergeant Ganier[15] of the 18th, who was also wounded whilst he had it in his possession. Lieut. Col. Clack[16] of this regiment was also mortally wounded, whilst fully one half of the officers were killed or disabled, the mortality of the men being in proportion.[17] Lieut. Col. Walker,[18] commanding the 28th, was mortally wounded at the head of his men; Capt. Blackman,[19] adjutant of Col. Gray, seized the regimental flag and led his old regiment forward until the victory was complete.

12. Colonel James H. Beard (CSR, Roll 376).

13. Major Mercer Canfield of the Consolidated Crescent Regiment (*ibid.*).

14. This was Lieutenant Arthur H. Martin, Colonel Gray's assistant inspector general, who had served as captain of Company C, 2nd Louisiana Infantry Regiment, and later as a drillmaster in the conscript camp at Monroe. At Mansfield, he had gone to bring the Consolidated Crescent Regiment up with the 18th and 28th Louisiana regiments following the initial charge. When he found that all of the field officers of the Crescent had fallen, he took the regimental colors and ordered the men forward. Almost instantly, an enemy bullet mortally wounded him (Colonel Henry Gray to Major E. Surget, April ?, 1864, typescript in Mansfield State Commemorative Area Museum library, Mansfield, La.; CSR, Roll 108).

15. Sergeant Elie Ganier, Company B (CSR, Roll 298).

16. Lieutenant Colonel Franklin H. Clack of the Consolidated Crescent Regiment (*ibid.*, Roll 377).

17. Captain Arthur W. Hyatt of the 18th Louisiana recorded in his diary that Mouton's division lost 762 men in the attack, most of them from Gray's brigade (Hyatt Diary, Entry of April 8, 1864, in Hyatt Papers).

18. Lieutenant Colonel William Walker (CSR, Roll 352).

19. Captain Wilbur F. Blackman. For a description of Blackman's actions in the attack, see Bartlett, "The Trans-Mississippi," in *Military Record of Louisiana*, 62.

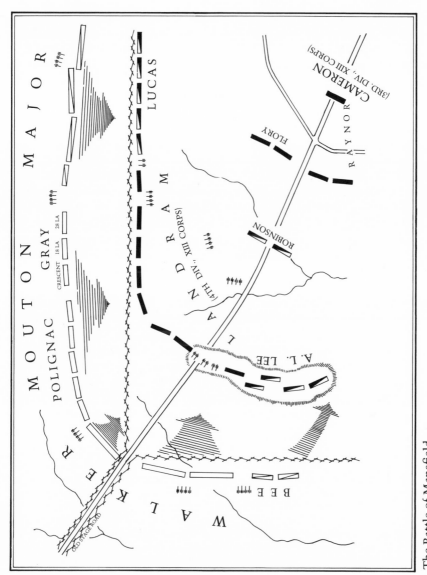

The Battle of Mansfield
Map by Bobbie Young

Col. Armant, the brave and youthful commander of the 18th, was instantly killed; Capt. J. T. Lavery was mortally wounded; Capt. S. A. Poche and Lieuts. Melville, Webre, and Becnel were wounded.[20] One half of our regiment was held in reserve and were ordered forward about the moment that the lines of the enemy were giving way.

During the engagement, our flag bearer, belonging to one of the St. James companies, was killed, when Private Emile Portier of our company picked up the flag and ever afterwards carried it, having been subsequently promoted to be an ensign for his conduct on this occasion. In our company, which was in reserve, Charles J. Barker was the only person injured, having received a wound in the foot, which subsequently necessitated amputation.[21]

But the greatest loss to us all on that day was the death of our noble General Mouton, who was dastardly killed in the moment of victory whilst striving to avoid any further loss of life to the enemy by some Federals who had thrown down their arms, but seeing him some distance from his own men, fired upon him, killing him instantly.

Another death occurred on that day which was much regretted by all who knew our former fellow citizen, Adam Beatty, Esq. He was serving as a volunteer aide on the staff of Col. Gray and passed through the fiercest of the contest unhurt.

As he and Capt. Poche[22] were about passing the fence to enter the woods out of which the enemy had been driven, he remarked to the captain "that there was a providence which had carried them safely through that contest," but in a moment afterwards he received a ball in his stomach which caused his death the next morning.

Col. Gray, apparently having a presentiment that his friend would be hurt, advised him not to enter into the charge about to be made. Speaking about this death, the general [Gray] frequently told me that he did not want him to go into the engagement, that he told

20. Lieutenant Thomas D. Melville, Company E; Lieutenant Septime Webre, Company E; and Captain Louis Becnel, Company A (CSR, Rolls 298, 300).

21. Barker lay on the battlefield for three days before being taken to an improvised hospital in Mansfield. There he lay on the floor for eight days before surgeons attended to him. About the middle of May, surgeons amputated Barker's leg, and he barely escaped dying (John Dimitry, "Louisiana," in *Confederate Military History*, ed. Evans, X, 334). The 18th Louisiana lost nineteen killed, seventy-five wounded, and one missing at Mansfield and Pleasant Hill (List of casualties, signed by Lieutenant J. B. Rosser, May 30, 1864, in Hyatt Papers).

22. Captain Felix Pierre Poche of Colonel Gray's commissary staff, temporarily serving as Gray's aide-de-camp (Bearss, ed., *A Louisiana Confederate*, 107).

him that it was unnecessary, and that at the moment the command was given by Gen. Mouton to advance he was meditating some order by which he could send him away from danger but the charge was made and a noble and gallant man lost his life.

Gen. John L. Lewis[23] of New Orleans, acting as aide to Gen. Gray, with his white and flowing locks, acted like a youthful cavalier on that occasion; he was struck on the head by a Minie ball, but binding up the wound continued in the engagement.

The charge of Mouton's Division at Mansfield was certainly a splendid one, and one that was not often excelled in vigor and impetuosity, and upon its brilliant result was decided the campaign of Gen. Banks up the Red River. Until this time the enemy had met with no obstacle to impede his progress. His loss this day was heavy in men, artillery, and transportation, and that night he turned back towards New Orleans.[24]

(I was not in the engagement, and only relate the above as I heard it from eyewitnesses at the time.)

Camp near Mansfield, April 9th, 1864. The army of Gen. Taylor, after obtaining a little rest from their bloody day's work, were aroused and sent forward at daybreak in pursuit of the enemy.

Gen. McCulloch's brigade of Missourians and Gen. Churchill's Arkansas brigade[25] reached the main army at night and moved forward with them this morning. Gen. Banks had been re-inforced by another corps of his army and taken up a position in front of the town of Pleasant Hill.[26] The attack was made in the afternoon.[27]

The right wing of our army, composed of Churchill's and McCulloch's troops, were met with a severe fire, lost Daniel's Battery,[28]

23. General Lewis had been a major general and commander of the First Division of the Louisiana militia (Glenn R. Conrad, ed., "John Lawson Lewis," in *A Dictionary of Louisiana Biography* [Lafayette, La., 1988], II, 511).

24. The Federals lost 113 men killed, 581 wounded, and 1,541 missing; 20 artillery pieces; nearly 200 wagons; and thousands of small arms (*OR*, Vol. XXXIV, Pt. 1, pp. 263–64, 452, 527).

25. See note 10 of this chapter for the correct identification of these units.

26. Banks had left Brigadier General Andrew J. Smith's two divisions of the XVI Corps at Pleasant Hill while he marched toward Mansfield with two divisions of the XIII Corps and one of the XIX Corps, plus the army's cavalry division. The XIII Corps bore the brunt of the battle of Mansfield, and Banks sent it, with the cavalry, to escort the army's trains to Grand Ecore (*OR*, Vol. XXXIV, Pt. 1, pp. 183, 452).

27. The Confederate attack began about 4:30 P.M. (*ibid.*, 567).

28. One gun of Captain Chambers B. Etter's Arkansas Battery and two of Captain James M. Daniel's Texas Battery fell into Union hands during the battle (Major

and were forced to fall back, but the enemy were repulsed by Mouton's and Walker's divisions.

At night, however, our lines were withdrawn some distance to obtain water, and the next day returned to Mansfield and encamped, the enemy falling back and fortifying themselves at Grand Ecore, four miles from Natchitoches on Red River, first burning all their stores at Pleasant Hill.

The result of these battles delivered the Red River country from the invader and furnished our troops with thousands of splendid rifles and several excellent pieces of artillery.

On the 11th, our brigade returned to the same camp they occupied previous to the battles. The Texas troops caught one of the Zouaves at Mansfield. He was clothed in red trousers and shirt, his pants belted around his waist, leg buckles over his knees, whilst the whole suit was hanging loosely about him. Besides he wore a red cap with a long tail hanging down his back. These backward Texans, never having seen such a looking creature, mistook him for some strange animal and were taking him out into the woods to shoot him, when someone informed them that he was only a man and saved his life.

April 13. This day Price's army commenced moving back towards Shreveport, whence they marched up into Arkansas and aided in the defeat of Steele's army at the Saline.[29]

Brig. Gen. Polignac was promoted to be a major general and placed in command of Mouton's Division, and Col. Henry Gray of the 28th, commanding our brigade, was promoted to be a brigadier general.[30]

By promotion, Lt. Colonel Joseph Collins became colonel, Maj. Wm. Mouton became Lt. Colonel, and Capt. Gourdain became Major of the 18th La. Regiment. The promotion of Capt. Gourdain was followed by the advancement of Lt. L. M. Hargis to the captaincy of our company and that of 2nd Lt. J. L. Aucoin to be a 1st lieutenant in the same company.

Joseph L. Brent to Major Eustace Surget, April 14, 1864, in Brent Papers, Jackson Barracks).

29. Churchill's divisions and Walker's division left Mansfield April 14, went to Arkansas, and fought in the battle of Jenkins' Ferry on April 30 (*OR*, Vol. XXXIV, Pt. 1, pp. 572, 782–83).

30. General Edmund Kirby Smith, commander of the Trans-Mississippi Department, appointed Polignac as a major general on April 13. Smith appointed Gray as a brigadier general on April 15 (*ibid.*, Pt. 3, pp. 764, 768).

The town of Mansfield was converted into one grand hospital, where the wounded were removed from the battlefield for treatment.

Capt. J. T. Lavery of the 18th died a few days subsequent to the battle, which caused the promotion of Lt. H. N. Jenkins[31] to be captain.

The boys serenaded Gen. Polignac and Gen. Gray and were favored with speeches from these gallant officers on the occasion. To-day the army was pained to hear of the fall of the great Texan officer Maj. Gen. Green, who was killed in a skirmish with some of the enemy's gunboats on the Red River.[32]

Camp near Mansfield, La., April 14th, 1864. This morning, under marching orders, we passed through Mansfield and moved on by the old Fort Jesup Road. I sent one of my clerks into town to hunt up all the wounded officers and pay them two months' wages.

I left the main road near the village so as to pass through the cemetery and take a look at the graves of the heroes who had fallen a few days previous on the battlefield. The cemetery was situated upon a high hill, and upon its crests were the tombs of General Mouton, Col. Armant, Major Canfield, Capt. Martin, and Adam Beatty. These brave and gallant gentlemen, who but a week previous were the leaders and pride of our brigade, were now sleeping quietly side by side, their graves being covered with flowers and bouquets by the hands of the gentle ladies of the village, whose preservation from pillage and ruin had cost them their life's blood.

On the 15th, we passed over the battlefield of Pleasant Hill, which showed evidence of having been hotly contested. In the town many of the houses had been pierced by cannon balls.

On the 16th, the march was continued along the old Shreveport and Natchitoches road. The enemy, in their flight, had cut down trees across the road and obstructed it in every manner possible. General Polignac, who now commanded all the forces in the front, had gone forward the day previous.[33] We encamped about 17 miles

31. Lieutenant Horatio N. Jenkins, Company E (CSR, Roll 299).

32. Green died on April 12 in an engagement with Union gunboats at Blair's Landing (*OR*, Vol. XXXIV, Pt. 1, p. 571).

33. Taylor ordered Polignac's infantry to Natchitoches to support the cavalry. Polignac held command of all of the troops in the field during Taylor's absence in Shreveport (*ibid.*, 572; General Order No. 35, Headquarters District of West Louisiana, April 14, 1864, in Letters Sent and Order Book, District of West Louisiana, Lou-

from Natchitoches; we had no forage for two days, but on the 17th my trains caught up with us, to the great joy of mules and horses. At the same time orders came to cook two days' rations, and one of those amusing scenes that occurred so often was enacted. Everybody was wondering what was going to be done; adjutants and quarter-masters and orderlies were galloping about giving directions, and everybody was inquiring what they thought was going to be done, and as soon as they received their answers, everybody was just as wise as he was at first, and then they all ate their supper and went to sleep without caring a straw what was in the wind.

The enemy had left Natchitoches on the 13th and were now en-camped in Grand Ecore, which was the landing point on Red River for Natchitoches and about four miles distant. We, however, re-mained quiet for several days.

Whilst waiting for marching orders, the following order was pro-mulgated for the re-organization of our brigade staff, emanating from Brig. Gen. Gray, who had just been promoted and assigned to duty in the same, viz.:

> Lieut. W. F. Blackman to be Captain and A. A. G.
> Lieut. L. Flournoy[34] to be Captain and A. D. C.
> and Inspector General.
> Capt. S. T. Grisamore to be Major and A. Q. M.
> Capt. C. T. Patin to be Major and A. C. M.
> Dr. McPheeters[35] to be Major and Chief Surgeon.
> Capt. A. F. Poche[36] to be Aide-de-Camp.

The 18th Regiment furnished the A. Q. M. and A. C. M. for the brigade.

Capt. C. M. Shepherd was appointed by Col. Collins as acting quartermaster of the 18th.

---

isiana Historical Association Collection, Special Collections Division, Howard-Til-ton Memorial Library, Tulane University Library, New Orleans).

34. Lucian Flournoy, former adjutant of the Consolidated Crescent Regiment (CSR, Roll 376).

35. Dr. W. A. McPheeters, former surgeon of the Consolidated Crescent Regiment (*ibid.*, Roll 378).

36. Probably Felix P. Poche.

Camp twenty miles above Natchitoches, April 18th, 1864. Remaining here for several days whilst the enemy were besieged at Grand Ecore, marching orders at length came, and we moved off through the piney woods, striking Cane River above Cloutierville. The army of Gen. Banks had passed down the day before,[37] crossing at Twenty-four Mile Ferry; we moved down near Cloutierville and encamped about the 25th April. The smoke of the burning buildings showed the route of the enemy. Some few dwellings and barns had been destroyed above this place, but from Cloutierville to Monett's Ferry, a distance of twelve miles, but one dwelling house was left standing. Everything in the shape of a building, from the mansion to the pig pen, was destroyed; every living thing was killed or driven away. A more complete scene of unnecessary or wanton destruction was never committed by barbarian or savage nations.[38]

On the 26th April we encamped near Monett's Ferry. It was at this point where the enemy were expecting to be met by a force of cavalry commanded by Gen. Bee of Texas. Why the attack was not made, or why some attempt to interfere with the crossing of the Federals was not made, has never been fully explained.[39] Near this ferry, about an acre of ground had been covered with wagons, carts, and carriages and burned. The Negroes had been made to hitch up all the teams, load them with everything they could lay their hands on, and follow their army. Arriving at this Ferry, they collected all their vehicles into one mass and fired them.[40]

This day the artillery company of Capt. Cornay was sent down Cane River to its junction with the Red, where they succeeded in capturing one of the enemy's transports after a sharp little fight; the

37. Banks's army left Grand Ecore on April 22 (*OR*, Vol. XXXIV, Pt. 1, p. 190).

38. Taylor reported on April 24: "The destruction of this country by the enemy exceeds anything in history. For many miles every dwelling-house, every negro cabin, every cotton-gin, every corn-crib, and even chicken-houses have been burned to the ground; every fence torn down and the fields torn up by the hooves of horses and wheels of wagons. Many hundreds of persons are utterly without shelter. But for our prompt attacks Natchitoches would have been burned to the ground, and also the little village of Cloutierville, both of them having been fired in several places" (*ibid.*, 581).

39. Grisamore is mistaken here. General Bee had contested the crossing with three cavalry brigades on April 23 but had fallen back when he imagined himself being outflanked (*ibid.*, 580).

40. This occurred, according to Taylor, on the night of April 22 (*ibid.*, 580).

only loss being their gallant Captain and the wounding of Lieut. Bourque[41] of Opelousas, who accompanied a detachment of our brigade in support of the artillery.

April 28th.   This morning we crossed Monett's Ferry and moved down Cotile Bayou and reached McNutt's Hill on the Rapides on the 29th.

This section of the country had been badly treated by the jayhawkers during its occupation by the Federals, who had stolen and carried off everything they could get hold of in the houses of the citizens.[42]

I visited the house of a friend in the vicinity which the Federals had fired in half a dozen places, but they were so hotly pursued that the ladies had time to quench the flames before they got beyond control. The army of Gen. Banks was in Alexandria, whilst our forces were on all sides of it. Several transports were captured below Alexandria trying to get up to his relief.[43] On the 1st and 2nd May, we moved out into the piney woods back of Alexandria, and about midnight I received orders to mount all the drummers in our brigade on mules and send them to headquarters. They were then sent to our advance picket line and distributed all around the enemy. At reveille they commenced beating the long roll, and long lists of soldiers' names were called and answered to, which caused the Federals to expect a general attack at daylight by our whole army.[44] It was something similar to the attack on the village of Jericho a few centuries ago, although the result was not precisely the same. The desire to terrify the enemy was, however, successful. A prisoner af-

41. Lieutenant Valery S. Bourque lost a leg in the skirmish (Bartlett, "The Trans-Mississippi," in *Military Record of Louisiana,* 44).

42. The Jayhawkers had begun to overrun the area after Taylor's army withdrew from Alexandria to Natchitoches. During the month of April, the depredations became so bad that the Union commander at Alexandria sent out troops to subdue them (*OR,* Vol. XXXIV, Pt. 1, p. 510; Dennis E. Haynes, *A Thrilling Narrative of the Sufferings of Union Refugees, and the Massacre of the Martyrs of Liberty of Western Louisiana* [Washington, D.C., 1866], 78).

43. Major's cavalry division captured the *Emma* on May 1 and the *City Belle* on May 3 (*OR,* Vol. XXXIV, Pt. 1, pp. 621, 622).

44. To keep the Federals in Alexandria on edge and ignorant of the weakness of his forces, Taylor was forced to "'eke out the lion's skin with the fox's hide.' On several occasions we have forced the enemy from strong positions by sending drummers to beat calls, lighting camp-fires, blowing bugles, and rolling empty wagons over fence rails" (*ibid.,* 590).

terwards captured, whilst talking with our men, said: "Yes, d—n you, you tried to drum us out of Alexandria, did you?" intimating pretty plainly that they were made a little nervous on the strength of the drumming to which they had been treated.

Our brigade was shortly after removed around near Lecompte and placed in position in rear of the cavalry near Bayou Lamourie.[45]

One night, as Gen. Gray and his staff were quietly snoozing under the trees, a soldier rode up: it was about 2 o'clock A.M. "Halloo," says he. No answer. "Halloo" again. Gen. Gray, who was half awake, replied by a grum "halloo yourself." "Do you know where Col. Likens' cavalry regiment[46] is?" "Yes," says the general, "it is about one mile up the road here, in line of battle, prepared to make an attack upon the Yankees at daylight. If you'll just hurry up, you'll get there in time to join in."

"Well, stranger, I've been riding all day and I am powerful tired. I guess I'll stop here and rest a little." "Oh," says the general, "that will never do. Col. Likens needs every man in the morning, and you must go on and assist him." "Well, look-e-here, stranger, I've rode about fifty miles today, I tell you what it is. I'm just about gin out," and down he got and was soon dreaming of hearing the "Angels sing."

Whether his halting at that time prevented the attack the next morning is a mystery that I have never investigated very closely but presume it did not.

Gen. Gray did not have a very exalted opinion of Trans-Mississippi cavalry. As we were coming down Cane River, General Wharton[47] placed a line of skirmishers in his rear to prevent straggling, and Gen. Gray had orders to allow no one to fall in the rear. One of the cavalry managed to evade Wharton's skirmish line and met General Gray. As he attempted to ride by, the general halted him and in-

45. Early on May 7, Polignac's division marched from Cheneyville toward Bayou Lamourie to support an attack by Bee's cavalry on Union forces near that stream. Polignac assumed command of all the troops on the field (Alwyn Barr, ed., "The Civil War Diary of James Allen Hamilton, 1861–1864," *Texana*, II [1964], 144; *OR*, Vol. XXXIV, Pt. 1, p. 589).

46. Colonel James B. Likens' 35th Texas Cavalry Regiment, which participated in the Confederate attack at Bayou Lamourie on May 7 (*OR*, Vol. XXXIV, Pt. 1, pp. 606, 611).

47. Major General John A. Wharton, who had previously served under Major General Joseph Wheeler in Tennessee, succeeded Green in command of Taylor's cavalry about April 22 (*OR*, Vol. XXXIV, Pt. 3, p. 782).

quired "what part of the army he belonged to." "I don't belong to the army, I belong to the cavalry." "That's a fact," says Gray, "you can pass on."

Lecompte, May 1864. In the early part of this month our little army moved gradually down Bayou Boeuf and by the 15th was encamped near Evergreen on the Bayou de Glaize.[48]

As we were moving along the hot and dusty road leading from Cheneyville to Evergreen, we met about 100 prisoners who had been captured a day or two previous by the 2nd Louisiana Cavalry, commanded by Col. Vincent.

The dust was about six inches deep, the sun was shining intensely hot as the squad filed along through our lines.

I noticed in the midst of the prisoners a man in citizen's dress, "with belly apparently with good fat capon lined," his hat drawn down over his eyes, the dust settling profusely over his face, through which streams of perspiration ran in little rivulets down his cheek, looking the very picture of despair as he was ruminating over the pleasant walk he was taking to Shreveport, only two hundred miles distant. Something about this individual appeared familiar to me, and upon taking a good look at him, he was recognized as the jolly, fat commissary that supplied our troops with beef and corn meal whilst we were in the neighborhood of Berwick's Bay in the autumn of 1862.

Finding the sale of beef to the Confederacy not profitable, he had turned his mercantile talents to speculating in cotton and was upon one of the ill-fated Red River boats when he was captured.

It was reported in camp the next day that upon arriving at Gen. Taylor's headquarters, the perspiration had turned into tears, which flowed so freely down the gullies formed through the dust upon his rubicund face that the dignified and tender-hearted commander of the Rebels had his sympathy so aroused that he liberated the old gentleman and told him to go in peace.

At all events, no serious harm happened to him, as I saw him a short time since on the cars of Morgan's Railroad, looking as if he had a lease of life for another quarter of a century.

The enemy had left Alexandria after burning the principal part of

48. Banks's army left Alexandria on May 13. Polignac's division had marched to Cocoville on the twelfth and moved to Mansura when the Federals left the city (*ibid.*, Pt. 1, p. 591; Bearss, ed., *A Louisiana Confederate*, 120).

town and was moving down the banks of Red River and had arrived at Marksville. Our command was too small to hope to stop him in his retreat, but all our artillery and infantry had met him in the prairie near Mansura, where an artillery duel of two or three hours was kept up during which time his trains had passed over the swamps to the Bayou de Glaize, when his whole force followed and retreated down that bayou toward Simmesport.[49] As he retreated, dwellings, corn houses, etc., were fired as usual. As our command arrived near Moreauville on the 17th May, about a hundred prisoners captured from the enemy's rear guard were brought in.[50] Among them was a lieutenant colonel[51] who was soon recognized by some of the citizens as having been instrumental in saving their houses from the flames. This fact being told to Gen. Taylor, this officer was immediately placed upon parole and allowed to pass through our lines and upon reaching New Orleans had himself exchanged for Lieut. Col. Blair[52] of the 2nd La. Cavalry, and then resigned in disgust and went home.

May 18th. At ten we were ordered to hitch up our trains instantly and await orders, whilst the infantry were hurried rapidly to the front. Parsons' brigade of cavalry[53] attacked the enemy's lines about one mile from Yellow Bayou and were repulsed with a loss of

49. Polignac's division occupied the Confederate left flank at Mansura, and thirteen artillery pieces were spread out on his front. Taylor reported, "The broad, open prairie, smooth as a billiard table, afforded an admirable field for artillery practice." When the Federals threatened to outflank the Confederate forces, the latter fell back toward Evergreen. The Federals then continued their retreat, and Taylor sent a cavalry division to attack them near Moreauville (*OR*, Vol. XXXIV, Pt. 1, p. 593).

50. Wharton's cavalry attacked the enemy's rear guard near Moreauville, and the Confederates captured a large number of prisoners (*ibid.*, 593–94; Theophilus Noel, *A Campaign from Santa Fe to the Mississippi*, ed. Martin H. Hall and Edwin A. Davis [Houston, 1961], 133; Spurlin, comp. and ed., *West of the Mississippi with Waller's 13th Texas Cavalry Battalion*, 11).

51. Attempts to identify this officer have proven unsuccessful. The memoirs of one Confederate soldier state that elements of Waller's 13th Texas Cavalry Battalion and the 5th Texas Cavalry captured a lieutenant colonel, two majors, eight other officers, and fifty-six enlisted men in Moreauville (Noel, *A Campaign from Santa Fe to the Mississippi*, 133).

52. Lieutenant Colonel James D. Blair had been captured at Henderson's Hill and was exchanged on June 2 (CSR, Roll 8).

53. Colonel William H. Parsons' Texas cavalry brigade joined Taylor's army from Texas on April 9–10 (Anne J. Bailey, *Between the Enemy and Texas: Parsons's Texas Cavalry in the Civil War* [Fort Worth, 1989], 169; *OR*, Vol. XXXIV, Pt. 1, p. 571).

50 to 70 men. The infantry division was then sent forward. The enemy were concealed in a strip of woods running from Bayou de Glaize to the swamps in the rear. Polignac's brigade, commanded by Col. Stone,[54] who had been promoted for gallantry at the Battles of Mansfield and Pleasant Hill, suffered severely, being repulsed with the loss of their heroic leader. The 28th Regiment lost one captain killed,[55] our regiment had but one death and few wounded.

This fight lasted two hours. The 18th was thought by Gen. Gray and the balance of the troops to be lost at one time.

It was placed on the extreme right of our line with directions to govern its movements by the remainder of the line, but upon getting into the woods, which were thick with undergrowth and briars, they did not perceive the retreat on the left[56] and continued to advance into the forest until they were met by a portion of the enemy, when a sharp firing commenced which soon cleared the ground in their front. Gen. Gray, seeing the perilous position of the regiment, sent Capt. F. P. Poche, his aide-de-camp, to recall them, little expecting to see them or his aide either upon that day.[57]

The 18th was soon discovered coming out of the woods in perfect order and marching back to their proper position in line. Gen. Wharton, who commanded the forces on that occasion, rode up and said that he "wanted to shake hands with the Colonel of such a regiment."[58]

Lieut. J. L. Aucoin of our company, as the commanding officer of

54. Colonel Robert D. Stone of the 22nd Texas Dismounted Cavalry Regiment was temporarily commanding Polignac's brigade. He was struck down by a Union minié ball. The brigade lost 208 men killed, wounded, and missing. Grisamore's reference to a promotion concerns Polignac, not Stone (Barr, *Polignac's Texas Brigade*, 42, 46).

55. Captain Benjamin F. Fort, Company K, 28th Louisiana Infantry, was captured and possibly wounded at Yellow Bayou (CSR, Roll 348).

56. When the enemy repulsed Polignac's brigade, the 28th Louisiana became disorderly, and Gray ordered his brigade to retreat (Bearss, ed., *A Louisiana Confederate*, 123).

57. Captain Felix P. Poche wrote in his diary that he found the 18th Louisiana "far back in the Woods, having entirely repulsed the enemy and who were in perfect Battle formation awaiting orders" (*ibid.*).

58. Because Colonel Collins was under arrest, Captain William Sanchez of Company C commanded the 18th on this occasion (Bartlett, "The Trans-Mississippi," in *Military Record of Louisiana*, 43).

a company composed of the Yellow Jacket Battalion,[59] acquitted himself very gallantly upon that occasion.

We held possession of the battlefield, and although the contest was severe, bloody, and well contested on both sides, the whole affair was unnecessary and utterly barren in its results. The enemy were retreating as rapidly as they could get away and would have left just as speedily without this attack. The losses were heavy on both sides.[60] More than fifty of our men were buried in one cemetery near a brick church, and others were interred near Moreauville. The enemy buried his dead in the trenches on the Yellow Bayou, and from the appearance, his loss must have been still greater.

The day was excessively hot, and the roads dusty, causing our men to suffer severely in the hurried march to the front, and then they were moved forward in line of battle for more than a mile across a field of standing cane from which the blades had been burnt. Gen. Polignac was strongly opposed to attacking and risking the lives of his men in an engagement that could not possibly result in any advantage to us.[61]

Camp on Bayou de Glaize, May 24th, 1864.   Today the army of Gen. Banks finished crossing the Atchafalaya River at Simmesport.[62] Our brigade was soon after removed near the spot upon which that little village stood, but the village was one of the things of the past.

A large quantity of wagons and carriages had been destroyed there, and our teamsters found many a chain and piece of gearing which they turned to good account afterwards.

We remained quietly encamped for several days, when we were ordered back into the woods near Moreauville,[63] at which camp a week or so was passed, when we removed into the woods some four

59. Company K.

60. The Federals reported losing 38 men killed, 226 wounded, and 3 missing (*OR*, Vol. XXXIV, Pt. 1, p. 311). Confederate losses are hard to determine. Taylor reported that casualties had totaled nearly 500 men, mostly captured (*ibid.*, 594).

61. A Texas cavalryman wrote home: "The enemy had decidedly the advantage in position, and Gen. Wharton is considerably censured for the manner in which he managed the fight" (John Q. Anderson, ed., *Campaigning with Parsons' Texas Cavalry Brigade, C.S.A.* [Hillsboro, Tex., 1967], 140).

62. The Federals actually crossed during the night of May 20–21 (*OR*, Vol. XXXIV, Pt. 1, p. 212).

63. This camp was on Bayou Black Water (Bearss, ed., *A Louisiana Confederate*, 125).

or five miles below Moreauville and encamped on a big lake[64] abounding in fish, of which our troops caught great numbers.

After a week or more rest on this lake, we were ordered into the woods to the rear of Marksville.[65]

The weather was excessively hot, the soldiers doing little but cooking, eating, and gathering blackberries.

About the 1st July orders came for us to move up by Alexandria to McNutt's Hill, on the Bayou Rapides. The troops left and marched up the Red River road to their destination.[66]

I obtained a leave of absence for a few days and rode down to Big Cane and Opelousas on a visit to my friends in those places.

On the 7th I left Opelousas and rode about forty miles into a prairie west of Chicot and passed the night at my friend C. Mayo's residence.[67] The next morning, after riding a few miles into the piney woods, I found myself outside of civilization and pretty much everything else.

Roads innumerable were met which were barely perceptible, and no one appeared to be more traveled than the others. Not a bird or animal was visible. The road which I was following appeared to be leading westward, which was not at all consoling, as I was fully aware that it was not many miles in that direction to the haunts of the Jayhawkers.[68] After traveling about twenty miles, a cabin became visible, and then the question arose whether that was the mansion of a set of pious Jayhawkers whose religious tenets would

64. Lake William. The Confederate camp was called Camp Eggling (*ibid.*, 127, 129; Hyatt Diary, Entry of June 9, 1864, in Hyatt Papers).

65. This camp was located one half mile east of Marksville (Bearss, ed., *A Louisiana Confederate*, 130).

66. Polignac's division left for McNutt's Hill on July 4 (*ibid.*, 136).

67. This was probably Claudius Mayo, who had served as a junior second lieutenant in Company B, 18th Louisiana. The 1860 census showed him as a twenty-three-year-old farmer (CSR, Roll 295; Eighth Census: St. Landry Parish, Roll 424).

68. As early as May, 1863, armed bands composed of Unionists, deserters, draft dodgers, and bandits began forming in the prairie and swamp regions west of Opelousas. Known as Jayhawkers, these groups included whites, free men of color, and runaway slaves. They plagued military and civil authorities as well as innocent civilians until after the end of the war. Their primary leaders were Ozeme Carriere, Martin Guillory, Billaut Guillory, and Dr. A. P. Dudley. Several campaigns by regular Confederate and home guard units failed to rid the area of this scourge (*OR*, Vol. XXVI, Pt. I, pp. 342, 778, Vol XXXIV, Pt. 2, pp. 962–66, and Vol. XLVIII, Pt. 2, pp. 718–19; Opelousas *Courier*, August 15, 1863, May 14, October 22, 1864, May 20, June 17, 1865).

not make it obligatory upon them to relieve me of the care of "Fanny" or perhaps give me a little elevation in such a manner as to render my feet of but little use or whether I would find friends therein.

Seeing but one man seated on the gallery, I hitched "Fanny" to the fence and marched up boldly, as a scared devil naturally would, and asked for a drink of water. Pointing to a bucket on the gallery, he told me to help myself. In so doing, I saw, through the open door, a man lying on the floor.

Inquiring if some of his family were ill, he replied that his son had just come from the army unwell. To what portion of the army does he belong? To Gen. Taylor's? I felt about fifteen years younger after this conversation, and ascertaining that I was on the right road to my destination, I bid him good evening and left. It was fifteen miles to the next house. Ten miles from this cabin, I met two soldiers of the 18th Regiment who had a furlough to go home, on Bayou Vermilion. They had left camp about 9 o'clock and had walked about forty miles and calculated to reach their home next day, a distance of about 125 to 150 miles from camp. There is no doubt they did so. It was not unusual for a soldier on furlough to walk seventy-five miles a day going home, but I do not remember ever having heard of such a feat being done on the return to duty.

The sun was going down as I reached the next house, having ridden nearly fifty miles since 8 1/2 o'clock. I inquired if I could remain over night and was informed that they had nothing to give me to eat. I then asked if I could get something for my horse and received a reply that they had no forage but was told that if I would go on to Paul's, five miles further, I might obtain accommodations. I didn't see the point exactly but rode on through a long lane with a large field of green corn on either side. Arriving at the end of the lane, I rode around the corner into a ravine, hitching "Fanny" to a fence, and got over in the field and cut down a couple of armsful of green corn, which furnished her with a supper, and then lay down and slept till daylight. I reached McNutt's Hill at 11 o'clock, where I found the command, and as I had nothing to eat for thirty hours, it is quite likely that I did justice to our dinner as soon as it was prepared.

McNutt's Hill was one of the most pleasant camping grounds we ever found during the whole war. Fine springs of cool water, a high, pleasant atmosphere, and a hospitable neighborhood made it a pleasant camp for the soldiers, whilst the Rapides Bayou contained abundance of fish for those who would take the trouble to catch them. We were in hopes of passing the summer here, but such was not the case.

Camp on McNutt's Hill, July 1864. Whilst at this point, Capt. Sanders, Chief Quartermaster at Alexandria,[69] promised me that if I would furnish two good wagons to be sent into Texas they should be returned to our division loaded with clothing. Two of my best teams were fitted up and started off, the prospect of a supply of clothing considerably brightening the hopes of our soldiers.

We were soon under marching orders and removed down on Beaver Creek, in the piney woods some twenty miles below Alexandria.[70] At this camp, Major Nugent,[71] Division Quartermaster, obtained a leave of absence, and I was assigned to duty in his place. In a week or two we removed our camps a few miles back into the piney woods, near the summer residence of the Compton family, where was one of the purest springs of fresh water I ever saw.

In this dwelling resided the family of J. S. Goode, and in the vicinity were the families of W. D. Burton and T. H. Ellis.[72]

The troops had but little to do but amuse themselves as they saw proper.

Our quiet did not long continue, and again on the move, we

69. Major R. W. Sanders, formerly acting assistant quartermaster of the 18th Louisiana and assistant quartermaster of Mouton's brigade, was now chief quartermaster of the District of West Louisiana (CSR, Roll 296; *OR, XV*, 177, and Vol. XXVI, Pt. 1, p. 216).

70. General Taylor had suggested an expedition into the Lafourche region following the conclusion of the Red River Campaign. Later, General Kirby Smith proposed to send Polignac's and Walker's divisions toward the Lafourche to force the Federals to reinforce their garrison at Morganza at the expense of an expedition being prepared to attack Mobile. Polignac's division stopped at Beaver Creek when orders arrived that it and Walker's divisions were to be transferred to the east side of the Mississippi River (*OR*, Vol. XXXIV, Pt. 1, p. 595, and Vol. XLI, Pt. 1, p. 90).

71. Major R. J. Nugent (CSR, M331, Roll 188).

72. Several Comptons lived in the area and had summer homes in the hills west of Bayou Boeuf. This may have been L. G. Compton, a thirty-nine-year-old planter. Joseph S. Goode, who was born in Alabama, was a lawyer in Terrebonne Parish. William D. Burton, also a lawyer, lived in Lafourche Parish and had served as lieutenant colonel of the Lafourche Regiment, Louisiana Militia, in the fall of 1862. Thomas H. Ellis operated a plantation in Terrebonne Parish and had been a lieutenant in the Lafourche Regiment under Burton. Many families from south Louisiana became refugees in southern Rapides and northern St. Landry parishes during the war (Eighth Census: Lafourche Parish, Roll 413, Rapides Parish, Roll 423, and Terrebonne Parish, Roll 425).

passed through Alexandria, crossed Red River, and camped in the rear of Pineville.[73] A circumstance occurred this night that proved to me that a soldier might disobey orders *some times* and not do wrong.

Acting as both division and brigade quartermaster, similar orders came to me from Gen. Polignac and Gen. Gray whenever any were issued that it was necessary for me to receive.

We had no forage for our stock although there were two steamboats at the landing loaded with corn for the Commissary Department. I made this fact known to Gen. Polignac and protested against leaving without feed for the teams, knowing that the route the next day was through a portion of piney woods, in passing which birds always carried rations. However, at dusk an order from brigade headquarters came commanding me to be ready to move at daylight.

Giving expression to my sentiments pretty freely seeing that nobody was about, I laid down and went to sleep, to be awakened about 10 o'clock by an orderly from division headquarters.

I had no light or fire near me, the night was as dark as vengeance, and, supposing it was a copy of the same order already received from the brigade commander, I stuck it under my pillow and passed off into the land of dreams once more. About three o'clock in the morning, I was again aroused by an orderly from Gen. Polignac with an order which I did not think advisable to stow away so unceremoniously, but taking both papers, I went off to a fire and read:

"The Gen. Commanding Division directs that the order issued to Maj. S. T. Grisamore at 9 o'clock be delayed until tomorrow morning as the division will remain another day."

Looking at the first order, I ascertained that I had been directed to take my forage trains over Red River and load them with corn from the commissary stores—an order that could have been executed that dark night with as much facility and ease as Henry Beecher could preach a sermon leaving out politics or Wendell Philips make a speech without bringing in the irrepressible Negro. I thought it was very kind in Gen. Polignac to rescind his first order, but always read any notice that I received on subsequent occasions.

Our route extended out by way of Catahoula Lake, over the dry and sandy bed of which we passed during one of the hottest days, I think, that I ever saw in Louisiana.

73. The division crossed the river and camped near Pineville on August 1 (Hyatt Diary, Entry of August 1, 1864, in Hyatt Papers).

Encamping for the night on the banks of Little River, we proceeded down the banks of the same stream the following morning.
Little River was low, and of all places for mean and nasty water, I
imagine there is none that can beat that section of country. It was,
both in the river and in the wells, too filthy for either man or beast,
our mules even refusing to drink it. We reached Trinity on Black
River about midday under a good deal of excitement, reports being
rife that the enemy were just over the river.

Quiet was restored during the day, the rumors proving false. We
remained there three or four days and then crossed Little River,
passed through Trinity, August 7th, a majority of whose buildings
were perforated by cannon balls from the enemy's guns in some of
their raids, and reached Harrisonburg, on the Ouachita, the same
evening. Here was evidence of the visit of the enemy also, the town
being pretty well peppered during an attack made by the enemy on
Fort Beauregard[74] (I think that was the name), which stood on a
high hill just above the village. Crossing the Ouachita on the 9th,
we moved up the bank of that stream, crossed Bayou Louis, and proceeded onward some ten miles to Lake Louis, where we remained
one day, and thence a few miles brought us to Sicily Island, where
we went into camp.

Sicily Island, August 12th, 1864.   We removed from Alexandria
to the Ouachita River with the design of being transported across
the river into the Army of the Tennessee.

Maj. Gen. Taylor passed several days with us previous to his departure.[75] The Louisiana troops were generally willing to make the
trip, and a large majority of the 18th were eager for the journey, but
a serious opposition was made by the Texans in Walker's Division
which was not confined to the men alone but was concurred in by
the officers. At one time, some two or three companies deliberately
walked off and started toward Texas but were arrested and brought
back. This disaffection extended, but to a less extent, to Polignac's
Brigade.[76]

74. Union forces had attacked Fort Beauregard on several different occasions, the
last occurring on March 4, 1864 (Edwin C. Bearss, "The Story of Fort Beauregard,"
Louisiana Studies, III [Winter, 1964], 330–84, and IV [Spring, 1965], 3–40).

75. Taylor crossed the Mississippi River about August 28 (Taylor, *Destruction
and Reconstruction,* 242).

76. Captain Poche recorded in his diary that four hundred men of Walker's division and over one hundred men of Polignac's Texas brigade deserted around August
19 (Bearss, ed., *A Louisiana Confederate,* 156).

The mutiny assumed such proportion that it was finally abandoned, if it ever had been seriously contemplated by the superior officers.[77] Many of the Texan troops and officers were court martialed, some of whom paid very dearly for their mutinous ideas.

Our brigade was encamped on Sicily Island near a clear, running stream of cool, fresh water. This Island is simply a tract of land somewhat higher than the surrounding alluvial lands east of the Ouachita River. My camp was on the top of a mound within 150 feet of Sicily Island Church. One Sunday morning,[78] I was sitting quietly under the shade of a tree when Maj. Patin, our commissary, called me over to his tent nearby and asked me to play a game of Eucher. Being a long ways from home, I yielded to temptation, and we were soon engaged in a contest for superiority in that scientific game. Before we had played a half dozen hands, I heard someone call my name, and by the time I could turn around, Rev. Dr. New, who used to reside here [Thibodaux], was inquiring about my health, and the game of cards was soon forgotten in a pleasant conversation of old times. I told the Reverend Doctor that I had been coaxed into a game on Sunday by my friend Maj. Patin, who had taken advantage of my inexperience in the ways of the world and persuaded me to violate precepts to which I ought to have shown more regard, but the Doctor looked as if he had some doubts on the subject.

We soon made amends by listening to an interesting sermon from the Doctor in the grove near the church, as the building had been taken possession of by our surgeons and used for a hospital.

The troops were paid two months' wages, and it being peach and melon time, everybody feasted upon those articles. Whilst wandering through the woods one day, I found myself in the midst of a pawpaw grove and for the first time in 14 years tasted of that fruit that I had so often run over the hills in search of in my youthful days.

On the 29th, we again resumed our march and proceeded towards Monroe.[79]

77. The large desertion rate and threat of further desertions were primarily responsible for the decision not to try to cross the river, but just as important was the fact that the Federals had tightened the security of their gunboats on the river (*OR*, Vol. XLI, Pt. 1, pp. 110, 112).

78. Probably August 14. Captain Poche recalled having dined with Grisamore and meeting Reverend New on that day (Bearss, ed., *A Louisiana Confederate*, 154).

79. Kirby Smith had abandoned the proposed crossing of the Mississippi River and ordered Polignac's and Walker's divisions to Monroe for an expedition into Arkansas (*OR*, Vol. XLI, Pt. 1, pp. 89, 117).

On the 31st, we reached the banks of the Boeuf River, a stream about the size of the Lafourche, and on the first of September, a pontoon was laid, over which we passed our teams at night.

Upon reaching Monroe,[80] we encamped in a pleasant grove above the town and immediately opposite Trenton, where we remained for about two weeks.

The troops had nothing to do but bathe in the clear water of the Ouachita and make pumpkin pies, gather wild grapes, and hunt wild honey, of which the surrounding woods furnished an abundant supply.

On the road leading from Bastrop, La., to Hamburg, Arkansas, and about midway between, stand two cabins built in the primitive style, with round logs and covered with clapboards, between which is a covered passage uniting the two buildings.[81] The line separating the two states passes through the passage, one cabin being in each state. It is represented as having once been a favorite place of resort for the inhabitants of many miles around in order to indulge in the innocent sports that were incompatible with the laws as expounded by the pious legislators of the two states. The sheriff of Louisiana, desiring to serve a writ, summons, or to make an arrest, following his man to this place would be politely invited into the Louisiana cabin and receive the hospitalities of the proprietor, whilst, by peeping through the cracks of the house, he could see the object of his search playing a game of "old sedge" over in Arkansas, and vice versa for the Arkansas sheriff, good care being taken against any collision that might occur in having both these officers to arrive at the same time.

On a hot day in the latter part of September 1864,[82] Polignac's Division, marching up into Arkansas, encamped a few miles beyond this place.

Going over to headquarters, we started a game of whist, which was kept up till the colonel played and insisted the Jack of Clubs

---

80. The troops reached Monroe on September 4, and they resumed the march toward Arkansas on the thirteenth (Hyatt Diary, Entry of September 14, 1864, in Hyatt Papers).

81. The following story is presented out of sequence. It was originally printed as one of Grisamore's initial installments but is placed here to take the place of an installment that is no longer extant.

82. The troops crossed the state line about 8 A.M., September 16, 1864 (Bearss, ed., *A Louisiana Confederate,* 164).

was the Queen of Hearts, which satisfied us that it was too dark to play, and we scattered around to enjoy ourselves as best we could. The brigade surgeon,[83] a huge mountain of flesh and jollity, familiarly known as "Big Medicine," having found what he facetiously called a pillow and taking the same in his arms, gave us some specimens of infantile music and education in a ventriloquial manner, lit his pipe, spread himself out, and surrounded his head with huge columns of smoke, the very picture of happiness and content.

Our Adjutant,[84] who was, perhaps, the only *Black-man* in the Trans-Mississippi Department who held an office in the Confederate army, was extended at full length on his blanket, with his heels resting against a sapling, four feet from the ground, brooding over the defeat he and his partner had just experienced in the game of whist against "Big Medicine" and myself. Musing how long his boots would last and finally bursting out peremptorily with "Major, when are you going to have my *boots* finished? I have worn this pair for nearly a *month*, and they have lasted *well*."

"Dog on your boots! They are eternally on your brain. Tell us a yarn, and may be I'll condescend to answer your question."

A general call around was made, and Black began by inquiring if we "had noticed the cabins" above mentioned. Having been satisfactorily answered, he proceeded: "In the early settlement of this section of country, those cabins were the only ones large enough for a ball anywhere within twenty miles. A fellow by the name of Jones was the happy possessor of the 'Chebang.' One day a traveller passing along here, aware that hotels were scarce, began to look out for a place to spend the night, and calling at a cabin, inquired if he 'could stay over night'; the proprietor told him he guessed he couldn't do anything of the kind, as they were all going down to Jones' to a ball. Proceeding, he came to another cabin and, seeing a man saddling his horse in front of his door, inquired what 'would be the chance of his remaining until morning.' 'Nary chance, we are all going to Jones' to the ball tonight.' Continuing his journey, he made another attempt with no better success. The sun was going down when he espied another house, and seeing the proprietor sitting on a stump in front of the door, he asked him if 'he could furnish him with a night's lodging.' 'Well, stranger, I don't know. If you will stay

83. Dr. W. A. McPheeters.
84. Major Wilbur F. Blackman.

without a bed I guess you can do so. A lot of the neighbors is coming over here tonight to have a dance, so that I will have no room for you.' 'Ah, you are Mr. Jones are you.' 'Yes, that's my name.' 'Well, show me where to put my horse, I reckon I'll stay.'

"The families began to come in. One horse generally sufficing for transportation. The man in the saddle, the wife behind, and the children hung on promiscuously. Everything went on smoothly until about 2 o'clock, when preparations were being made for the final reel. One room had been devoted to the ball, and the other dedicated to the use of those who were too young to indulge in such sports. Blankets had been spread over the floor, and the babies laid along in platoons and were sleeping as soundly as all well regulated babies were expected to on occasions of that kind.

"Our traveller did not participate in the closing dance, and passing by the door of this latter room, which was ajar, he noticed the condition of things through the glimmerings of an expiring tallow candle. The spirit of mischief got the better of his good manners, and he slipped into the room and began changing the positions of the sleepers. Blue dress in the east corner exchanged places with blue dress in the south corner, red head in the north with red head in the west, curly head at one point took the berth of curly head in another point, striped gown in the center was exchanged for striped frock on the outside, and so on until every one had been removed from the position in which it had been deposited by its owner.

"The reel finished, the fathers made a rush for their horses, the anxious mamas for the babies, and soon all were securely arranged upon horseback, each family taking his own cow path through the woods to his residence. Taking a short nap on his chair, our traveller settled his bill and left at sunrise. Coming to a house, he inquired 'if he could not get some breakfast.' 'No, you can't do anything of the kind. We were up at Jones' at the ball last night, and somehow or other my wife has brought home somebody else's baby, and she is too mad to get any breakfast for *me*, and *you* can bet high she will not bother *her* head with strangers.' Proceeding, he came to a second cabin, and making the same inquiry, he was informed that 'nothing could be had as they had been up to Jones' to the ball last night, and this morning their little daughter had been changed into a son, and somebody else's son at that.' A third trial was equally unavailing, and a fourth succeeded no better. Our traveller was satisfied that everybody who had been to Jones' ball had a good time, and coming to the conclusion that he was not hungry anyhow, he rode on quietly till he came to a tavern out of reach of the influence of Jones' balls. Whether the lost babies ever found their real papas is a question I never have investigated."

"Well, Black, you shall have a new pair of boots as soon as this march is over, and red topped ones at that."

The tatoo was beating, and we separated each to his own private room under his own pine tree.

In 1864 when we were marching from Monticello to Camden in Arkansas, we encamped one evening about six miles from the Saline River. From this camp to the river was a low, flat country, over which there had once been a road, but at that time it was covered with soft mud and water at depths ranging from four to fourteen feet. It was not long before half of the wagons of the train were bogged down, and such a cracking of whips was never heard before in that valley, accompanied by that loud and refined language which army teamsters are accustomed to use in talking to their "mools."

Whilst busily engaged in riding around contemplating the beautiful spectacle thus presented and exercising my skill in mud navigation so well that only twice had I been under the necessity of dismounting in order to enable my horse to extricate himself from the mire, Willy, the orderly, came up to me with an order from the major general commanding, directing me to report forthwith to headquarters.

Knowing that there was no enemy within 100 miles, I rode on to Warren, fully impressed with the idea that some wonderful information was to be imparted, something upon which the safety of the Trans-Mississippi Department depended. Finding the general and staff quietly reposing under the shade of some trees in the outskirts of the town of Warren, I alighted, scraped a few chipfulls of mud off my clothes, and advanced with all due dignity and decorum into the presence of those officials. Waiting some time to learn what was wanted without avail, I finally inquired of the general if he wished to see me. "Ah, yes, Major, we will remain in camp at this place until day after tomorrow." Thanking him for this extraordinary information, I remounted my horse and rode back five miles to see about the wagon trains, which were brought into camp and parked about 9 o'clock P.M. Lying down, I went to sleep, gratified with the thought that I would obtain a day's rest on the morrow, to be awakened at 3 A.M. with the long roll ringing marching orders into my ears.

After a long and tedious march of 24 miles, we reached the Bayou Moro. Finding the train stopped, I rode forward to find the ordnance wagons all bogged in a deep hole, scarcely anything visible above water but the mules' ears and the bewildered drivers standing on stumps nearby, cracking their whips and addressing the half-drowned mules in their own peculiar language, not laid down in any of the modern catechisms. After a good deal of *persuasion*, the wagons were finally piloted through in safety and got into camp. Willy had been back to inform me that one of the headquarters wagons was broken and that the general desired me to send the carpenter up to repair it. I requested him to inform the general that the mechanics were behind repairing broken wagons and could not possibly reach camp that night, but that I would send a wagon forward in the morning to take the place of the one broken. Partaking of a cup of sassafras, I lay down and was quietly taking a journey into the land to which Cain emigrated after he had had a little family difficulty at home, when an orderly rode up and gave me an order similar to this: "The major general commanding directs me to inform you that one of the headquarters wagons is broken and directs you to forward mechanics to repair it without delay, J. H. M., A. A. G."[85] Endorsing on the back the same message I had already sent, I prepared to complete the aforesaid journey. About an hour afterwards, I was again awakened and another order given me. "I am directed by the major general commanding to instruct you to forward the mechanics to these headquarters without delay to repair one of the broken headquarters wagons, O. V., A. A. & I. G."[86] Placing the same indorsement on this as on the other, I lay down wondering how the general and his brilliant staff supposed that men could work in a night as dark as that one and how I could send up mechanics that were 25 miles in the rear.

85. Major John Conway Moncure served as assistant adjutant general on Polignac's staff (Dimitry, "Louisiana," in *Confederate Military History*, ed. Evans, X, 512–13; *OR*, Vol. XXXIV, Pt. 1, p. 631).

86. Major O. Voorhies was assistant adjutant and inspector general to Polignac (Crute, *Confederate Staff Officers*, 153).

To help the matter, the rain began to fall slowly, and rolling my-self up in my blanket, musing over what would become of the head of our army in case the fool killer would pass along, I was about getting to sleep when I heard someone calling for the major.

Another order, "Major, the sheneral directs me to say that one of the headquarters wagons ish broke and you must shend up some-body to fix 'em. Jack O'Diamonds, Aide-de-C."[87]

"Orderly, you just go and tell the general, his adjutants, inspec-tors, and aide-de-camps to go to the bottom of ———. Hold on, I had better endorse it on the back of this order." After making the same response as upon the others, I handed it to the orderly, who re-mounted his horse and, riding off about ten paces, stopped. "Major, shall I deliver your message to the general?"

"Dog on your skin, you'd better hurry back to your position, or I will report you for neglect of duty," and away he galloped, whis-tling "down in Dixie." Rolling myself up in my blanket, I dreamed that all the generals and all the ornamentals were in a big mud hole, with all the broken wagons piled up on top of them, and was just getting myself comfortably seated in an elevated position to enjoy the scene, when the reveille broke my slumbers and informed me that another day's march through the mud was before me.

October, 1864. Crossing the Ouachita River, our division was encamped some three miles from Camden,[88] but in a few days we were ordered back within a mile of the town, where we went into camp. The men were ordered to build cabins and prepare to remain for some time. Since the first of July we had marched over 500 miles without being at any time within 100 miles of any enemy. Our di-vision was in a deplorable condition, not less than 200 men were barefooted, 100 had no pants and were marching in their drawers, others had no coats, some were without hats, and some had no signs of a blanket, yet we had been kept on this long march and hurried about the country at the rate of 15 to 25 miles per day; our mules and horses half the time without corn, and for fodder, depending entirely upon the grass the teamsters could gather out of the field during the day.

87. See note 101 following.

88. Polignac's division left Monticello, Arkansas, on October 2 and arrived at Camden on the sixth (Roy O. Hatton, "Prince Camille de Polignac: The Life of a Soldier" [Ph.D. dissertation, Louisiana State University, 1970], 174–75).

As soon as we went into camp, attempts were made to procure clothing for the more destitute soldiers, and a fair supply of shoes, pants, jackets, and blankets were issued to us by the post quartermaster.

In receiving these blankets, a curious coincidence occurred, developing the extent to which the art of getting things without permission had reached in the army.

I received 250 blankets one evening; I counted them carefully twice in the store and a third time as they were loaded on the wagon; putting a man on top of the wagon to see that none might drop overboard, I rode back with it to my camp, which was reached about sundown. Spreading a big Sibley tent over the wagon, completely covering everything, I then marked with a pencil the points of the wagon bed to which the edges of the tent reached so as to render it impossible to be moved without detection.

Placing a guard over the property, I had a fire kept up all night and slept within ten feet of the wagon. The next morning I examined my private marks, congratulating myself that all was right as there was no evidence that the covering had been touched, but at 9 o'clock, in making a distribution to the regiments, all the counting that I could do never would find over 245 blankets.

One evening I walked over to the quarters of the 18th Regiment, and upon arriving near the camp, I noticed an old man drive up with a light wagon containing two or three barrels of apples; I bought a dozen and stepped back a few rods to see how long it would take the boys to buy him out. The wagon was surrounded in less than two minutes, when the farmer perceiving that the apples were going faster than the money was coming in, he gave his horses a touch of the whip, which started them in a hurry, but from some unaccountable reason, they slipped loose from the wagon. The old man jumped out and caught the horses, but during the 60 seconds necessary to effect that, the crowd had dispersed, leaving the poor victim of misplaced confidence to hitch up and return home with his empty wagon, a sadder if not wiser man.

It was during our stay at Camden that two or three boxes of clothing reached our quarters for the use of the 18th Regiment, which that noble and patriotic man, Governor Henry W. Allen, had sent to them; these, with what we had received from the post at Camden, put our men in a tolerably comfortable condition again.

Camden, Arkansas, Nov. 1864. Whilst at this camp, Gen. Polignac made a trip to Shreveport and succeeded in obtaining a pretty
good supply of clothing for his men,[89] who had built themselves cabins and huts, endeavoring to make their winter quarters as comfortable as possible. Gen. Magruder was in command of all the forces
about Camden[90] and kept the men busy fortifying on the top of every hill in sight of that hilly city, from no point in which can more
than one half of the town be seen.

It was during our encampment here that a Texas captain was
court martialed and found guilty of mutiny when an attempt had
been made to cross the Mississippi River.[91] Gen. Magruder ordered
the whole of the four divisions[92] out on the plain above the town to
witness his execution.

Our stay in Camden was pleasant, as we had plenty of provisions,
but it kept our teams busy to supply provision and forage which had
to be hauled some 40 or 50 miles.

Joseph Roper, a member of our company, died and was buried in
the cemetery of Camden.

About the 15th of November our brigade was put on the march
towards Walnut Hill on Red River; the roads were heavy, making the
march a slow and toilsome one.[93] The third night, I parked my wagons in an old field, and during the night it rained heavily so that the
next morning when we started off every wagon was bogged, and it
took nearly half the day to get them in the road, which road was a
mixture of mud and water that only Arkansas can produce to
perfection.

At night, we encamped and laid up for two or three days. It was
at this place that an innocent deer was impelled by curiosity to ven-

89. Polignac left for Shreveport to get supplies on October 13, picked up clothing
for the division on the twentieth, and arrived back at Camden on the thirty-first
(*ibid.*, 175–76).

90. Major General John B. Magruder, former commander of the District of Texas,
New Mexico, and Arizona, had assumed command of the District of Arkansas, with
headquarters at Camden, on August 4 (*OR*, Vol. XLI, Pt. 2, p. 1039).

91. On October 12, Captain John Guynes, Company F, 22nd Texas Infantry, was
shot at Camden (Blessington, *The Campaigns of Walker's Texas Division*, 279).

92. The four divisions were those of Polignac, Parsons, Churchill, and Major General John H. Forney (formerly Walker's).

93. The men reached Walnut Hill on November 18 (Hatton, "Prince Camille de
Polignac," 178).

ture within the limits of the camp of our brigade; the boys soon raised a yell and surrounded him and taught the curious creature not to go promenading about a soldiers' camp.

In a couple of weeks, without anything of note transpiring, we passed by Walnut Hill, and moving down into Louisiana, we arrived at Minden and went into camp about three miles from that village.[94]

Joseph Guyot, who had been left behind sick, died about this time.

Minden, La., Christmas 1864. All of us remember that no matter what may have been the state of the elements previous to our arrival at this little town, we had a decided "spell of weather" at this camp. Several times it was impossible to get into town on account of a small branch that would spread itself a 100 yards in width and become 10 or 15 feet in depth during a rain of an hour's duration.

On Christmas day, I was one of a few invited guests at General Polignac's headquarters, where we partook of an excellent dinner and had a good time generally.

About one o'clock, my wagons, which had been gone four days to get some whiskey for a general treat to the men, came in, and the precious liquid was immediately forwarded to the different commands.

Anticipating a lively time, I returned to my quarters as soon as we finished our meal. By this time the treat was being distributed, and in a half hour afterwards the whole division was the liveliest body of men in the Trans-Mississippi Department. There was more singing, more yelling, more dancing, than was ever witnessed any time in the woods about Minden.

Arriving at my quarters, I inquired if they had received their treat yet. Schexnaydre[95]—that's the way his name was spelled—you can pronounce it to suit yourself. Some of the boys called him "Shake." I called him "Snyder" for short. Schexnaydre, he was my cook, said that Larry had gone after it, but Larry did not come and then they sent another one and he did not come—by this time Schexnaydre began to get thirsty, and I advised him to go over to Maj. Patin's quarters and get it himself and see what had become of the other messengers.

94. Polignac's and Forney's divisions received orders to go to Minden for the winter, and they arrived there on November 26 (*OR*, Vol. XLI, Pt. 4, pp. 1052, 1082; Hatton, "Prince Camille de Polignac," 178).

95. Private C. Schexnayder, formerly of Company B, now a wagoner for Grisamore (CSR, Roll 300).

In about a quarter of an hour, someone was heard yelling over towards Maj. Patin's quarters, and a couple of the men went and found Schexnaydre spread out on the road with an empty bottle lying alongside of him. I finally started off somebody else, who managed to return bringing in safely the rations and the three mules the other messengers had ridden. Poor Schexnaydre often heard how he boasted of being able to go to Major Patin's quarters and return without getting tight—and didn't do it.

I gave Paul Thibodaux, who had gone foraging a few days previous, some money to purchase a Christmas turkey. He had succeeded in getting five of them for fifty dollars. Four I gave to the company, and the other was kept for a dinner to be given by myself during the week. I knew very well that if my turkey got out of his cage any night he would run away, so that I could never find him again, and, therefore, to make things secure, Schexnaydre was directed to cause a separation of his head from his body. This was done, and having him nicely cleaned and prepared for the oven, Schexnaydre put the body in his wagon, carefully stowed it away under his mattress, and went to sleep over it. During the night, Schexnaydre was aroused by someone slipping his hand under the wagon cover and getting hold of the turkey, but Schexnaydre got his grip on him and hung to him until the fellow pulled him to the edge of the ravine and jumped down, a distance of 25 feet.

Schexnaydre did not jump after him, but the next morning picked up his hat, which had dropped from his head during the leap.

That chap never called for his hat afterwards, although it was hung up conspicuously on a sapling for several days.

Our turkey was none the worse for this little romance, and if the unfortunate victim had made himself known, he should have had a piece and no questions asked.

Minden, La., January 1865. Whilst at Minden, a spirit of theatrical genius seized hold of some of the officers, and a few of the intellectual ladies of that thriving little village, until nothing but a public performance could satisfy those afflicted sons and daughters of Thespis.

Accordingly, the large reception hall belonging to the Female College[96] was obtained for the exhibition, and preparations in the way

96. The Minden Female College had been incorporated in 1854, and its average attendance was 150 (Prichard, ed., "A Tourist's Description," 1184).

of rehearsals and suppers were rapidly made. (To the latter I attended very punctually.)

Claude Melnotte[97] was the play in which the performers were to distinguish themselves and to excite the admiration of the army and the dignified citizens in the piney woods about Minden.

Col. Collins was to do up Claude; Lieut. St. Martin was Mr. Deschapelles; Miss McF.—— personated Pauline; and Miss J.—— was the Lady of Lyons; the other characters were properly represented. The very important part which I had to personate was to hoist the curtains and holler "hurrah for the Prince!!"

The large hall was crowded, and the play was well-executed by all the performers.

A comic scene followed in which the principal actors were Capt. Blackman and Miss L.——, which kept the audience in a continual roar. *Box and Cox*[98] followed and was admirably acted, bringing "down the house."

Songs filled up the interludes, and a band furnished music for the occasion.

Upon the whole, the Thespians deserved credit for a pleasing and entertaining evening's enjoyment.

The necessary rehearsals and consultations, however, came very near leading to serious consequences and breaking the hearts of some of the susceptible young gentlemen and ladies of the village, and had not marching orders come in opportunely, there is no telling what might have been the result.

Shortly after our arrival at this camp, I made a trip to Shreveport, which was about forty or fifty miles distant. I confess that I was a little surprised at the appearance of the town but not much from the officers who were at the head of the Quartermaster Department in that city. From them I expected but little and did not go away disappointed in the least.

Gen. Polignac here left us on a visit to Shreveport, whence he

97. The proper name of this play was *The Lady of Lyons*. Set in the period of the French Revolution, it was written by Edward E. Bulwer-Lytton (1803–73), British novelist and politician. Claude Melnotte is the hero of the play (The Earl of Lytton, K. G., *Bulwer-Lytton* [London, 1948], 70–71).

98. Written by John M. Morton (1811–91) in England, this farcical play was "a hit on both sides of the Atlantic" (Joseph T. Shipley, *Guide to Great Plays* [Washington, D.C., 1956], 129).

departed shortly afterwards to France via Mexico.[99] Brig. Gen. King[100] of the Texas brigade assumed command of the division.

Gen. Polignac had a German on his staff who signed himself A. D. C., but who was generally known as "Polignac's orderly," and whom the Texans had given the name of "Jack O'Diamonds."[101]

He had led himself to believe that the general could not do without him, and when he learned that he had gone to France and left his right bower behind, the "Jack O'Diamonds" was inconsolable.

For several days he wandered about with downcast looks and woebegone countenance, until ordered to Alexandria, when he got lost in the piney woods, took the wrong road, went to Monroe, and drowned all his sorrows in matrimony, and furthermore, deponent knoweth nothing.

Pineville, La., January 1865. In the early part of this month, our brigade was ordered from Minden to Alexandria.[102] Gen. Gray, having been elected a member of the Confederate Congress, left us at Camden, leaving Col. Collins as senior and commanding officer of the brigade.[103] In three days' pleasant marching, the troops arrived at Campti, on Red River, whence they proceeded down the river by steamboat, leaving the wagon trains to move down by land; these arrived at Pineville on the 21st, in the rear of which picturesque village the command was encamped.

99. The Confederate government sent Polignac to his native France to try to persuade Napoleon III to intervene in favor of the Confederacy. He left Shreveport on January 10, 1865 (Warner, *Generals in Gray*, 242; Hatton, "Prince Camille de Polignac," 182).

100. Kirby Smith assigned Colonel Wilburn H. King, 18th Texas Infantry, to the rank of brigadier general on April 16, 1864. He became commander of Polignac's brigade on October 8 (Arthur W. Bergeron, Jr., "Wilburn Hill King," in *The Confederate General*, ed. William C. Davis [Harrisburg, Pa., 1991–92], VI, 186–87).

101. Possibly Captain Sainville Cucullu or Lieutenant William Eggling (*OR*, Vol. XXXIV, Pt. 1, p. 156).

102. On January 1, 1865, Polignac received orders to be ready to move his division to Alexandria. His old brigade went to Texas, however, while Gray's did go to Alexandria (*ibid.*, Vol. XLVIII, Pt. 1, p. 1309, and Pt. 2, p. 93).

103. Gray was elected to represent the 5th District on October 17, 1864, defeating General John L. Lewis by 1,078 votes to 233. Gray left on October 31. Colonel Collins assumed command of the brigade in the absence of Colonel Abel W. Bosworth of the Crescent Regiment, senior colonel (Opelousas *Courier*, October 29, 1864; Hatton, "Prince Camille de Polignac," 176; Bartlett, "The Trans-Mississippi," in *Military Record of Louisiana*, 43).

On the 22nd, the brigade was removed across Red River and put into camp about one mile from town on the Opelousas road, on Kelso's plantation.[104]

The rain fell in torrents all that night, and the next morning but little dry ground was to be seen. In four years' service, I do not believe that I ever saw as mean and pitiable a camping place, and *some* of the troops expressed themselves much more expressive than polite.

I was more fortunate, however, than my companions, as Gen. Thomas, who was commanding the forces about Alexandria,[105] stopped me in that town, ordering me on duty as quartermaster of all the forces in that vicinity, and for the first time in my term of service, I occupied a house and would have gotten along exceedingly well had I not, in a moment of unguarded good nature, suffered flattery to beguile me from the path of discretion and take into my mess Capt. Louis Guion and Lieut. Jim Martin,[106] who, after eating all the chickens and eggs I could get hold of, grumbled because I did not feed them on blackberry pies and oyster soup.

About the first of February our brigade, which had been formed into a division with Thomas' brigade,[107] was removed up on Bayou Cotile, where they had fine camping grounds, but I remained in Alexandria.

One day I received from the Quartermaster Department in Shreveport about 3000 yards of calico, with directions from Major Haynes,[108] Chief Q'r-M'r, to exchange the same with the people about the country for homespun. I endeavored to get permission to

104. John Kelso was born in 1830 and was educated at Princeton University. During the war, he served as a captain, commanding Company B, 2nd Louisiana Infantry Regiment, and Company E, 12th Louisiana Infantry Battalion, before going on staff duty in late 1863. After the war, he was a parish judge and served briefly in the state senate. Kelso died December 4, 1870 (Catherine Baillio Futch, *The Baillio Family* [Baton Rouge?, 1961], 394; CSR, Rolls 107, 281).

105. Brigadier General Allen Thomas, commander of a brigade of Louisianians paroled after their capture at Vicksburg, held command of Alexandria and Pineville, where his troops were camped (Bartlett, "Army of the West," in *Military Record of Louisiana*, 51).

106. Captain Louis Guion, Company D, and Lieutenant James B. Martin, Company C, 26th Louisiana Infantry, of Thomas' brigade (CSR, Roll 336).

107. Thomas assumed command of the new division (Bartlett, "Army of the West," in *Military Record of Louisiana*, 51).

108. Major W. H. Haynes headed the Clothing Bureau in Shreveport (James L. Nichols, *The Confederate Quartermaster in the Trans-Mississippi* [Austin, 1964], 30).

go down in the prairies about Opelousas to effect the exchange, without effect, and made preparations to distribute the calico among the troops for them to manufacture into shirts. One morning I received a letter from Major Haynes notifying me to send the calico back to Shreveport, as they had made arrangements to exchange it for other material in that vicinity.

Knowing that that "other material" would never gladden my eyes, I did not feel in the proper mood to return Major Haynes anything more substantial than my compliments. After breakfast, I went over to Gen. Thomas' office, and upon his inquiry if there were any news, I handed him my letter. Those persons who had the pleasure of his company know that the general had a peculiar way of expressing his thoughts in a manner that was easy to understand.

After reading the letter, he remarked, "Well, that's Hell," which was a peculiarity of the letter that I had not perceived but kept silence however. "Well, Major, what are you going to do about it?"

"General, will you give me written orders to return the calico to Shreveport?" "No, I'll be d—d if I do." "Well, then, general, I shall be under the disagreeable necessity of informing you that Major Haynes will never see these articles of feminine apparel again. Good morning, general."

In less than three hours, the calico was in wagons and on the way to the command, with written orders to the quartermasters to distribute forthwith. If Gen. Thomas should have been seized with a fit of repentance, I was determined that it would have to get hold of him quickly to do any good. The next morning, the general asked me what I was going to do with my calico. I told him I did not have any, but I could show him receipts for it if he wished to see them.

Alexandria, April 1865.   A residence at this place was not very agreeable so far as the article of food was concerned. Nothing but rations was to be obtained, save an occasional chicken that wandered into town and was sold at from one to ten dollars.

To destroy the monotony of our life, I was persuaded by Capt. Blackman to make a call one evening upon some ladies. The night was moderately dark for a cloudy night, and the captain, who was the guide, soon piloted us into a mudhole about knee deep, which had the effect of making us decline a visit to some more suitable occasion.

Another amusement afforded us was the musical entertainment given twice a week by Gen. Thomas' band of musicians, who came into town for that purpose. Occasionally a joke was perpetrated upon individuals and sometimes upon regiments. One evening, a young and festive lieutenant of Thomas' brigade, upon retiring to bed, suddenly imagined that he was getting up and undertook to put on his vest for his pants and was horror struck to find that the legs of his pants were missing as he ran his foot through the sleeve of his vest. (I did not see this operation, but Capt. G—— was ever ready to swear that the allegations contained therein were true.)

One day the 18th Cavalry Regiment[109] was ordered up to Cotile and encamped near Gray's brigade. Some of the infantry inquired of the men why they were sent up there. The cavalrymen, thinking it would be a good joke, replied that they supposed it was "to assist the infantry in crossing the Mississippi River." The joke was not so amusing the next morning when our enterprising horsemen awoke and the mists of the morning cleared up so as to enable them to open their eyes and see the infantry camp perfectly quiet and unconcerned, looking as innocent as lambs and as if they would not do the least harm to anybody in all this wide world; nor did they appear the least troublesome until some of the cavalry evinced a disposition to take a morning ride, when they were notified that early riding was unhealthy in the blustering winds of March. During the forenoon they were dismounted and converted into infantry. News began to come in daily of the disasters befalling our armies over the river, and a gloom began to settle upon our minds that was far from pleasant.

Confederate money was almost worthless. I gave eight hundred and fifty dollars for eighty dollars in greenback, with which I bought a horse, and with nine hundred dollars another one for Dr. Dejarnets. Anything that came into town for sale would find purchasers at any price. A country man brought in ten chickens, which brought him one hundred dollars, and they would have been sold ten times later for three-times that amount. Desertions began to become frequent; the men, seeing no future prospect before them, deliberately went to their homes.[110]

109. This was Colonel Benjamin W. Clark's 8th Louisiana Cavalry, which was assigned to Gray's brigade (Bartlett, "The Trans-Mississippi," in *Military Record of Louisiana*, 43).

110. Major General Harry T. Hays, who later assumed command of the Louisiana division, wrote to the cavalry commander in south Louisiana: "I am mortified to have to tell you that my own division, though at a much greater distance from the enemy than your command, are becoming—have become disgracefully demoralized. Last night one hundred & fifty men, mostly from the 29th Regt left in a body with their arms in their hands" (Major General Harry T. Hays to Brigadier General Joseph

And not much blame should be attached to them for it. The troops paroled in the armies of the Cis-Mississippi were returning by hundreds into Louisiana and Texas, rendering the facts certain that the war was rapidly drawing to a close and that it would be futile for the Trans-Mississippi Department to attempt to remain in the field.[111] To help this feeling, steamboats laden with cotton were sent to the mouths of Red River, and others came up loaded with all sorts of luxuries that were not requisite supplies for an army.

I remember one day, when a boat laden in this style arrived at the wharf, and soldiers were not even allowed to buy any of these luxuries, which were designed for headquarters at Shreveport, that it would only have required one or two officers to have said the word, when the whole stock in trade would have been sold out in about 30 minutes.

Mansfield, La., May 1865. No sooner were we encamped on the Lower Shreveport road,[112] than the fact became apparent that the war was concluded and that a grand tableau of dissolving views was about to be exhibited without any admission fees. The next day information came to me that my quarters were to be overhauled by the troops and the mules and wagons were to be appropriated by them.[113] What was to be done in order to save my baggage and that of the dozen detailed men who were with me was the great question to be decided by us.

A consultation was held and the decision made that each detailed

---

L. Brent, May 12, 1865, in David F. Boyd Civil War Papers, 1861–1865, Louisiana and Lower Mississippi Valley Collection, Special Collections, Hill Memorial Library, Louisiana State University, Baton Rouge).

111. Word of General Robert E. Lee's surrender reached the division on April 20 (Hall, *The Story of the 26th Louisiana Infantry,* 128).

112. On May 13, the division took up its march to Mansfield from Natchitoches, arriving four days later. It camped on the Kingston Road about five miles from Mansfield (Colonel Robert Richardson to Captain Samuel Flower, May 22, 1865, quoted in "The Commander's Report on How Hays' Confederate Division Ended Its Career," North Louisiana Historical Association *Newsletter,* VIII [February, 1968], 16–17; Hays to Brent, May 11, 1865, in Boyd Papers).

113. Colonel Richardson reported: "The Division became a mob and rabble, disregarding the authority of their superiors and governed alone by a spirit of lawless plunder and pillage. Predatory bands were formed, and in many instances led by officers, for the seizure and appropriation of all public property. The Quartermaster, Commissary, and Ordnance depots, both with the Division and in Mansfield, were sacked, the mules and wagons forcibly taken and appropriated" ("The Commander's Report," 16–17).

man was to "flank" one mule, and then the boys took one of the wheels off each of two wagons and sunk them in the little bayou on which we were encamped. The bright idea was originated that some of our horses and mules might be hid in the woods until we were ready to start, and a teamster, residing in Mansfield, named Clark,[114] told me privately that he knew all the ravines in the country and that if I would give him a mule, he would show the boys where to conceal theirs so that nobody could find them. I told him to pick out his "animule" and started off Jim Collins[115] and Paul Thibodaux with him with a lot of mules and one of my own horses. Clark fulfilled his promise, and then went to his home in Mansfield and had the gratification of learning, the next morning, that his mule had been stolen out of his stable. Major Wedge,[116] our commissary, sent his team into the woods, and the next day his horse was sent into camp with the information that his "trusty friend," who had been sent out in charge, had gone home with *his* mule.

The last I saw of the major, he was following his wagon, drawn by hired oxen, with a countenance as long as a text in moral law.

I managed to save mules enough to transport the papers and baggage of the colonel and his aide-de-camp. I had a box of clothing and some stationery that I was intending to distribute as soon as we got into camp and was preparing to make a distribution when about a dozen fellows came up and expressed a very anxious desire to see into the box. As I had all my own papers and baggage in another wagon, I was peculiarly solicitous to attract their attention from it and became quite spunky, telling them that they should not see into the box and that it was none of their business what was in it, etc. Gathering around the wagon like a gang of hungry wolves preparatory to a charge, I got myself in a good position, and, after a good deal of talking, I turned my head, when they pitched into the box and began relieving it of its contents. I threw about half the articles over my head into the hands of my detailed men, who took good care of them.

Notwithstanding the universal pillage of the departing soldiers, I have always commended them for one generous trait. Not a private horse was taken, nor a trunk or anything that was not government property was disturbed.

I had several hired wagons belonging to good men which I was

114. Private Findley Clark, Company B, Consolidated Crescent Regiment, had been detailed as a teamster (CSR, Roll 277).

115. Private James H. Collins, Company D, 18th Louisiana (*ibid.*, Roll 298).

116. Major D. J. Wedge, formerly of the 4th Louisiana Infantry (*ibid.*, Roll 137).

anxious to save. They were taken possession of to transport the men's baggage, but so far as I have been able to learn, they were all left in possession of their owners.

Gov. H. W. Allen paid us a visit and advised us all to go peaceably to our homes, as there was no longer any hope of continuing the war.[117] The 18th Regiment, to which myself and most of my detailed men belonged, had been left at Natchitoches, where they surrendered and came home by river.

We were so few that we did not dare to go to Natchitoches alone and were not certain of finding our friends there if we did. The 26th Regiment was nearby with two Lafourche and one Terrebonne company, and we concluded to accompany them by way of the piney woods to Opelousas.

For two days, the men of north Louisiana had been leaving, and the day before the one we had fixed upon for leaving, we fished up our wagon wheels, collected together our mules, hitched up one six- and one four-mule wagon, and drove over to Col. Lagarde's[118] camp. I think that was about as refreshing a night as I ever had the pleasure of passing.

The colonel had guards around his camp to watch his teams, and during the night, prowlers came into his limits for the purpose of picking up things promiscuously. The way some of them got the benefit of leather straps, ramrods, etc., was a caution to all persons who are desirous of purchasing property during the absence of the owners. How many of these fellows were paid for their labor that night I never have ascertained, but every time I awakened, I could hear amusements of that kind going on.

When the next day arrived at Mansfield, we found a few men who had been put on guard about the commissary stores, out of which they had saved a few pieces of bacon during its pillage.

We found a little corn, and, bidding an everlasting farewell to Mansfield, we started towards our home, four hundred miles southward, with forage for about two days and bread for the same length of time. Passing down the old military road, we arrived at Fort Jesup just in time to see the last wagonload of corn leave the depot.

117. Governor Allen's sister wrote after the war that he had urged the troops to remain loyal. Other sources indicate that on May 19, 1865, Colonel Richardson issued an order for the division to disband (Sarah A. Dorsey, *Recollections of Henry Watkins Allen* [New York, 1866], 295; "The Commander's Report," 17; Hall, *The Story of the 26th Louisiana Infantry*, 135–36).

118. Major Cleophas Legarde, 26th Louisiana Infantry (CSR, Roll 338).

It only required two minutes to convince the owner of the cart that he was too heavily loaded for his half-grown ox team and to transfer his corn into our wagons, and then *he* went his way rejoicing, and *we* did the same.

As we arrived at Michael Paul's, we were again out of corn; some of us stopped to see if we could not get some forage. The old man declared that he had no corn, that he had been eaten out of house and home, &c. There was a cherry tree at the end of his gallery with round, ripe cherries.

Pulling a couple of this delicious fruit, which I had not tasted for 20 years, I said, "Now, Mr. Paul, look here. We are all going home and never in all this wide world will you see any of us again. Let us have a few barrels of corn to carry us to the Bayou Boeuf country." The old man did not appear to see the point, when I continued, "We have a few pounds of coffee; now how much do you want in exchange for four barrels of corn?" The old man's eyes brightened, and a bargain was soon made.

The old man's heart and corn crib both opened at the magic sound of coffee. We were soon on our way, and, passing down the Bayou Boeuf, a few of us were furnished with a nice breakfast at the house of Dr. Winn,[119] at Holmesville, who had been with us during our late journeyings.

Nothing of much importance occurred to us afterwards, and in a few days, we reached Opelousas, where I took up my quarters at the ever hospitable mansion of Col. Bush.

Opelousas, June 1865.   When we arrived at Opelousas, we found that the whole country between the Bayou Teche and the Lafourche was covered with water from crevasses on the river. The men, however, did not allow such a fact to prevent them from going to their homes and started off in squads to obtain boats, rafts, and any means of transportation that could be devised to carry them over this immense waste of water.

The men whom I had with me, who resided in the prairies, left immediately on their mules, leaving myself, Paul Thibodaux, and three others from New Orleans behind. I believe the five of us had about two bits in silver, and neither gold nor greenbacks had we any.

We, however, sold one wagon and four mules for some $200.00 in

119. Dr. W. H. Winn had been surgeon of the 28th Louisiana Infantry and acting brigade surgeon of Gray's brigade (*ibid.,* Roll 347).

silver, and I subsequently disposed of the other wagon we had for about $40.00.

There were no Federals near us, and we remained for several days before any came to whom we might surrender ourselves.

Finally a boat reached Washington, and in a couple of hours, we had our paroles in our pockets. The men found opportunity to go home by steamer, and I, sending my horse around with Paul, awaited a few days to come through with Col. Bush. It was on the 23rd of June that we went out to Washington, and in company with three ladies, we embarked on a little steamer and started down the Courtableau Bayou and thence by the Atchafalaya and lakes to Brashear, at which place we arrived before daybreak the next morning.

Removing on to another boat, we were transported up to Tigerville, where we found the whole surface of the earth covered with water to the depth of four feet. Skiffs were our only remedy, and loading some four or five with our baggage and ourselves, we started, reaching the rear of the Tanner plantation,[120] whence the colonel and the ladies footed it out to Mrs. Winder's,[121] where they obtained means to reach Thibodaux. After enjoying the pleasures of a heavy shower of rain, a hand car came and carried our baggage to the station at Terrebonne, when I obtained transportation from the Quartermaster Department to Thibodaux, at which place I arrived about sunset and enjoyed the hospitality for the first time for two years at the residence of my friend W. H. Ragan,[122] on the corner of St. Philip and St. Bridget streets.

Remaining in quiet for two or three days, the colonel and myself went down to New Orleans, where we met our former fellow officer Major Sanders, and all three of us took the oath of allegiance together.

We both returned in a day or two, being truly loyal citizens.

120. Mrs. C. Tanner and her son Washington Tanner both owned plantations on Bayou Lafourche in northern Terrebonne Parish (Eighth Census: Terrebonne Parish, Roll 425).

121. Ducros plantation was owned by Mrs. Martha Grundy Winder, widow of Van Perkins Winder and daughter of a former attorney general of the United States. It was on Bayou Terrebonne near present-day Schriever (Paul F. Stahls, Jr., *Plantation Homes of the Lafourche Country* [Gretna, La., 1983], 59–60).

122. The 1860 census gave New York native W. H. Ragan's occupation as collector (Eighth Census: Lafourche Parish, Roll 413).

5 "Our Officers"

Henry Gray[1]

Gen. Henry Gray, of the C. S. A., died a few days ago,[2] at the house of his daughter in Coushatta, on Red River.

The deceased was in his earlier years a remarkable man. Born in South Carolina,[3] at manhood he removed to Mississippi and was the contemporary and close friend of Jefferson Davis and Sergeant S. Prentiss. He occupied, during his residence in that state, a prominent position as an orator, politician, and lawyer.

Later on, he removed to Bienville Parish in Louisiana and very quickly established himself at the head of the bar and on the political arena in north Louisiana, that was, at that date, noted for its lawyers and orators. In the contest for United States Senator, he was beaten by the great Judah P. Benjamin by only one vote.[4]

At the beginning of the war, he joined the Confederate forces as a private in a Mississippi regiment, but on reaching Virginia he was ordered by his friend, President Davis, to return to Louisiana and organize a regiment of infantry.

He did so and became colonel of the 28th Louisiana Infantry, which did effective service in the Trans-Mississippi Department. In 1862 it was attached to and formed part of Mouton's brigade, with the 18th Louisiana Regiment, composed of companies raised in Lafourche, New Orleans, and the Opelousas countries. On the death of Gen. Mouton at Mansfield, previously promoted to the command of his own and Polignac's brigades, Col. Gray was promoted to brigadier general and given the command of his brigade.

1. This sketch was not one of Grisamore's original installments but appeared after Gray's death. It is included here because of Gray's connection with the 18th Louisiana.

2. December 11, 1892 (Warner, *Generals in Gray*, 115).

3. January 19, 1816, in Laurens District (*ibid.*).

4. In January, 1859, the Louisiana general assembly reelected Benjamin to the United States Senate. On the final ballot, Benjamin received fifty-seven votes to Gray's fifty. Know-Nothing party candidate Randall Hunt received five votes (Robert D. Meade, *Judah P. Benjamin, Confederate Statesman* [New York, 1943], 119).

Gen. Gray was not famous for his expertness as a commander of troops but was brave and fearless as a lion and distinguished himself for boldness and fearlessness in the bloody charge of his brigade at Mansfield, in which the commanders of each of his regiments were killed—Armant of the 18th; Beard, Clack, and Canfield of the Crescent; and Walker of the 28th.

After the war, the general has been living a very quiet life. The loss of an only son, who died in 1864, and that of his wife subsequently, weighed heavy on the old man's mind and removed from him all the charms of life.

The general was small in stature and not prepossessing in appearance, and when mounted on his famous big horse, Cesar, the "boys" used to call him "baby on a monument." Shortly after the battle of Mansfield, the writer asked him "if he did not think that the Yankees would get him during the fight"; the reply was that "he was afraid that they might get Cesar."

He was averse to everything in the way of display and always grumbled when he was required to make his appearance in full uniform.

He was social, kind, careful of his soldiers, attentive to their wants, and possessed of a keen, black eye that could dance when he got his anger aroused. In 1864, he was elected a member of the Confederate Congress and left the army when his command encamped at Camden, Arkansas.

The general was 76 years of age at his death.

He is buried in the valley of the Red River, which he loved so dearly and where he will rest until the resurrection do come.

Louisiana has produced many great men, but few have possessed more of the elements of greatness than Henry Gray. It required one to know him closely and intimately as did the writer to understand and appreciate the noble qualities and generous attributes of the man and to learn the varied talents and wonderful knowledge that was treasured in his mind.

Alfred Mouton

Upon the organization of the 18th Regiment, Capt. Alfred Mouton of Lafayette Parish[5] was elected colonel. He was a son of the vener-

---

5. Mouton was born February 18, 1829, at Opelousas (William Arceneaux, *Acadian General: Alfred Mouton and the Civil War* [2nd ed.; Lafayette, La., 1981], 11).

able ex-Governor Mouton,[6] who still resides in the vicinity of Vermilionville in the above parish. The colonel was a graduate of West Point,[7] but not having any desire to be a soldier in peace, he resigned from the army and became a planter in the prairies in which he had been born and raised.

During the troubles among the inhabitants of the Attakapas and Opelousas countries previous to the war, he had taken an active part on the side of honesty and justice in the effort to disperse the organized band of scoundrels who roamed over the prairies robbing and pillaging in defiance of law and its officers.[8]

He was one of the finest looking officers I ever saw, having a large, robust form, fully developed, with a strong, commanding voice.

As a drillmaster, he had few, if any, equals. I have seen him drill the regiment for an hour in a square, the sides of which were equal to the length of his line of battle, without once throwing a company outside or recalling a command when given.

He was a strict disciplinarian and allowed no deviation from orders either by officers or soldiers.

Whilst off duty, he mingled freely with his soldiers and was exceedingly proud of his regiment, always greeting any member kindly whenever he met him, even after he had been promoted to a higher position. He always insisted on having the 18th under his command.

In the first skirmish we had with the enemy at Pittsburg Landing on the 1st day of March 1862, he convinced his soldiers that he was equally as brave and gallant under fire as he was efficient and capable in camp.

During the terrible days of Shiloh when he was under the command of a brave but unskilled officer, his anxiety for the safety of the men under his command was very evident to us all, and the bad management of the brigade seemed to annoy and worry him exceedingly.

And when at last our regiment was ordered to charge the enemy and leave almost half of our strength upon that bloody hill, seeing

6. Alexandre Mouton.

7. Mouton graduated from West Point in 1850 (*ibid.*, 21).

8. In 1859, bands of outlaws plagued the Attakapas region. Citizens organized Committees of Vigilance to combat these bandits, and Alfred Mouton was in command on September 3 when the vigilance men routed without a fight the collected forces of the outlaws at Bayou Queue Tortue (Alexandre Barde, *The Vigilante Committees of the Attakapas*, ed. David C. Edmonds and Dennis Gibson [Lafayette, La., 1981], 330–33).

that we had not been supported by the other regiments who were sent forward one by one to meet a fate similar to ours and realizing the destruction of his men when a proper movement would have proven a victory, driven the enemy away, and saved hundreds of our gallant men who had fallen before our eyes, his emotions overcame him, and he wept like a child. Gathering his scattered remnants together, he watched over them during the night and again the next day led them into the midst of the battle, when he was wounded and compelled to leave the field. He was but a few feet behind his men when he fell from his horse.

The wound was apparently but trifling, but on returning to our camp at Corinth, Erysipelas set in and he was compelled to return to New Orleans, where his life was in imminent danger for several days. The city fell, and he escaped over the river in sight of the Federal fleet coming to take possession of New Orleans.

It was not until October that he became sufficiently recovered to take the field, having in the meantime been promoted to a brigadier generalship.[9]

He met the 18th in October, a few days after our return to this side of the Mississippi River, and the first military duty he performed was in command of a detachment from his old command. I remember how warmly he expressed his gratification at being with his old regiment when he rebuckled his sword for the contest.

He was in command of the Lafourche District in 1862 when Gen. Weitzel made his triumphant march down our bayou. On the day the fight took place at Winn's road, he was suffering so severely with rheumatism that he could not participate.

After the retreat, he remained in command of the Teche country during the winter and in February 1863 fought the first fight at Bisland's, driving the enemy back.

In April the retreat from Bisland occurred and continued as far as Natchitoches.

When the Federals fell back, he took command of cavalry and proceeded down the Calcasieu country towards Niblett's Bluff and thence to Opelousas and New Iberia. Following up the retreating Federals to this place [Thibodaux], he was in active duty whilst we remained here in 1863.

After the Lafourche had been evacuated, he was placed in com-

9. Mouton received his promotion to brigadier general to rank from April 16, 1862 (Warner, *Generals in Gray*, 222).

mand at Vermilionville and afterwards shared all the ups and downs of the army until the fatal day at Mansfield, where he fell, basely murdered by men whose lives he had just saved after one of the most brilliant charges made during that extraordinary campaign and in the moment that victory was crowning him with her laurel wreaths. He was buried in the cemetery at Mansfield by the side of the heroic Armant, Martin, and Beatty, who had fallen at the same time. Since the war his remains have been brought to the family cemetery at Vermilionville, where they now repose in quiet by the side of those he loved so well and where his tomb is daily freshened by the gentle gales of his native land.[10]

He who stands by the grave of Alfred Mouton looks upon the dust of an honest man and an upright citizen, a hero and a patriot.

Of all the glorious dead of Louisiana, who for their country's freedom gave up their lives and "passed over the river to rest under the shadow of the trees," in the Lost Cause none deserves a brighter niche in the Temple of Fame than does this gallant son of Attakapas. May the memory of his virtues and heroism be ever embalmed in the hearts of the sons of Louisiana.

No officer in the Confederate service was more universally beloved by his soldiers, whilst living, nor more sincerely mourned when he passed from earth in the discharge of his duty at the very moment when he was conscious that the day was his and that he and his own cherished division were the victors of the bloody battle of Mansfield.[11] The line of the enemy had been broken from left to right, Nims' famous and boasted battery had been captured,[12] two thousand prisoners had thrown down their arms, and the general had, by that quick, peculiar glance of his brilliant eye, seen that the day was won and had sent his aides in different directions with the necessary orders to secure the fruits of the victory and arrest further destruction of life. Notwithstanding he had witnessed the fall of the gallant Armant, the chivalric Canfield, the intrepid Beard, the fearless Clack, and brave Walker, the daring Martin, the cool and heroic Beatty, and hundreds of his own valiant troops as they surmounted

10. Relatives of Mouton removed his remains from the cemetery at Mansfield and reinterred them on April 24, 1867, in the St. John the Evangelist Catholic Church Cemetery in Lafayette (Arceneaux, *Acadian General*, 141–42).

11. This account of Mouton's death is taken from a separate issue of the *Sentinel*.

12. Six guns of Captain Ormand F. Nims's 2nd Massachusetts Light Battery fell into Confederate hands when the cannoneers abandoned them during the battle (*OR*, Vol. XXXIV, Pt. 1, p. 462).

every obstacle in their path, yet to save the lives of those men who had slain his beloved soldiers, he had ridden forward alone, calling upon them to throw down their arms, as being surrounded, they could not escape. Passing near a bunch of brambles in which some Federal soldiers had concealed themselves and thrown down their arms, they, perceiving the general to be alone, picked up their guns and treacherously fired upon him. Falling from his horse, pierced through the breast and heart with seven balls, the noble and gallant hero breathed his last before any of his friends had reached his side.

ALFRED ROMAN

At the reorganization of our regiment at Corinth in April 1862, Lieutenant Colonel Alfred Roman was chosen Colonel.

He was a son of the popular and well-known A. B. Roman, ex-Governor of this state. A native of St. James Parish, reared and educated among the ancient Creole population of Louisiana, all the ease and dignity of manner peculiar to that race of people were exhibited in the character and bearing of the colonel.

After completing his education, Mr. Roman studied law, and at one time, about 1848 or '50, he had an office in this town [Thibodaux], but for a short period only, having secured a sufficient practice in the river parishes near his residence.[13]

At the beginning of the late war, he raised a splendid company, composed principally of the sons of the wealthiest and most refined families in St. James and St. John parishes, and upon the organization of the 18th Regiment at Camp Moore on the 5th of October 1861, this officer was unanimously elected lieutenant colonel. Always taking an active part in promoting the welfare of his soldiers and in effecting a thorough and perfect organization of the regiment, he rendered himself popular both with the officers and men.

He was an excellent drill officer and spared no pain in instructing those under his command in the maneuvers and movements which they were soon to test in actual strife with the enemy.

When in command, the strictest obedience and discipline were required, but when off duty, he was social, kind, and indulgent, mixing freely with his subordinates and enjoying the hilarity and sports incidence to a camp of soldiers.

13. Roman was born in St. James Parish on May 24, 1824. Educated at Jefferson College, he was admitted to the Louisiana bar in 1845 (Conrad, ed., "Alfred Roman," in *Dictionary of Louisiana Biography*, II, 693).

At the beginning of the engagement with the gunboats at Pittsburg Landing on March 1st, 1862, Col. Mouton was absent reconnoitering the position.

Col. Roman skillfully disposed of the troops, made all the preparations necessary, and was in the midst of the engagement when his superior arrived and assumed command. During this little battle, the colonel impressed the fact upon the regiment that they could rely safely upon his judgment, ability, and coolness in any emergency that might arise. During the Battle of Shiloh, the colonel bore himself gallantly and was in the thickest of the fight during the two days in which we were engaged, having command of the regiment, or what was left of it, subsequent to the wounding of Col. Mouton. On arriving at Corinth, the health of Col. Roman became so bad that he was compelled to obtain a leave of absence and, subsequently, to forward his resignation.

After his resignation had been forwarded as lt. col., he was elected colonel at the reorganization of his regiment on the 15th April 1862, but in the meantime his resignation had been granted on account of ill health, and he retired from service. Subsequently, he returned to the army and was appointed by Gen. Beauregard as Inspector General of his army and served with that gallant officer throughout the siege of Charleston and during the campaign at Petersburg until the surrender at Appomattox.

Since the war, the colonel has resided in St. James, following the profession of law and also, we believe, engaging in planting.

The colonel is still in the prime of life and vigor of manhood. He has lately taken a lively interest in the construction of a railroad from his parish by way of Napoleonville to Thibodaux and a few weeks since spent a day in this place, endeavoring to interest our citizens in the enterprise and in talking over old times with his former comrades in arms.[14]

It is to Col. Roman to whom the writer is indebted to a position in the service which relieved him from many of the fatigues and severe duties he would otherwise have, perhaps, been called upon to perform. Whilst acting as colonel at Corinth and during the absence of Capt. Sanders, our assistant quartermaster, wounded at Shiloh, he gave me the temporary appointment of A. Q. M. which was afterward made permanent by a regular appointment to that position by the President of the Confederate States.

14. Roman died in New Orleans on September 20, 1892 (*ibid.*).

LOUIS BUSH

The second company raised in this parish in 1861 was enlisted and commanded by Capt. Louis Bush. At the organization of the 18th Regiment at Camp Moore, September the 5th, 1861, Capt. Louis Bush was elected major without any opposition. The major was a strict disciplinarian, an excellent drill officer, and always had a paternal solicitude for the welfare of the men under his command. Always found at his post of duty, he had the unlimited confidence of both officers and men, which confidence was ratified in gallantry and skill in the fights at Pittsburg Landing and during the two days' engagement at Shiloh. During the siege of Corinth, the major was unwell and had to retire to the rear to recuperate. On the 15th of April 1862, upon the reorganization of his regiment, he was unanimously elected lieutenant colonel, and after the resignation of Col. Roman, he was promoted to the colonelcy.

The army had fallen back to Tupelo before the health of the colonel permitted him to return to the field, when he assumed command of the 18th. Doubtful concerning his health, he sent in his resignation, which was accepted, and much to the sorrow of the regiment, he left us at Tupelo.

Subsequently, he served in the Trans-Mississippi Department as A. A. G. to Gen. Mouton until the latter part of 1863, when he succeeded in raising a regiment of cavalry, which he commanded for some time, when he was appointed as one of the judges of the Military Court in the Trans-Mississippi Department, stationed at Shreveport, which position he occupied until the close of the war.[15]

The colonel is a native of Iberville Parish but emigrated to this town when quite young.[16] He was for many years clerk of the district court, during the occupancy of which position he studied law and in a short time became one of the most successful practitioners in this section of Louisiana.

He served also several terms as a member of the popular branch of the legislature and was senatorial delegate from this parish and St. Charles to the convention which passed the Ordinance of Secession.

15. Bush became presiding officer of the court by orders issued on January 7, 1865 (*OR*, Vol. XLVIII, Pt. 1, p. 1318).

16. Bush was born in Iberville Parish in 1820, the son of Reuben Bush and Marie Ludivine Brasset (Conrad, ed., "Louis Bush," in *Dictionary of Louisiana Biography*, I, 134).

During the session of this convention, the colonel was one of the ablest and most eloquent opponents of said ordinance, advocating what was known as the cooperation policy.

But finding that the Ordinance of Secession was a foregone conclusion, he voted for and signed the same, being determined to stand by his people and his state in the great step which the course of human events forced upon us at that time.

At the close of the war, the colonel returned home and resumed the practice of his profession. Upon the request of Gov. Wells,[17] he accepted the position of colonel of the militia and was in process of effecting a thorough organization of the same when military authority overthrew and superceded the state government.

The colonel is a successful planter as well as lawyer and also takes a hand in politics occasionally.

He is now in fine health, with the prospect of many years before him.

With his family, he is now luxuriating in the north and west.[18]

Leopold L. Armant[19]

Leopold L. Armant was a native of St. James Parish and had all the advantages of education and culture that wealth could bestow upon him.[20]

To complete his education, he spent some time in Europe, traveling and studying the customs and manners of the people of the old world and contrasting the laws and governments of resplendent and imperial royalty with the plain and simple characteristics of Republican rulers.

17. James Madison Wells served as governor of Louisiana from March 4, 1865, until removed by Major General Philip H. Sheridan on May 3, 1867 (Joe Gray Taylor, *Louisiana Reconstructed, 1863–1877* [Baton Rouge, 1974], 58, 140).

18. Bush died on August 10, 1892, in Palmyra, Wisconsin, but his body was brought back to New Orleans for burial (Conrad, ed., "Louis Bush," in *Dictionary of Louisiana Biography,* I, 134).

19. This account is a combination of the original installment and a subsequent biographical sketch.

20. Born in St. James Parish on June 10, 1835, Armant graduated from Georgetown College (now University) in 1855 and from the University of Louisiana in 1858. His father, John S., had served as adjutant general under Governors Alexandre Mouton and Isaac Johnson (Conrad, ed., "John S. Armant" and "Leopold L. Armant," in *Dictionary of Louisiana Biography,* I, 19).

Returning to his native home, he was elected by his neighbors and friends as their representative to the legislature of the state, a high compliment in St. James, within which parish there was so much ability and talent. This position was filled by the young representative with credit to himself and to the satisfaction of his fellow-citizens who had entrusted their interests to his care.

But the tocsin of war banished the gentle pursuits of peace, and the songs of a happy and contented people were silenced by the fierce rattling of the drum and fife, arousing their martial spirit and inviting them to act in defense of what they believed to be their inalienable rights.

Young Armant united, with the energy and zeal that was characteristic of all his actions, in the formation of a military company known as the St. James Rifles. Alfred Roman, subsequently colonel and later historian and judge, was the captain of this company, Armant being elected 2nd lieutenant.

The company was composed of the wealthy and educated young men of St. James Parish, which made the election of Armant a compliment of which he had reason to be proud.

At the organization of the Eighteenth Louisiana Regiment at Camp Moore on October 5, 1861, Captain Roman was elected lieut. colonel, which by promotion gave Armant the office of first lieutenant of his company.

He was one of the most efficient lieutenants in the 18th Regiment and soon became popular in the command both as an accomplished officer and as an agreeable, social gentleman. The young lieutenant first became conspicuous in March 1862. Our regiment was stationed on picket duty in front of Corinth, at which point the army that fought the battle of Shiloh was then in process of organization, and encamped near Monterey, some five miles from Pittsburg Landing.

The Federal forces were being debarked at this landing and placed in position in the forests between that point and Shiloh Church.

Col. Alfred Mouton desired to obtain some accurate information of the movement of the Federal forces, their position, and probable strength. He summoned Lieut. Armant, requested him to make an investigation, and to procure the requisite information. Although the mission was fraught with danger, requiring boldness, tact, and audacity to accomplish, the young officer accepted the duty assigned him without a moment's hesitation.

The following night, using the screen that the darkness afforded him in the dense woods amid which the hostile troops were encamped, he approached sufficiently near the Federal lines to hear the soldiers talking and, by climbing into trees, obtained, by the dim light of the camp fires that were visible, a fair enumeration of the number of regiments that had debarked at Pittsburg Landing and been placed in position, and at dawn of day, stood at the door of the tent of his commander, ready to render to his chief a satisfactory report of his nocturnal feat.

For this gallant, daring, and successful deed, he was officially thanked in special orders read to the regiment at dress parade.

This at once gave prestige to the youthful lieutenant as a bold, reliable, and gallant officer. Lieut. Armant passed unhurt through the two days' fighting at Shiloh which proved so disastrous to the Eighteenth Regiment.

He was at all times at his position, gallantly leading his men through those bloody days and faithfully performing all duties incumbent upon him as an officer and soldier.

At Corinth, in April 1862, a reorganization of the companies took place under directions from the government at Richmond. Lieut. Armant was elected captain of his company, and in May 1862, at the reorganization of the field officers, Roman was elected colonel, Bush lieut. colonel, and Armant major.

For gallant services at Shiloh, Col. Mouton had been appointed brigadier-general and was at home in Attakapas, chafing under the sufferings of disease that kept him in the rear.

The sufferings of the Confederate army at Corinth in 1862, the sickness and privation to which they were subject, require no repetition here. They were indelibly impressed upon the memory of the half-sick and scantily-clothed troops who remained to the end and made the long, weary, and hungry retreat to Tupelo.

Ill health had forced Col. Roman to offer his resignation, and having had the same accepted, he bade farewell to the soldiers to whom he had endeared himself by his urbanity, dignity, and kindness and left the command regretted by both rank and file. On July 15, 1862, Lieut. Col. Bush received the acceptance of his resignation, which he had forwarded to army headquarters for reasons similar to those given by Col. Roman.

He immediately left the command at Tupelo and came over to

the Trans-Mississippi Department. These resignations, it was supposed, made, by promotion, Major Armant colonel, Capt. Joseph
Collins lieut. colonel, and Capt. Wm. Mouton major.

In August 1862, the Eighteenth La. Regiment received orders to
remove to Pollard, Alabama.

My duties required me to travel across the mountains of Alabama
to Chattanooga, at which point Gen. Bragg was organizing his army
and putting it on the march into Kentucky. On my arrival at Pollard
in September 1862, I learned that the Confederate government refused to sanction the promotion of field officers as above mentioned
and had directed that an election should be held to fill the vacancies,
the election then taking place.

Absent for more than a month, I was surprised at this order. An
effort was being made to elect Maj. Wm. Mouton in place of Armant.

I, at once, visited the colonel to ascertain the facts. I inquired
whether he was aware that he had opposition. He replied that he was.

I then asked if he was not a candidate for the colonelcy. His answer was "that he was not; that if his brother officers saw proper to
select him as their colonel he would accept the position with thanks
and gratitude, but that he had not sought the vote of any officer nor
did he propose to do so."

His manner and his language impressed me very favorably. Leaving his tent, I went to the polling booth and cast my vote for him.
He was elected by a handsome majority.

In October, orders required us to remove to the Trans-Mississippi,
our first halt being in New Iberia.

The regiment was delighted to find themselves once more under
the immediate command of their beloved colonel—now brigadier
general—Mouton, who was commander-in-chief of all the forces in
the Attakapas country. On his staff were our former lieut. col., Bush,
as chief of staff and Lieut. Watts as aide-de-camp.

Headquarters were soon removed to Thibodaux. The Federal
forces were reported to be moving down the bayou from Donaldsonville. Col. [Gen.] Mouton was afflicted with rheumatism and was
compelled to place the troops on the west side of the Lafourche under the command of Col. Armant.

The Confederates, consisting of the 18th La. and Crescent regiments of infantry, badly armed—less than 400 men—and Ralston's
Battery were in the woods at Georgia Landing awaiting an attack on

October 27. The Federals were descending on the opposite side of the bayou but crossed three or four regiments over about two miles above.

The Confederates were placed in line behind the fence along Winn's road, which led to the Texas Brusly. Bayou Lafourche was on one flank and an impenetrable swamp on the other, so that the impending battle would be a square one, face to face, no room being found for strategy.

The Federal regiments moved down in echelon, partly concealed by fences and high roads, exercising great caution, deferring their attack for some time. The engagement lasted about six hours. The ammunition of the battery was finally exhausted and Capt. Ralston wounded, when the order to retreat was given.

Col. McPheeters, of the Crescent Regiment, was killed and some 10 or 12 men fell in that engagement, whilst about 100 were made prisoners. Weitzel was in command of the Federal troops. When he ascertained that such a small force had kept him in check almost an entire day, he complimented the prisoners on their gallantry and paroled all the file on their own parole of honor.

Col. Armant was conspicuous throughout the engagement, encouraging the men and leading them into the fight.

Falling back to Labadieville, he collected his scattered forces, and, in charge of the rear, he kept the enemy at bay until they had safely reached Morgan City and encamped on the opposite bank of Berwick Bay.

In the campaign on the Teche which followed and the fights at Bisland, the colonel always was found at the head of his regiment and bore himself gallantly whenever occasion presented. In the long marches which the 18th Regiment made in northern Louisiana, Colonel Armant accompanied his men, sharing with them the privations and sufferings to which they were subject.

Finally, the retreat toward Shreveport before Banks' army was made. At Mansfield, on April 8, 1864, the collision took place which sent the Federals to the rear covered with defeat and disgrace. On that morning, Col. Armant's regiment was placed on the extreme left of the infantry forces.

He was ordered to hold back one half of his regiment as a reserve, when the command to charge rang out along the Confederate line. Instead of remaining with his reserve, he left it under the command of Lt. Col. Collins and went into the fight with that vim and soldierly pride that he ever exhibited when danger was to be encountered.

The gallantry of that heroic charge and the tenacity with which the Federals held their position formed one of the brightest pages of the War of Secession. Like leaves before the chilling blasts of the autumnal winds, the men on both sides fell before the prowess of their adversaries. The Federals finally yielded and abandoned their position to their victorious foes.

But the victory, however brilliant, was gained at a fearful sacrifice. Mouton, Beard, Clack, Walker, Armant, Canfield, Beatty, Lavery, Martin, and many other heroes went down in that fearful charge, adding another wreath to the Confederate escutcheon and sealed it with their life's blood.

In the thickest of the fight, Armant's horse was shot from under him. At the same moment, his color bearer went down; Armant rushed forward and, seizing the flag, received his death wound whilst gallantly waving the flag in the shower of bullets in which he was placed. When last seen alive, he was prostrate, trying to hold up his flag and bidding defiance to his destroyers. Thus closed the young life of a true patriot, a heroic soldier, and a noble man.

Col. Armant was generally a strict disciplinarian, although there were occasions in which he did not enforce all his orders with that promptness a superior officer should exhibit. But there were periods in which he would relax the reins and overlook breaches that upon other occasions he would not permit and occasionally inflicted punishment for an infraction of an order that had been for some time practically a dead letter. This was the occasion of some unpleasant feelings among the officers and men, but generally the best of feelings were entertained for him, satisfied that if he committed errors or mistakes they were faults of the head and not of the heart.

One of his peculiarities was that those who were his most intimate friends socially were subjected to the most rigid discipline. He was ambitious and yearned to win honor and fame upon the field. No danger was shirked, no opportunity of meeting the enemy was lost. He could have remained honorably with his reserve at Mansfield but declined to do so and accompanied his soldiers into that bloody action with a hero's martial spirit and a heart bounding with a laudable desire to win renown.

Socially, Col. Armant was pleasant, genial, agreeable. He was possessed of good conversational powers that had been polished by study and travel. To all he was affable and kind, firm in his decisions, honest in his dealings with other men. His leisure hours were occupied with the study of such literature as could be had.

During the afternoon before the Battle of Mansfield was fought, I called upon the colonel to get some papers signed in his tent, in which I found him reading. After my business had been transacted, we conversed together for some time, speculating upon the probable prospect of a fight before the army reached Shreveport, which would be in a few days.

As I rose to leave, the colonel said to me, "Major, we are going to have a bloody battle ere many days; I owe one of my officers— naming him—$800.00 dollars. There are several months' salary due me. If I should fall, I desire you to collect that amount and pay it over to him."

His looks and language impressed me deeply, and the idea that he had a presentiment of his fate was firmly fixed in my mind.

The friends of Col. Armant do not claim that he was a perfect man. He was subject to the same errors, liable to commit the faults that other men were prone to commit.

His official acts were frequently the subject of warm criticism by both rank and file. These wayward errors, had Col. Armant lived, would have been softened by the heavy polishing of experience. They emanated not from the heart, and once convinced that he had done an injustice, willingly and promptly was that injustice repaired.

The whole command had always the most unbounded confidence in his ability and gallantry in battle, and this confidence was ever ably sustained by his valor and heroism.

His remains were interred on the topmost height of the Mansfield Cemetery, side by side with Mouton, Martin, Beatty, Walker, and others who gave up their lives on that fatal day.

Subsequently, loving friends have transported the remains of the dead soldier to his family cemetery in St. James and placed them by the side of his ancestors and friends.

JOSEPH COLLINS[21]

When the 18th Regiment was removed from Camp Roman to Camp Benjamin below New Orleans, then composed of eight companies,

21. Born in New Orleans in 1837, Collins was educated at Spring Hill College near Mobile, Alabama. Prior to the war, he was a bookkeeper for D. H. Holmes's dry

we were joined by a new company, which had been for several months organized and kept on duty guarding public property in that city, commanded by Capt. Joseph Collins, who then became our senior captain. The captain was soon found to be a genial, social companion, a good officer, and was not long in making himself a favorite among the officers of the regiment.

He commanded his company in the battle of Pittsburg Landing, and during the arduous duties of the regiment previous to the battle of Shiloh, he was ever ready to accomplish any orders that were given or perform any duties that were required for him to consummate.

In the battle of Shiloh and during our charge upon the enemy on the evening of the first day, the captain was wounded and compelled to leave the field. He subsequently procured a leave of absence and returned to New Orleans, where he remained but a few days, being obliged to leave when the city fell into the hands of the enemy. He remained during the summer on the line of the Jackson Railroad until sufficiently recovered to resume active duty, when he rejoined the command at Pollard, Alabama. Upon the promotion of Major Armant to be colonel, Capt. Collins by seniority became lieutenant colonel, but as the government at Richmond ignored this proceeding, at an election held at Pollard, he was elected lieut. col. over Capt. Wm. Mouton by a small majority. The lieut. col. made an efficient field officer, was a good disciplinarian, and took an active interest in the welfare of the men under his command, and by his pleasant and sociable habits, he rendered himself popular with the soldiers. At the battle of Winn's road above Labadieville, Col. Armant being in command of all the forces, the command of the regiment devolved upon Col. Collins, and during the engagement, the scabbard of his sword was struck and considerably bent by a ball, which, had it not met with this obstruction, would in all probability have put an end to his military career. Col. Collins served for a long time on a court martial sitting in Alexandria, but afterwards rejoined the command, and at the battle of Mansfield was left behind

---

goods house and a partner in the firm of Collins, Hepp & Co. of the Pelican Cotton Press. He returned to his business pursuits after the war, served in the Constitutional Convention of 1879, was a member of the city school board, and was the city's Administrator of Improvements. At the time of his death, Collins was a cotton weigher. He died on the morning of April 4, 1886, at his home on Annunciation Street after a long illness. His body was buried in the Army of Tennessee tomb in Metairie Cemetery (New Orleans *Daily Picayune,* April 5, 6, 1886).

with one half the regiment as a reserve, being ordered forward just as the enemy gave way. Col. Armant having fallen, he assumed command of the regiment and was with it the next day at Pleasant Hill, although not warmly engaged.

During our march in pursuit of the enemy, as we were in the neighborhood of Cheneyville, the col. discovered a half dozen men of his regiment who had attached themselves to some cavalry and had them arrested.

For this, he was placed under arrest during which time the fight at Yellow Bayou took place, Capt. Sanchez commanding the 18th. The colonel was soon released without either trial or reprimand. During our march through Arkansas, Gen. Gray, having been elected a member of the Confederate Congress, resigned his position in the army, when Col. Collins, as senior officer in the command, assumed the position of acting brig. gen. until we reached Alexandria in January 1865, when Col. Bosworth, being his senior, rejoined the brigade.

Col. Collins was with his regiment at the surrender of Natchitoches and accompanied his men down the river to his home in New Orleans.

Since his return, the colonel has been quietly endeavoring to recover his losses, performing the duties incumbent on him as a good citizen, and confining himself to the management of his private business.

He is still in the prime of life, and we hope to meet him many a time in the future and talk over past scenes and trials which we have undergone in times in which neither of us regret having participated.

WILLIAM MOUTON [22]

William Mouton was 1st lieutenant in the company raised and organized by Capt. Alfred Mouton, and upon the election of the cap-

---

22. Christened Guillaume Cesaire, William Mouton was born in St. Landry Parish on June 21, 1831. His father, Cesaire, was a brother of Governor Alexandre Mouton. After graduation from Yale University, William practiced law in Vermilionville. It was said that he was not only an eloquent orator but he also "'had a wonderful memory and could quote the British poets, including Shakespeare and Byron, off hand without previous preparation.'" He died in New Iberia on January 19, 1885 (J. Franklin Mouton, III, comp. and ed., *The Moutons: A Genealogy* [Lafayette, La., 1978], 16; Harry Lewis Griffin, *The Attakapas Country: A History of Lafayette Par-*

tain to the colonelcy of the 18th Regiment, he became captain of the company.

He is a native of Attakapas and a lawyer of some eminence in Vermilionville.

He was gifted with all the qualities requisite for a good companion at any social gathering, having a pleasant conversation and possessing notoriety as an orator in either French, Spanish, or English.

He was almost too good natured to be a strict disciplinarian or a severe officer and did not take very kindly to the tactics of Hardee.

On our departure to Corinth in February 1862, Capt. Mouton was sent with his company as an escort to some 500 prisoners captured at Manassas and confined in New Orleans for several months, who were being removed to Salisbury, North Carolina.

He met the command, after having performed this duty, at Corinth and participated in all the movements in which the 18th Regiment made in front of that place, participating in the fight at Pittsburg Landing and the battle of Shiloh. During the siege of Corinth, Capt. Mouton, owing to sickness of so many officers, was in command of the regiment for the last 15 or 20 days that we remained in front of that place. After our retreat to Tupelo, the captain became major by promotion and was subsequently elected by the officers to that position when the above promotion was declared null. Shortly after the retreat from Corinth, Capt. Mouton obtained leave of absence on account of ill health and came to his home in Louisiana.

He returned to his command at Pollard, Alabama, but a few days previous to the reception of orders removing our regiment to the Trans-Mississippi Department. When we reached Berwick's Bay, the major was ordered to Camp Pratt near New Iberia for the purpose of obtaining conscripts sufficient to fill up our regiment. It was during this period that the campaign on the bayou took place. He was with his regiment the greater portion of the time in all its wanderings over Louisiana and Arkansas. He was too unwell to participate in the battles of Mansfield and Pleasant Hill. The fall of Col. Armant and the promotion of Lieutenant Colonel Collins was followed by the promotion of Major Mouton to be lieutenant colonel, which rank he held until the surrender at Natchitoches.

---

ish, Louisiana [Gretna, La., 1974], 44; Rev. Donald J. Hebert, ed., *Southwest Louisiana Records: Church and Civil Records* [Cecilia, La., 1978], XVII, 452).

After the surrender, he resumed the practice of law in Vermilion-ville, but afterwards removed to New Orleans. He has, however, re-turned to his old home in the prairies and is now in the vigor of manhood with the prospect of many happy days before him.

The colonel will no doubt remember one evening in front of Cor-inth when our regiment was ordered out on the Farmington road and placed in front of the enemy. The whole army was drawn up in line of battle along the skirmish line. Sickness had reduced the regiment a few men. The major was in command and I, a 1st lieutenant, was second, which fact will give an idea of the condition of our effective-ness. Night came, and about 11 o'clock the major and myself made our coach in an empty wagon, which was done by spreading one blanket on the floor and another on ourselves. We conversed a long time on the prospect of the next day's chances and, wondering where our bed on the following night would be, finally dropped asleep. When we awoke, the sun was up; I remarked "that everything was quiet, and it did not look much like there was going to be a fight." "Well, Lieutenant, let's get up and try and get one more cup of coffee before the ball opens." We did so, and lay around in the shade all day, when we were sent back to camp.

At another time, our men, who were in camp, were nearly all unwell, and about half of them were on duty every day; the major, having been over to see Gen. Ruggles' headquarters, told me that he had obtained a few days' rest for his men.

We were congratulating ourselves on this pleasant information when an orderly rode up and presented the major with an order to remove his whole regiment out on picket duty that evening on the Monterey road. A sweet time we had that night with the minnie balls passing through the trees and whistling around our ears every few minutes.

The next day, I was sent by the major to accompany Major New-man of the 21st Regiment and Lt. Levi Hargis to ascertain why there was no connection between our pickets and that on our right. We soon found the reason and ascertained how much pleasure a man can have in being deliberately shot at by one of his own friends—and missed.

J. KLEBER GOURDAIN

This officer was first lieutenant in our company when it was orga-nized, but upon the election of Capt. Bush as major of the 18th Regiment at Camp Moore on the 5th of October 1861, he was elected captain of his company.

Capt. Gourdain was a strict disciplinarian and always enforced a rigid obedience to orders and was equally prompt and obedient to orders from his superiors.

The interests and welfare of his men were objects of care, and no efforts were every spared to secure for them all the supplies to which they were entitled and privileges which were allowed to others.

At our first skirmish with the enemy's gunboats, an amusing scene occurred that none of the men with us is likely to have forgotten. Our company was encamped in a shallow ravine about 100 yards from the river bank and almost in a line with the enemy's boats and the battery upon which they were firing. The shells, therefore, very nearly passed over our heads.

Capt. Gourdain, who very often gets a little excited, ordered his men to form into line as soon as the first shot was heard and ordered them to count off by twos. The head of the company began, one, two; one, two; one, two; but before they would get half through a shell would come whizzing along over our heads, and by some peculiar coincidence, each one of us imagined that that identical shell was going to hit us at the root of the right ear, which idea at once stopped the counting, and every fellow would first bend his head as far out of the way as possible and then drop down on his knee, whilst the shell would pass in perfect safety two or three hundred feet above us.

The captain tried to count off three or four times but was finally compelled to give up the attempt.

At the Battle of Shiloh, Capt. Gourdain received a wound in the right arm on Sunday evening and was compelled to go to the rear.

Subsequently obtaining a leave of absence, he came to his home with the other wounded of his company. He again returned to his regiment when it was stationed at Pollard, Alabama, and accompanied it to this side of the Mississippi River and was in the fight at the Texana road above Labadieville, where he was again slightly wounded in the arm but not enough to cause him to leave the field.[23] After our retreat across Berwick's Bay, he was detailed on duty as provost marshal at Franklin for a short time, when he was made

23. This wound in his right arm was "almost similar and nearly on the same spot as the one received at Shiloh" (*Weekly Thibodaux Sentinel,* March 13, 1875).

commander at the post of New Iberia, on which duty he continued until our retreat, when he assumed command of his company until our return to Thibodaux in June 1863, when he was detailed as post commander there.

After our retreat, he was again stationed at New Iberia and subsequently at Alexandria, at which station he continued until the close of the war.

Upon the fall of Col. Armant at Mansfield, he became major of the 18th Regiment by promotion, being senior captain.

As a Captain he was emphatically a commander of his Company, but whilst exacting rigid discipline from his soldiers, he was studiously careful of their lives and health, and no comforts which his supervision and energy could obtain were ever wanting.[24]

Apparently at times imperious in his orders, he required nothing that was not sanctioned by good discipline and asked nothing of his men, which military duties did not sanction.

His men were asked to occupy no position to which he would not lead them, nor to incur any danger that he did not partake of, to its utmost extent.

As was the case with many a good officer in the volunteer service, at the commencement of his military career, he acquired that species of unpopularity among his men, which was the natural result of the enforcement of a rigid discipline and prompt obedience, but which ere the war closed proved to be the great traits which made the successful commander, and secured the appreciation of those who at first chafed under its exactions.

Major Gourdain was a native of Donaldsonville or that vicinity and was raised in the family of the late Capt. A. J. Powell,[25] who was always his warm and devoted friend.

With him he studied practical engineering and located in Thibodaux for the purpose of following that occupation. He was, however, a few years later elected parish recorder, to which position he was

24. This and the succeeding three paragraphs were taken from a subsequent article about Gourdain (ibid.).

25. The sixty-five-year-old Powell was living in New Orleans in 1860. He was a land agent and had been born in Mississippi. Powell served early during the war as quartermaster of the 1st Division, Louisiana Militia, with the rank of colonel. In June, 1861, he selected the site for Camp Lewis near Carrollton (Eighth Census: Orleans Parish, Roll 416; Casey, Encyclopedia of Forts, 104–105).

re-elected several times and was in the possession of that office
when he left in 1861.[26]

After the surrender, he was appointed parish recorder by Gov.
Wells and remained in that office until the first election under the
new constitution. Previous to that time, however, he had engaged in
planting, having leased the Scuddy Plantation, some twelve miles
below this place. Three years since, he removed to New Orleans and
went into the commission business, and about one year later formed
a co-partnership with one of his former soldiers, and now the [illeg-
ible] house of Sevin and Gourdain 111 Decatur [illegible].[27]

Clerville T. Patin[28]

Among the first acquaintances I formed in the 18th Regiment was
the gentleman whose name appears above. He was orderly sergeant
of Capt. W. Mouton's company. He is a native of the Attakapas country near the town of Vermilionville.

A short time after the organization of the regiment, he was recommended as assistant commissary by Col. A. Roman, and whilst
at Corinth in 1862, he received his commission as such.

Capt. Patin, as all commissaries of the C. S. Army who desired to
perform their duty, had a hard commission to fill, the execution of
which required all the energy of which he was possessed.

That this officer did everything that a man could do under the

26. Gourdain was born in St. James Parish on August 20, 1826. He participated in
the Mexican War and worked as a surveyor in Donaldsonville after his return. He
moved to Thibodaux in November, 1847. In 1859, he opened a grocery store with
Cleophas Gautreau (*Weekly Thibodaux Sentinel,* March 13, 1875).

27. In New Orleans, Gourdain set up a store with Felix P. Sevin. He was one of
the "martyrs" of the Battle of Liberty Place on September 14, 1874. Gourdain had
attended the mass meeting at the Henry Clay statue on Canal Street and was on his
way back to his business when killed. He met a fleeing Metropolitan policeman on
Chartres Street near St. Louis and a fight ensued. The policeman shot him in the
back. Gourdain was buried three days later in Thibodaux. He left a widow and six
children (*ibid.;* Stuart Omer Landry, *The Battle of Liberty Place* [New Orleans, 1955],
210–11).

28. Clerville Toussaint Patin was born in December, 1826, and later operated a
plantation near Lafayette. He was president of the White Man's Club, a White League
organization in Lafayette Parish, in 1874 (Hebert, ed., *Southwest Louisiana Records,*
II [1974], 707; Griffin, *The Attakapas Country,* 66–68).

circumstances, no one will badly dispute, and the men of his regiment and brigade should ever remember him kindly.

The captain was ever at his post, except when disabled by disease, never obtaining but one leave of absence for a short time to visit his family. He remained with his regiment until regimental commissaries were abolished, when he was selected as brigade commissary, which post he retained until the close of the war in the old brigade. The captain was a jovial, pleasant companion and maintained his equanimity in a remarkable manner, considering the daily reasons he had for testing his temper.

The boys used to tell some hard stories on their commissary, however, and there was doubtless some truth in them, sometimes.

I recollect when we were on the march from Monroe to Alexandria in January 1864, it was currently reported in camp that every evening Major P. used to lay down a six inch pole and have his herd driven over it, and the first beeves that fell in stepping across it were killed and issued to the soldiers.

We never watched this process, but the beeves, after being driven for weeks from 15 to 25 miles per day and pastured at night in barren fields, were not in a condition to jump over fences, and the chances are that if the herdsmen had driven the whole herd over the six inch pole, there would have been none left for the next day's rations.

My associations with Major Patin were always of the most agreeable character; we both entered the services as sergeants, were promoted to be staff officers about the same time, both became majors by the same order of promotion, were always on duty in the same command, and, during the most of the marches, travelled together. Major Patin possessed the good will of the officers and men under his command and undoubtedly merited their esteem, as but few officers exercised as much skill and energy in promoting the comfort of those who looked upon him for their daily rations.

The major is now residing at the old homestead near Vermilionville, where it is hoped he is enjoying the comforts and pleasures of a well-to-do farmer, surrounded by his family and friends.

OUR SURGEONS

Our first surgeon was Dr. Littlell of Opelousas. He came to the regiment and entered upon the discharge of his duties whilst we were stationed at Camp Roman. It was not long before the doctor received the usual fate of surgeons, the ill will of nearly all the officers and men.

He was naturally of a surly, morose disposition, and in attempting to strictly comply with the army regulations, he met with opposition on all sides. The men were not accustomed to such a discipline, and perhaps if the surgeon had not come into the regiment for a couple of years later, he would have given more satisfaction, as it is well known that the best officers at the beginning of the war were always the most unpopular.

Dr. Littlell was a good physician and fully capable of making a good army surgeon, but he was not possessed of a disposition to render himself popular. At Corinth, his health became bad, and for some time he was not able to leave his tent, still he continued to prescribe for the men who were able to visit him. Obtaining a leave of absence before the retreat, the doctor returned to his station at Tupelo but still in bad health. My associations with Dr. Littlell were always very pleasant, and in all our personal affairs, we got along together quite smoothly.

The doctor is a practicing physician in Opelousas at present, where he possesses the reputation of being among the most skillful practitioners in that portion of the state.

Dr. Gourrier of the parish of Iberville was appointed assistant surgeon of the regiment and came to his position also at Camp Roman.

It was not long before the harmony existing between the two surgeons became a thing of the past, which state of affairs did not promote the comfort of the sick and ailing. Dr. Gourrier also obtained leave of absence at Corinth and retired to the rear.

In the meantime, we had the services of Dr. Ballard of Assumption for a few days, who finally had to leave on account of ill health, and of Dr. Wiescher, or some other outlandish name, from some of the Baton Rouge parishes, who distinguished himself by drinking all the brandy and eating all the jellies which had been sent to us by the ladies for the use of the sick and wounded, when he left, to the gratification of everybody.

Next came a young physician, Dr. Key, son of the late P. B. Key, who died on the Cecadia plantation just below Thibodaux, who performed his duties well, was with us during the retreat, and left reluctantly and to our regret whilst we were at Tupelo.

A few days after encamping near this little town, Dr. Gourrier came, armed, as he said, with a surgeon's commission and an assignment to the 18th La. Volunteers, fitted up a big Sibley tent, and entered upon the discharge of his duties. A couple of days afterwards, Dr. Littlell returned to assume his position. We were at that time decidedly rich in surgeons and were, consequently, edified at the maneuvers which took place between the two doctors.

One of them would ride over to Tupelo in the morning and come back during the forenoon, to be followed by the order. What miseries the chief surgeon had to undergo to reconcile the disputants history does not mention, but in about a week Dr. Littlell received his discharge,[29] and Dr. Gourrier was assigned to some other post,[30] and we were minus all physicians.

Dr. Bonsall,[31] a Mississippian, was then assigned to duty as assistant surgeon of our regiment and immediately entered upon the discharge of his duties. This surgeon soon acquired the friendship of both officers and men, was attentive to duty, genial and pleasant in conversation, kind to the ailing, causing us all to be thankful that we were so fortunate to obtain the services of one who was satisfactory and skillful. He was promoted to a full surgeon after we came to this side of the river and remained with us during all our wanderings and trials until we arrived at Minden, La., in January 1865.

Here he obtained a leave of absence to visit his family near West Point, Mississippi, and bade us all farewell. The war was soon closing; he never returned. I have never heard of him since the war, but wherever he may be it is to be hoped that his path may lie in pleasant places. Dr. Allen[32] of St. Mary was for some time our assistant surgeon, who was a clever gentleman and a good physician. Dr. Vernon[33] of Avoyelles was also for a time assistant surgeon of the 18th. He was assassinated at or near his home a year or two ago.

29. Littlell resigned on July 31, 1862 (CSR, Roll 294).

30. Gourrier was detached on June 29, 1862. He later served on several hospital staffs and with other military units, the last being the 34th Alabama Infantry Regiment (ibid., Roll 293; Joseph Jones, "Roster of the Medical Officers of the Army of Tennessee," Southern Historical Society Papers, XXII [1894], 209).

31. Dr. W. B. Bonsall. Mustered in as assistant surgeon on June 23, 1862, and appointed regimental surgeon on December 17, 1862, Bonsall eventually received his parole at Columbus, Mississippi, on May 23, 1865 (CSR, Rolls 290, 298).

32. Dr. C. E. Allen was appointed assistant surgeon on December 9, 1862 (ibid., Roll 290).

33. Dr. M. P. Vernon was appointed assistant surgeon on December 17, 1862 (ibid., Roll 297).

Bibliography

Unpublished Sources

Manuscripts

Eugene C. Barker Texas History Center, University of Texas, Austin
    Raney Greene, Jr., Papers.
Loretta Gilibert, Aurora, Colorado
    Diary of Elphege LeBoeuf, 1861–1862.
Hill Memorial Library, Louisiana State University, Baton Rouge
    Louisiana and Lower Mississippi Valley Collection, Special Collections
        David F. Boyd Civil War Papers, 1861–1865.
        John A. Harris Letters, 1861–1864.
        Arthur W. Hyatt Papers, 1861–1865.
        Frederick R. Taber Papers, 1861–1862.
Howard-Tilton Memorial Library, Tulane University, New Orleans
    Special Collections Division
        Louisiana Historical Association Collection.
Louisiana Adjutant General's Library, Jackson Barracks, New Orleans
    Joseph L. Brent Papers, 1862–1865.
Louisiana State Archives, Baton Rouge
    Confederate Pension Files.
    Secretary of State's Register of Appointments, 1856–1865.
Mansfield State Commemorative Area Museum, Mansfield, La.
    Letter, Colonel Henry Gray to Major E. Surget, April ?, 1864 (typescript).
National Archives, Washington, D.C.
    Compiled Service Records of Confederate General and Staff Officers and Nonregimental Enlisted Men. National Archives Microcopy No. 331.
    Compiled Service Records of Confederate Soldiers Who Served in Organizations from the State of Louisiana. National Archives Microcopy No. 320.
    Compiled Service Records of Confederate Soldiers Who Served in Organizations from the State of Texas. National Archives Microcopy No. 323.

Eighth Census of the United States, 1860: Population Schedules. National Archives Microcopy No. 653.

Louisiana State Records in the War Department Collection of Confederate Records. National Archives Microcopy No. 359.

Nicholls State University Library, Thibodaux, La.

Manuscript Collection

William Littlejohn (Litt) Martin Collection.

Other Materials

Hatton, Roy O. "Prince Camille de Polignac: The Life of a Soldier." Ph.D. dissertation, Louisiana State University, 1970.

Moseley, Cynthia Elizabeth. "The Naval Career of Henry Kennedy Stevens as Revealed in His Letters, 1839–1863." M.A. thesis, University of North Carolina, 1951.

Published Works

Books

Anderson, John Q., ed. *Campaigning with Parsons' Texas Cavalry Brigade, C. S. A.* Hillsboro, Tex., 1967.

Arceneaux, William. *Acadian General: Alfred Mouton and the Civil War.* 2nd ed. Lafayette, La., 1981.

Bailey, Anne J. *Between the Enemy and Texas: Parsons's Texas Cavalry in the Civil War.* Fort Worth, 1989.

Barde, Alexandre. *The Vigilante Committees of the Attakapas.* Edited by David C. Edmonds and Dennis Gibson. Lafayette, La., 1981.

Barr, Alwyn. *Polignac's Texas Brigade.* Houston, 1964.

Bartlett, Napier. *Military Record of Louisiana.* Baton Rouge, 1964.

Bearss, Edwin C., ed. *A Louisiana Confederate: Diary of Felix Pierre Poche.* Natchitoches, 1972.

Bergeron, Arthur W., Jr. *Guide to Louisiana Confederate Military Units, 1861–1865.* Baton Rouge, 1989.

Black, Robert C., III. *Railroads of the Confederacy.* Chapel Hill, 1952.

Blessington, J. P. *The Campaigns of Walker's Texas Division.* 1875; rpr. Austin, 1968.

Boatner, Mark M., III. *Civil War Dictionary.* New York, 1959.

Brewer, Willis. *Alabama: Her History, Resources, War Record, and Public Men.* Montgomery, 1872.

Casey, Powell A. *Encyclopedia of Forts, Posts, Named Camps and Other Military Installations in Louisiana, 1700–1981.* Baton Rouge, 1983.

Casey, Powell A. *The Story of Camp Moore.* Baton Rouge, 1985.

Connelly, Thomas L. *Army of the Heartland: The Army of Tennessee, 1861–1862.* Baton Rouge, 1967.

Davis, William C., ed. *The Confederate General.* Vol. VI of 6 vols. Harrisburg, Pa., 1992.

DeForest, John W. *A Volunteer's Adventures: A Union Captain's Record of the Civil War.* New Haven, 1946.

Dorsey, Sarah A. *Recollections of Henry Watkins Allen.* New York, 1866.

Duffy, John, ed. *The Rudolph Matas History of Medicine in Louisiana.* Vol. II of 2 vols. Baton Rouge, 1958, 1962.

Eakin, Sue. *Rapides Parish: An Illustrated History.* Northridge, Calif., 1987.

Eakin, Sue Lyles, and Patsy K. Barber, eds. *Lecompte: Plantation Town in Transition.* Baton Rouge, 1982.

Evans, Clement A., ed. *Confederate Military History.* 17 vols. 1899; rpr. Wilmington, N.C., 1987.

Fortier, Alcée. *Louisiana.* Vol. II of 3 vols. Atlanta, 1914.

Futch, Catherine Baillio. *The Baillio Family.* [Baton Rouge?], 1961.

Griffin, Harry Lewis. *The Attakapas Country: A History of Lafayette Parish, Louisiana.* Gretna, La., 1974.

Hall, Winchester. *The Story of the 26th Louisiana Infantry in the Service of the Confederate States.* Edited by Edwin C. Bearss. [1890s?]; rpr. Gaithersburg, Md., 1984.

Hartje, Robert G. *Van Dorn: The Life and Times of a Confederate General.* Nashville, 1967.

Haynes, Dennis E. *A Thrilling Narrative of the Sufferings of Union Refugees, and the Massacre of the Martyrs of Liberty of Western Louisiana.* Washington, D.C., 1866.

Herzberg, Max J. *The Reader's Encyclopedia of American Literature.* New York, 1962.

Hughes, Nathaniel C. *General William J. Hardee: Old Reliable.* Baton Rouge, 1965.

Landry, Stuart Omer. *The Battle of Liberty Place.* New Orleans, 1955.

Lonn, Ella. *Salt as a Factor in the Confederacy.* New York, 1933.

Lord, Francis A. *Civil War Collector's Encyclopedia.* New York, 1963.

Lytton, K. G. (the earl of Lytton). *Bulwer-Lytton.* London, 1948.

Meade, Robert D. *Judah P. Benjamin, Confederate Statesman.* New York, 1943.

Mouton, J. Franklin, III, comp. and ed. *The Moutons: A Genealogy.* Lafayette, La., 1978.

Nichols, James L. *The Confederate Quartermaster in the Trans-Mississippi.* Austin, 1964.

Noel, Theophilus. *A Campaign from Santa Fe to the Mississippi.* Edited by Martin H. Hall and Edwin A. Davis. Houston, 1961.

Owen, Thomas M. *History of Alabama and Dictionary of Alabama Biography.* Vol. IV of 4 vols. Spartanburg, S.C., 1978.

Roman, Alfred. *The Military Operations of General Beauregard.* Vol. I of 2 vols. New York, 1884.

Rowland, Dunbar, ed. *Jefferson Davis, Constitutionalist: His Letters, Papers and Speeches.* Vol. VI of 10 vols. Jackson, Miss., 1923.

Spurlin, Charles, comp. and ed. *West of the Mississippi with Waller's 13th Texas Cavalry Battalion, CSA.* Hillsboro, Tex., 1971.

Stahls, Paul F., Jr. *Plantation Homes of the Lafourche Country.* Gretna, La., 1983.

———. *Plantation Homes of the Teche Country.* Gretna, La., 1979.

Stanyan, John M. *A History of the Eighth Regiment of New Hampshire Volunteers.* Concord, N.H., 1892.

Still, William N., Jr. *Iron Afloat: The Story of the Confederate Armorclads.* Nashville, 1971.

Taylor, Joe Gray. *Louisiana Reconstructed, 1863–1877.* Baton Rouge, 1974.

Taylor, Richard. *Destruction and Reconstruction: Personal Experiences of the Late War.* Edited by Richard B. Harwell. New York, 1955.

Thompson, Jerry D. *Henry Hopkins Sibley: Confederate General of the West.* Natchitoches, La., 1987.

Warner, Ezra J. *Generals in Gray.* Baton Rouge, 1959.

Warner, Ezra J., and W. Buck Yearns. *Biographical Register of the Confederate Congress.* Baton Rouge, 1975.

Articles

Barr, Alwyn, ed. "The Civil War Diary of James Allen Hamilton, 1861–1864." *Texana,* II (1964), 144.

Bearss, Edwin C. "The Story of Fort Beauregard." *Louisiana Studies,* III (Winter, 1964), 330–84, and IV (Spring, 1965), 3–40.

Browne, P. D. "Captain T. D. Nettles and the Valverde Battery." *Texana,* II (1964), 6–7.

"The Commander's Report on How Hays' Confederate Division Ended Its Career." North Louisiana Historical Association *Newsletter,* VIII (February, 1968), 16–17.

Jones, Joseph. "Roster of the Medical Officers of the Army of Tennessee." *Southern Historical Society Papers,* XXII (1894), 209.

Lathrop, Barnes F. "The Lafourche District in 1862: Confederate Revival." *Louisiana History,* I (1960), 317–18.

———. "The Lafourche District in 1862: Invasion." *Louisiana History,* II (1961), 175–201.

Peters, Martha Ann. "The St. Charles Hotel: New Orleans Social Center, 1837–1860." *Louisiana History,* I (1960), 191–211.

"Polignac's Diary, Part I." *Civil War Times Illustrated*, XIX (August, 1980), 14.

Prichard, Walter, ed. "A Forgotten Louisiana Engineer: G. W. R. Bayley and His 'History of the Railroads of Louisiana.'" *Louisiana Historical Quarterly*, XXX (1947), 1148, 1155.

———, ed. "A Tourist's Description of Louisiana in 1860." *Louisiana Historical Quarterly*, XXI (1938), 1151.

Ragan, Cooper K., ed. "The Diary of Captain George W. O'Brien, 1863." *Southwestern Historical Quarterly*, LXVII (January, 1964), 432.

Weinert, Richard P. "The Confederate Regulars in Louisiana." *Louisiana Studies*, VI (1967), 55–56.

Newspapers

Lucy (La.) *Le Meschacebe*, 1861–1862.
New Orleans *Daily Crescent*, 1862, 1868.
New Orleans *Daily Delta*, 1862.
New Orleans *Daily Picayune*, 1861–1862, 1886.
New Orleans *Morning Star and Catholic Messenger*, March 8, 1868.
Opelousas *Courier*, 1862–1864.
St. Charles *L'Avant-Coureur*, March 22, 1862.
Weekly Thibodaux Sentinel, May 23, 30, 1868, September 26, 1874, March 13, 1875.

Government Documents

Official Records of the Union and Confederate Navies in the War of the Rebellion. 30 vols. Washington, D.C., 1894–1922.

Official Report Relative to the Conduct of Federal Troops in Western Louisiana, During the Invasions of 1863 and 1864. 1865; rpr. Baton Rouge, 1939.

War of the Rebellion: A Compilation of the Official Records of the Union and Confederate Armies. 128 parts in 70 vols. Washington, D.C., 1880–1902.

Other Materials

Conrad, Glenn R., ed. *A Dictionary of Louisiana Biography*. Vol. II of 2 vols. Lafayette, La., 1988.

Crute, Joseph H., Jr. *Confederate Staff Officers, 1861–1865*. Powhatan, Va., 1982.

Federal Writers' Project. *New Orleans City Guide*. Boston, 1938.

Gardner, Charles, comp. *Gardner's New Orleans Directory, for 1861.* New Orleans, 1861.

Goodwin, R. Christopher *et al. The Battle of Fort Bisland: Historical Research and Development of an Archaeological Research Design.* New Orleans, 1988.

Hebert, Rev. Donald J., ed. *Southwest Louisiana Records: Church and Civil Records.* Vols. II and XVII of 36 vols. Cecilia, La., 1974, 1978.

Pritchard, Dr. Peter C. H. *Encyclopedia of Turtles.* Neptune, N. J., 1979.

Shipley, Joseph T. *Guide to Great Plays.* Washington, D.C., 1956.

INDEX

erate), 84, 169, 181, 193, 197, 203
Trenton, La., 132, 133, 137, 166
Triche, Dorville, 5, 80
Triche, Joachim, 125, 126
Trinity, La., 164
Trone, Joseph, 5, 104, 125
Tucker, Joseph P., 4, 6, 7
Tunnel Hill, Tenn., 78–79
Tupelo, Miss., 60, 61, 62, 63, 64, 68, 70,
    73, 79, 94n5, 193, 196, 203, 209, 210
Turgis, Francois Isidore, 36n76
Tuscaloosa, Ala., 73
12th Connecticut Infantry Regiment,
    99n18
12th Louisiana Infantry Battalion, 96n7,
    103, 114n47, 119n58, 121n62,
    127n71, 178n104
20th Louisiana Infantry Regiment, 56,
    57n29, 61, 62n35
21st Louisiana Infantry Regiment, 47n4,
    54, 204
22nd Texas Dismounted Cavalry Regi-
    ment, 121n63, 129n75, 158n54
22nd Texas Infantry Regiment, 173n91
25th Louisiana Infantry Regiment, 47n4
26th Louisiana Infantry Regiment,
    29n61, 64, 93, 138, 178n106, 183
27th Tennessee Infantry Regiment,
    34n72
28th Louisiana Infantry Regiment, 104,
    108, 111n41, 114, 116, 119, 137, 146,
    158, 184n119, 186
29th Alabama Infantry Regiment, 82n61
29th Louisiana Infantry Regiment, 1n3
20 Mile Creek, 58, 60, 61, 62
24 Mile Ferry, 118, 153
Tyler, Tex., 128
Tyler (Union gunboat), 20n38, 22n43

Valverde (Texas) Battery, 108, 111n41
Van Dorn, Earl, 45n100, 48n5, 49n9,
    55n24
Van's Valley, Ga., 74
Vedroz, Antoine, 5, 43, 125
Vermilionville, La., 106–107, 115,
    125–26, 190, 203, 204, 207, 208
Vernon, La., 137
Vernon, M. P., 210

Vicknair, Felix, 77
Vickner, Valery, 1n1, 42
Vicksburg, Miss., 64, 93, 111n40, 125,
    138n85, 178n105
Ville Platte Prairie, 107
Vincent, William G., 97, 114, 156
Voorhies, O., 170
Voorhies' Ferry, 130

Walker, Dr., 122
Walker, John G., 134n83, 141, 145, 150,
    162n70, 164, 165n79, 173n92
Walker, John L., 132
Walker, Lucius M., 57n29
Walker, William, 146, 187, 190, 199, 200
Wallace, Lew, 26n52
Waller, Ed, Jr., 108n34
Walnut Hill, Ark., 173–74
Warren, Ark., 169
Washington, La., 118n56, 126, 128, 185
Watt, Andrew J., 22, 197
Webre, J. Septime, 56, 58, 83, 148
Wedge, Daniel J., 182
Weitzel, Godfrey, 96, 98, 99n17, 101,
    102, 189, 198
Wells, James Madison, 194, 207
West Point, Ga., 79
West Point, Miss., 210
Wharton, John A., 155, 157n50, 158,
    159n61
Wheeler, Joseph, 155n47
Whitaker, William A., 25
White, William, 5, 40, 41
Wiescher, Dr., 209
Winder, George W., 6, 40, 41, 72, 114,
    125
Winder, Martha Grundy, 185
Winder, Van Perkins, 185n121
Winn, W. H., 184
Winnfield, La., 131–32, 137
Wood, John D., 3, 12, 25, 36, 71

Yellow Bayou: battle, 157–59, 202;
    mentioned, 141
Yellow Jacket (10th Louisiana) Infantry
    Battalion, 96, 103, 111n42, 113n45,
    119n58, 129, 159
Young, John M., 36